THE FIRST
AMERICAN
WOMEN
ARCHITECTS

Williams, Emily (1869–1942)

Young, Helen Binkerd (1877–1959)

Adams, Ruth Maxon (1883–1970)

Almy, Mary (1883–1967)

Barney, Nora Stanton Blatch (1883–1971)

Bethune, Jennie Louise Blanchard (1856–1913)

Bridgman, Lilian (1866–1948)

Brunson, Emma F. (1887–1980)

Budd, Katharine Cotheal (1860–1951)

Butterfield, Emily Helen (1884–1958)

Chapman, Josephine Wright (1867–1943)

Coit, Elisabeth (1892–1987)

Colter, Mary Jane Elizabeth (1869–1958)

Connor, Rose (1892–1970)

Craig, Mary (1889–1964)

Darling-Parlin, Maude (1885–1979)

Deakin, Edna (1871–1946)

Dozier, Henrietta Cuttino (1872–1947)

French, Helen Douglass (b. 1900)

Fritsch, Margaret Goodin (1899–1993)

Furman, Ethel Madison Bailey (1893–1976)

Gannon, Mary Nevan (b. 1867)

Greely, Rose Ishbel (1887–1969)

Griffin, Marion Mahony (1871–1961)

Hall, Leola (1881–1930)

Hands, Alice J.

Hayden, Florence Kenyon (1882–1973)

Hayden, Sophia Gregoria (1868–1953)

Henley, Frances Evelyn (d. 1955)

Hicks, Margaret (1858–83)

Hill, Esther Marjorie (1895–1985)

Holman, Emily Elizabeth (fl. 1892–1915)

Hook, Mary Rockwell (1877–1978)

Howe, Lois Lilley (1864–1964)

Irwin, Harriet Morrison (1828–97)

Johnson, Alice E. (1862–1936)

Keichline, Anna Wagner (1889–1943)

Kellogg, Fay (1871–1918)

THE FIRST AMERICAN WOMEN ARCHITECTS

Sarah Allaback

McCain, Ida B. 1884?
Mead, Marcia (1879–1967)
Mercur, Elise (1869–1947)
Moody, Harriet I. (1891–1966)
Morgan, Julia (1872–1957)
Morrow, Gertrude E. Comfort (ca. 1892–1987)
Mother Joseph of the Sacred Heart, Sister of Providence [Esther Pariseau] (1823–1902)
Muir, Edla (1906–71)
Nedved, Elizabeth Kimball (1897–1969)
Nichols, Minerva Parker (1863–1949)
Northman, Edith Mortensen (b. 1893)
Parker, Marion Alice (1875–1935)
Pattee, Elizabeth Greenleaf (b. 1893)
Peddle, Juliet (1899–1979)
Peters, Nelle Elizabeth Nichols (1884–1974)
Pfeiffer, Alberta Raffl (1899–1994)
Pierce, Marjorie (1900–1999)
Pope, Theodate (1867–1946)
Power, Ethel Brown (1881–1969)
Raymond, Eleanor (1888–1989)
Rice, Lillian Jeanette (1888–1938)
Riggs, Lutah Maria (1896–1984)
Roberts, Isabel (b. 1874)
Rockfellow, Anne Graham (1866–1954)
Rogers, Eliza Jacobus Newkirk (1877–1966)
Ryan, Ida Annah (1873–1950)
Salomonsky, Verna Cook (1890–1978)
Sawyer, Gertrude (1895–1996)
Schenck, Anna Pendleton (d. 1915)
Spencer, Margaret Fulton (1882–1966)
Steinmesch, Harriet Mae (1893–1979)
Waterman, Hazel Wood (1865–1948)
Whitman, Bertha Louise Yerex (b. 1892)
Wilburn, Leila Ross (1885–1967)
Williams, Emily (1869–1942)
Young, Helen Binkerd (1877–1959)
Adams, Ruth Maxon (1883–1970)

University of Illinois Press
Urbana and Chicago

Library of Congress Cataloging-in-Publication Data
Allaback, Sarah
The first American women architects / Sarah Allaback.
p.   cm.
Includes bibliographical references and index.
ISBN-13: 978-0-252-03321-6 (cloth : alk. paper)
ISBN-10: 0-252-03321-3 (cloth : alk. paper)
1. Women architects—United States—Biography—Dictionaries.
I. Title.
NA736.A48   2008
720.92'273—dc22 [B]   2007036187

Furman, Ethel Madison Bailey (1893–1976)
Gannon, Mary Nevan (b. 1867)
Greely, Rose Ishbel (1887–1969)
Griffin, Marion Mahony (1871–1961)
Hall, Leola (1881–1930)
Hands, Alice J.
Hayden, Florence Kenyon (1882–1973)
Hayden, Sophia Gregoria (1868–1953)
Henley, Frances Evelyn (d. 1955)
Hicks, Margaret (1858–83)
Hill, Esther Marjorie (1895–1985)
Holman, Emily Elizabeth (fl. 1892–1915)
Hook, Mary Rockwell (1877–1978)
Howe, Lois Lilley (1864–1964)
Irwin, Harriet Morrison (1828–97)
Johnson, Alice E. (1862–1936)
Keichline, Anna Wagner (1889–1943)
Kellogg, Fay (1871–1918)
Luscomb, Florence Hope (1887–1985)
Manley, Marion Isadore (1893–1984)
Manning, Eleanor (1884–1973)
Martini, Elisabeth A. (b. 1886)
McCain, Ida (b. 1884)
Mead, Marcia (1879–1967)
Mercur, Elise (1869–1947)
Moody, Harriet J. (1891–1966)
Morgan, Julia (1872–1957)
Morrow, Gertrude E. Comfort (ca. 1892–1987)
Mother Joseph of the Sacred Heart, Sister of Providence [Esther Pariseau] (1823–1902)
Muir, Edla (1906–71)
Nedved, Elizabeth Kimball (1897–1969)
Nichols, Minerva Parker (1863–1949)
Northman, Edith Mortensen (b. 1893)
Parker, Marion Alice (1875?–1935)
Pattee, Elizabeth Greenleaf (b. 1893)
Peddle, Juliet (1899–1979)

As I said
about the Atlanta Courthouse,
this work was refused me
because I was not a voter,
so they said.

—

HENRIETTA C. DOZIER, AIA

CONTENTS

ACKNOWLEDGMENTS

The initial research for this book began when I lived in Washington, D.C., and discovered an archive devoted to women in architecture at the headquarters of the American Institute of Architects (AIA). This collection was organized by the AIA's archivist, Tony Wrenn, who assisted me in gathering material on the earliest female practitioners. Many years after Wrenn's retirement, Nancy Hadley, by then the AIA archivist, went out of her way to send new information and to connect me with other scholars working on similar topics. Nancy provided research materials throughout my project and contributed a comprehensive list of female AIA members up to 1950 (Appendix 2). At the University of Illinois at Urbana-Champaign, William J. Maher, university archivist, sent me copies of alumni records and helped identify several student architects. Glenda Insua, research assistant for the Bentley Historical Library at the University of Michigan, Ann Arbor, found new information about graduates of that university and provided photographs that enhance the book. In addition to efficiently answering many questions, Melanie Bourbeau of Hill-Stead Museum in Farmington, Connecticut, sent me an important letter by Theodate Pope Riddle and several excellent photographs. The Hill-Stead Museum's curator, Cynthia Cormier, and the museum's archivist, Polly Huntington, reviewed and improved the Pope Riddle biography and building list.

I am grateful to J. Norman Dizon of the Providence Archives in Seattle for editing the entry on Mother Joseph and to Martin Wachadlo for reviewing my transcription of his list of buildings designed by Louise Bethune. Two anonymous peer reviewers for the University of Illinois Press gave insightful comments on the text. I am also deeply indebted to Carol Betts at the University of Illinois Press for her many contributions and improvements to this book.

The following archivists and archives were helpful in providing photographs: Laura Schiefer, Buffalo and Erie County Historical Society; Colleen L. Hyde, Grand Canyon National Park Museum; J. Norman Dizon and Peter Schmid, Providence Archives, Seattle; N. Adam Watson, State Library and Archives of Florida; Laura Knott, MIT Museum; International Archive of Women in Architecture, Blacksburg, Virginia; Julie Tozer and Janet S. Parks, Avery Architectural and Fine Arts Library, Columbia University; Glenda Insua, Karen L. Jania, and Laura Schmidt of the Bentley Historical Library, University of Michigan; Sophia Smith Collection, Smith College Archives; Jennifer McDaid of the Library of Virginia, Richmond; Library of Congress, Prints and Photographs Division; Ken Kenyon, Special Collections, California State Polytechnic University; David W. Jackson, Jackson County Historical Society, Independence, Missouri; Mary Daniels, Loeb Library, Harvard University; Michael Redmon, Santa Barbara Historical Museum; and Wilma Slaight, Wellesley College Archives. Tibby Storey of the San Francisco Public Library; Maria Allen of Westover School, Middlebury, Connecticut; and Bhavaprana of the Vedanta Society of Southern California also graciously provided photographs.

Although I have mentioned in my text numerous buildings that are on the National Register of Historic Places or designated as National Historic Landmarks, I have not attempted to note all buildings by American women architects that have received these designations. Readers may consult the comprehensive lists maintained by the National Park Service at www.nps.gov/nr/ and www.nps.gov/history/nhl.

This book is dedicated to James F. O'Gorman. Jim inspired me with his lectures at Wellesley College and guided me in my later work. His faith in me over the years, and the example of his own scholarship, resulted in this book. My mother, Patricia Manuras, encouraged me to finish the project, helped with research, and remained enthusiastic to the end. My husband, Ethan Carr, assisted in countless ways, and my daughter, Marion Carr, witnessed the writing process with interest and offered a cover illustration. I am especially grateful to Ethan and Marion for their many personal sacrifices that gave me the time to write this book.

INTRODUCTION

Among AIA members, where the other names have no handle, my name should not be entered with prefix "Miss." In vain have I indicated my great desire to be known as above [Katharine Cotheal Budd, Architect] . . . will the AIA do it? No. When you write to me of course say: "Miss K. C. B." It might please your paternal relative to know that half my letters come addressed—"K. C. B., Esq.," or "Mr."

KATHARINE COTHEAL BUDD TO MR. WHITAKER,
August 21, 1926

Katharine Budd had been practicing architecture for over thirty years when she wrote to a Mr. Whitaker demanding to be identified as herself.[1] A registered architect with professional training in several offices, Budd was the first female member of the New York chapter of the American Institute of Architects (AIA) (1924) and the designer of Hostess Houses, sponsored by the Young Women's Christian Association (YWCA), in the South and Midwest. Today, she is hardly more than a footnote in a handful of sources on women in architecture, but when she is mentioned it is without the "Miss." Budd's struggle for professional identity, in light of her expertise, is typical of a woman's experience in the architectural profession. Two years after Budd joined the AIA, an accomplished architect from Florida became the institute's thirteenth female member. Her acceptance letter was addressed to Mr. Marion Manley.[2]

By 1920 more than two hundred women were practicing architecture in the United States, and in the course of their careers, they designed thousands of buildings throughout the country—including apartments in Kansas City, hotels in the nation's national parks, churches in Michigan, and mansions on the coast of California. Like Budd and Manley, nearly all these practitioners have been forgotten. The present book includes biographical sketches of more than seventy-five women architects, with partial lists of their works and references for further research. The architects profiled were either practicing or attending architectural schools by 1920 and commenced practice within the decade. A significant number of women who were just beginning their architectural education or design practice in the 1920s are not included. I considered this group as beyond the pioneering "first" generation. During their careers, the majority of the women discussed in this book were architects of actual buildings, and the few who may not have had independent commissions contributed to the growth of the profession in other significant ways. The lists of each architect's work are rarely complete, but they have been included to demonstrate the range and extent of buildings designed by women and to guide future researchers in the development of more comprehensive records.

Research on this topic shares the challenges of women's history: women's achievements often slip through the cracks, unrecorded; records that remain are difficult, if not impossible, to locate; and the women themselves often preferred to remain anonymous. The career challenges encountered by early woman architects caused some to disguise their gender for professional advancement. This was true of C. [Charlotte] Julian Mesic, a drafter in the office of Julia Morgan. Henrietta Dozier called herself "Cousin Harry," "Harry," or "H. C. Dozier." In a case of unintentional deception, Lois Lilley Howe became the second woman voted into the AIA because the electing members assumed "Lois" was a man. It is impossible to know how many women architects went by initials, pseudonyms, or nicknames. The difficulty of tracing married names is an additional complication, and while many women did stop working as architects after marriage, others simply took their husbands' names and continued to practice. It is necessary to investigate records by searching for both the birth names and married names of the architects. In my texts, I have noted both names of each woman, but I refer to each person primarily by the name under which she worked. Finally, the historian's effort to describe the professional situation of the early female architect is colored by the fact that the majority of practitioners chose to blend into the traditional office as much as possible. They were architects who happened to be women.

During the late nineteenth and early twentieth centuries, the architectural profession in America was closely tied to the studio or atelier. It need hardly be noted that this setting—an office run by a famous architect—was the ultimate "old boys' club." A few extraordinary women were able to gain apprenticeships, but most were excluded from the atelier and the professional network it represented. Once it became possible to receive a university degree in architecture, some women were able to open their own offices, to hire other women, and to receive commissions from female patrons. The biographical sketches that follow describe a handful of aspiring female architects who found space in the studio and many others who gained their education and experience in more unusual ways. It should be assumed that significant numbers of women were discouraged from becoming architects or remained in menial positions. As a close look at the history of women in the architectural profession indicates, many of the stereotypes that surrounded the first female architects are still significant factors in the failure of women to advance at the rate of their sisters in professions such as medicine and law. For over a decade, Kathryn H. Anthony, a professor of architecture at the University of Illinois, has been studying the fate of women in the architectural profession, their struggles and accomplishments, and has used oral history interviews to document a consistent pattern of discrimination in the workplace. Despite a growing number of successful firms owned by women at the time of Anthony's study (2001), the typical woman architect still earns less, and advances far more slowly, than her male peer.[3]

The role of women as wives and mothers has always been at the heart of debates involving female architects, the lack of them, and their failure to achieve long-term success. While it is true that most early female architects were single, several married women practiced, including the pioneering professional Louise Blanchard Bethune, FAIA (fig. 1). Bethune worked as a drafter for Richard A. Waite before opening her own office in 1881 and marrying her former coworker Robert Bethune. The birth of their son a few years later seems to have had little effect on Louise's career. Other husband and wife teams include Gertrude and Irving Comfort, who ran a firm in northern California, and Verna and Edgar Salomonsky, who founded a successful practice in New York. Upon the death of Edgar in 1929, Verna Salomonsky continued the firm on her own. A woman's effort to pursue an architectural career was certainly made easier if she was well established in the profession before marriage; such was the case of Marion Mahony, who married her coworker Walter Burley Griffin, and Nora Stanton Blatch Barney, who earned a civil engineering degree from Cornell in 1905, married in 1919, and had two children before returning to work as a developer in Greenwich, Connecticut. Eliza Newkirk married at midcareer and split her time between New Hampshire, where her husband was headmaster at Phillips Exeter Academy, and Boston, the location of her business. Hazel Wood Waterman and Ella Mae Ellis League both became architects after the deaths of their husbands left them with young children to support. Louise Caldwell Murdock began her professional career the year after her husband died. The California architect Mary Craig worked in the shadow of her husband until his death in 1922, when she took over the firm and furthered the Spanish revival style on the West Coast. As these examples illustrate, there were as many different ways for women architects to manage their personal and professional lives in the early twentieth century as there are today. However, the decision to end any architectural aspirations upon marriage was undoubtedly more common a

FIGURE 1. Jennie Louise Blanchard Bethune. Courtesy Buffalo and Erie County Historical Society.

hundred years ago. Mary Gannon, an early practitioner, gave up her successful New York architectural career to help her husband with his tailoring business in Spokane, Washington. An unknown number of trained female architects took the path of Helen McClellan-Wilson Atwater, the first female graduate of what is now Drexel University and a member of Paul Cret's studio, who settled down to a traditional family routine after marriage.

If early women architects were able to establish themselves in professional practice, most labored under the assumption that they were naturally suited to design houses. Historians have consistently described the nineteenth century as a time when women were mired in a "cult of domesticity" that gave social value to domestic roles thereby keeping them from entering the public workforce. Considering the power of this concept, it is not surprising that many early women architects developed exclusively residential practices. In the case of Josephine Wright Chapman, a Boston architect, this choice developed after she had entered the public forum. After designing a Harvard dormitory (1897), a church, and two women's clubs, Chapman decided to focus exclusively on domestic architecture because she felt women were inherently better home designers. Leila Ross Wilburn, architect of hundreds of homes and apartment buildings in Georgia, advertised women's natural taste and affinity for residential work, and she did so at a time when the Atlanta suburbs were the most marketable prospect in town. The architect Eleanor Raymond also promoted her practice as residential, which was obviously a good business decision as her work was much sought after throughout New England. In its 1919–20 catalog, the Cambridge School of Domestic Architecture and Landscape Architecture consciously made "domestic" part of its name in an effort to encourage women professionals and to soften any negative response from the public. An accomplished graduate of the school, Raymond believed that men "in general do not want to design houses (they say mostly for financial reasons, because they can't afford to). I think it is because they can't bother with the hundreds of little things that have to be considered in making a house primarily livable as well as distinguished in design."[4] Regardless of any inherent suitability for residential design, women architects usually found themselves in private practice, which meant that commissions other than residential were hard to come by. With this in mind, it is surprising to see the scope and variety of buildings produced by women of the late nineteenth and early twentieth centuries (figs. 2 and 3). They designed not only hotels, churches, factories, warehouses, and public buildings, but also apartment buildings and large housing tracts. In fact, the choice of building type seems to have been dictated in large part by the economy,

FIGURE 2. Providence Academy, Vancouver, Washington, designed by Mother Joseph. The main building, at right, was completed in 1873. The auditorium wing was added in the 1880s. Courtesy Providence Archives, Seattle.

FIGURE 3. Lookout Studio by Mary Colter, view north, front entrance and stairway down to observation area, ca. 1915. Santa Fe Railroad photograph. Courtesy Grand Canyon National Park Museum Collection.

and, of course, by the fact that architects in private practice are rarely able to compete against larger firms for major building commissions.

Louise Bethune demonstrated not only that a woman could run a successful architectural firm, but that she might design all manner of public buildings. The firm she established in 1881 went on to produce at least eighteen public schools in Buffalo, New York, and boasted examples of almost every building type. In a speech announcing the opening of her firm, Bethune challenged those who would limit possibilities for women architects and urged that any qualifications suggested by gender be removed from the job description. "There is no need whatever of a woman architect. No one wants her, no one yearns for her and there is no special line in architecture to which she is better adapted than a man. . . . [The woman architect] has exactly the same work to do as a man. When a woman enters the profession she will be met kindly and will be welcome but not as a woman, only as an architect."[5]

By refusing to praise her gender's "natural" affinity for residential architecture, she gave talented women the opportunity to perform every aspect of the job. At this early date, Bethune believed that women architects would be accepted if they followed her advice and focused on their work rather than their gender. Her own success was based on such practice, and her early acceptance to membership in both the Western Association of Architects (1885) and the American Institute of Architects (1888) proved the point.

Bethune was the first female member of the AIA, and a pioneer in the field on many levels, but researchers who pursue the study of early women architects discover that each is considered a pioneer. Even in the twenty-first century, the female designer is usually described as unique, the first, or one of only a handful of her sex with a career in architecture. Designers who became well known for major commissions in the 1950s and 1960s, such as Marion Manley, are brought forward as pioneers in the field (fig. 4). This situation can be explained, in part, by the lack of historical records and the difficulty contemporary historians encounter doing the necessary research. It is also attributable to the isolation experienced by individual women who attempted to become successful architects. In the nineteenth century, each had to struggle to make her own way, often unaware of any who came before. Those who succeeded did so on their own merit, usually by blending into the masculine professional world as Bethune recommended, even if that meant taking on the least glamorous commissions and receiving less money than they deserved. No real advancements were made until the early twentieth century, when women had the opportunity to meet other female architec-

FIGURE 4. Marion Manley (left) with the conservationist Marjory Stoneman Douglas (1890–1998) in Miami, Florida, n.d. Courtesy State Library and Archives of Florida.

tural students in universities, to open their own firms, and to attract female patrons. Once such networks were established during the 1920s and 30s, progress was still tenuous; although more academic opportunities were open to women, the barriers to professional advancement remained daunting. At the end of World War II, women architects found opportunities limited by the return of men from the war and the "patriotic" sentiment that women should be waiting in houses, not designing them. In general, women like Manley, who became successful after World War II, flourished because they had already earned the respect of other professionals.

The stereotype of the architect is the almost mythological figure of Frank Lloyd Wright, the self-assured genius who developed an original modern architectural style that appealed to a Victorian sense of the past. Women architects are too rare to warrant a stereotype, but independent female professionals were often described as solitary, eccentric spinsters. As the following biographical sketches illustrate, however, women architects of the late nineteenth and early twentieth centuries cannot be so easily characterized. Several were recent immigrants, and one was African American.[6] Their family backgrounds, financial status, and training varied considerably. By 1920 many had college degrees in architecture or engineering and some had even earned master's degrees (see Appendix 1). But a traditional apprenticeship in an office was the means of advancement for Agnes Ballard, who received her education in the firm of Percy Dwight Butler in La Crosse, Wisconsin. Hazel Wood Waterman enrolled in an International Correspondence School course before working for the modern architect Irving Gill. Although the majority of successful women architects were single, in several cases they continued to work after marriage, and some marriages clearly occurred because husband and wife shared a common occupation. While the architectural profession was a difficult career path, most successful female practitioners claimed they received no special treatment or encountered any significant barriers to success. And yet few were without stories of unfair treatment. In addition to designing buildings, most women architects were well traveled, literate, interesting people who enjoyed a range of activities outside of their work. As a group, they were much like their male counterparts—sociable, civic-minded community members, often leaders in historic preservation and local business organizations. A glimpse into their lives provides an unusual window into what was possible for a woman over a hundred years ago.

During the course of my research for this volume, I discovered many women who could not be identified extensively. Nothing is known but the office addresses of Caroline E. Ashley and Laura H. Charsley, two New York City architects practicing in 1899.[7] Although Mrs. Ellen M. Goodrich is listed as an architect in early twentieth-century Portland, Oregon, no record of her work has been found.[8] Florence Chauncey Rice, an architect for the New York firm of George Martin Huss, was born in 1873, but details of her life, including her death date, have not been discovered. The career of Agnes Ballard, the first licensed female architect in Florida and an AIA member, remains largely undocumented. Alice Pardee, who graduated from the University of Michigan in 1910, became an AIA member in 1945 on the strength of a flourishing independent practice since graduation. Because she was working under her married name, the student records that might reveal more about her professional identity cannot be located. On her 1927 AIA application, Alice Walton listed ten years of practice as an architect in Kansas City; the president of the Kansas City chapter recommended her for membership without qualification because of "the character of her work" and her education at the University of Minnesota.[9] Efforts to learn more about Walton's successful architectural career have been fruitless. These examples of little-known women architects, as well as a longer list of names with even less personal information, suggest that the participation of women in the architectural profession before 1920 is only beginning to be explored. Future researchers have the exciting opportunity to contribute to a greater understanding of women's experience as architects and to develop a more complete picture of the growth of the architectural profession in nineteenth- and twentieth-century America.

|||||||||||||||||||||||||||

Nineteenth-Century Women Writers on Architecture

|||||||||||||||||||||||||||

If early nineteenth-century women could not imagine becoming architects, they could offer opinions and criticism of the built environment through fictional descriptions, historical essays, etiquette books, travel accounts, and contributions to popular journals. Writing, or "taking up the pen" as some modest practitioners put it, was one of the few means of financial self-sufficiency available to women during the first half of the nineteenth century. The popular stereotype of the literary woman—the bluestocking—suggests that plenty of spinsters and widows availed themselves of this opportunity, both for fund raising and self-expression. Despite the persistent image of Victorian matrons as domestic ornaments, women achieved considerable freedom in the nineteenth century. Political activists successfully passed the married women's property act in 1848, a landmark in the long road toward gaining suffrage. The outspoken activist Florence Luscomb (fig. 5), a 1909 architecture graduate from the Massachusetts Institute of Technology (MIT), recalled the work of her mother's generation in radical movements for social justice. Such unconventional women may have been treated as social outcasts in some circles, but they also made the domestic achievements of their literary compatriots seem appropriately feminine.

The search for American women's views of architecture begins not with the builders' guides and stylebooks produced in the early nineteenth century, the starting point for traditional studies of architectural literature, but with writing more suitable for fireside reading. Although women did not have experience in architects' offices or on construction sites, they were free to observe the changing urban scene and to record what they saw. In *Sketches of a New-England Village,* Eliza Buckminster Lee describes the meetinghouse, the parsonage, "old fashioned houses," and other buildings characteristic of what was already becoming a nostalgic setting in 1838. Catharine Sedgewick, author of the popular historical romance *Hope Leslie* (1827), writes about domestic attachment in *Home* (1835). Sedgewick dwells on philosophical contrasts between European and American feelings about home, explaining that, in contrast to European domiciles, American homes are not "consecrated

FIGURE 5. Florence Luscomb with "Votes for Women" flag. Courtesy MIT Museum.

by the memories of centuries," and therefore Yankee associations of home extend to the unexplored western forests.[10] Lee's and Sedgewick's sentimental depictions of New England villages were a reaction to increased urban development transforming the countryside and a growing sense of nationalism, as American artists and writers attempted to define a native style in the arts.

Descriptions of American architecture were an important part of travel writing, an anecdotal form of literature that was often published in letter form and considered acceptable for women. By the 1830s, literary Americans were familiar with the works of a host of female travelers, including Frances Wright and Frances Trollope, both of whom wrote well-publicized accounts of their experiences as tourists in American cities. According to Wright, Philadelphia's "public buildings are all remarkable for neatness and some for pure classic elegance. . . . I trust the citizens will never swerve from the pure style of architecture to which they seem at present to have attached themselves."[11] Wright lectured throughout the country after the publication of her book, and in 1830 Trollope was among the audience attending one of her talks in Philadelphia. Trollope agreed that the city was particularly "neat" in appearance but considered the "coup-d'oeil" . . . "everywhere the same" and the civic spaces rarely as impressive as those of her native England.[12] Although Wright's liberal political views and Trollope's comparisons may have alienated some readers, the mere circulation of their work, both in publication and through public lecture circuits, helped to establish women travelers as perceptive urban critics.

The works of the English art historian Anna Jameson (1794–1860) and Madame de Staël (1766–1817) influenced the American transcendentalist Margaret Fuller (1810–50) and Louisa Tuthill (1798–1879), author of the first history of architecture published in America. Fuller, one of the few Bostonians able to translate German, read de Staël in the original. She began writing about national aesthetics in the late 1830s and contributed to the transcendentalist journal *The Dial* before she became its editor in 1841.[13] Beginning in 1839, Fuller hosted a series of "Conversations for Women" on art and related subjects that incorporated the philosophies of Jameson and de Staël.[14] The same year, in her hometown of New Haven, Louisa Tuthill published *The Young Lady's Reader*, which included excerpts from *Corinne* and "Semiramis" by Mrs. Jameson. Tuthill believed that in addition to such literature, a knowledge of architecture "ought to be acquired by every well-informed lady."[15] Despite the intellectual chasm between the participants in the conversations and the audience of young ladies, Fuller and Tuthill both found inspiration in the work of earlier female philosophers who considered no aesthetic topic off limits to their sex.

It is not surprising, then, that in the 1840s, when Louisa Caroline Tuthill wrote her architectural history, she did not see herself as the solitary woman in the field. Tuthill wrote, "I am happy to say I am not the only lady who has written on This Art," and mentioned the translation work of Mrs. Edward Cresy (Eliza) as one example.[16] Tuthill's *History of Architecture from the Earliest Times* (1848) traces the evolution of architecture from prehistory to the present, with chapters on construction, cemeteries, and qualifications for architects (fig. 6). Almost twenty years earlier, Tuthill had written a textbook for young people about the history of ancient architecture (fig. 7), and some of the research from this work was incorporated into the introductory chapters of her larger text.[17] The architectural studies were influenced by Tuthill's use of the architect Ithiel Town's library, the largest of its kind in America and housed conveniently down the street from her home in New Haven.[18] Tuthill relied on hundreds of histories, travelers' accounts, and builders' guides to write the historical sections of the history, but she based much of the criticism about contemporary American buildings on her own observations of cities throughout New England.

Despite her unique decision to produce an architectural history, Tuthill was a practical writer rather than an intellectual, and her principles remained solidly within the boundaries acceptable for a society woman. The dedication of the *History of Architecture* to "the Ladies of the United States of America, Acknowledged Arbiters of Taste," gave women an influential position with respect to American architecture, but did so within a popular contemporary effort to promote aesthetic reform. By simplifying architectural scholarship and condensing the lengthy histories by Prescott and Bancroft, Tuthill was both appealing to women and making difficult texts accessible to a "common" readership that included "the painter, the poet, the sculptor, the novelist, the

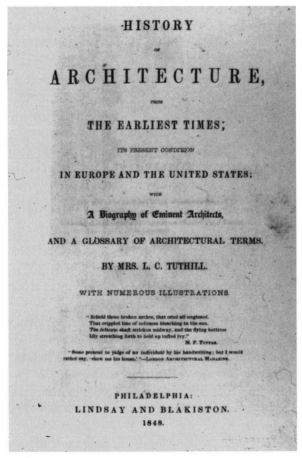

FIGURE 6. Title page of Louisa Tuthill, *History of Architecture from the Earliest Times* (Philadelphia: Lindsay and Blakiston, 1848).

FIGURE 7. Title page of Louisa Tuthill, *Architecture. Part I. Ancient Architecture* (1831).

traveler, the reader and the writer of books of travels and history"; in other words, "readers of all classes" were expected to profit from it.[19] After the publication of the history, Tuthill continued to write juvenile fiction intended to educate young people in the principles of art and architecture. Her anthology of John Ruskin's work, *The True and the Beautiful in Nature, Arts, Morals, and Religion* (1858), was the first anthology of the English critic's writings published in America.[20]

Tuthill's contemporary, the educator and writer Catharine Beecher, chose to introduce architectural topics in etiquette books or domestic guides, which were widely available to middle-class housewives. In 1841, Beecher published *A Treatise on Domestic Economy, For the Use of Young Ladies at Home and at School,* a manual intended to train young women in self-discipline as well as domestic tasks. She described the power a woman might exert over her family's domestic environment by redesigning her home for improved efficiency and better health. As many modern critics have pointed out, Beecher's emphasis on increasing women's power in the home may have decreased their ability to escape from it and enter the public workplace. Although her work must be included in any history of women involved in the architectural profession, Beecher's strategies for domestic management are more closely related to the development of home economics. Nevertheless, Beecher's book included the first published architectural plans designed by an American woman. In a second book, *The American Woman's Home* (1869), written with her famous sister Harriet Beecher Stowe, Beecher anticipated the growth of a new industry in the education of female "domestic scientists." Helen Campbell, and later Christine Frederick and Lillian Galbraith, would go on to build a domestic empire for women that incorporated the latest in scientific management but moved increasingly further from architectural design.

In their writings of the 1840s, Catharine Beecher and Louisa Tuthill declared women the moral overseers of the home, responsible for influencing architecture by "arbitrating" standards of taste and decency. Considering the limited professional roles for women of their day, Beecher and Tuthill were enlightened; they devised a way for women to claim some power over their environment without stepping outside of the home. This effort at enlarging women's career opportunities would continue into the late nineteenth century, as temperance advocates strove to create a more homelike world, and domestic engineers attempted to design a more efficient, scientific home "laboratory" for women. However, once women gained access and acceptance in the professions, the elevation of the domestic realm appeared more and more oppressive and far less innovative than it must have earlier in the century.

The year Tuthill's history was published also marked the beginning of the design school movement, wherein schools were started in Philadelphia and other major cities to train women in industrial design arts. School administrations included female founders, board members, patrons, teachers, and, after the first classes graduated, many former students. Although these schools were intended to train middle-class women in the industrial design arts, they also created new audiences for female art instructors, such as Mary Ann Dwight. A teacher and writer from New England, Dwight lectured on "the necessity of cultivating taste in the arts of design" at the Philadelphia school before advertising her own drawing academy in New York.[21] Over the next few years, Dwight wrote regularly for Henry Barnard's periodical, the *American Journal of Education,* emphasizing the importance of design education for women and children. Her *Introduction to the Study of Art* (1856) was intended as a primer in art history.[22] Elizabeth Palmer Peabody, also an active advocate of design schools for women, published instructional books appropriate for school use—*A Method of Teaching Linear Drawing, Adapted to the Public Schools* (1841) and *Aesthetic Papers* (1849).[23]

In the aftermath of the Civil War, American women wrote on a range of topics that contributed to the development of art and architectural criticism. The world traveler and art historian Clara Erskine Clement (Waters) (1834–1916) published *A Handbook of Legendary and Mythological Art* (1871) and *Painters, Sculptors, Architects, Engravers, and Their Works* (1874), among other catalogs on art and its practitioners (fig. 8). Even as she published dozens of books, Clement managed to explore foreign cultures, climbing the great pyramid at the age of sixty-six. Caroline W. Horton carried on the tradition of writing textbooks with *Architecture for General Students* (1874). Five years later, both Clement's *American Artists of the Nineteenth Century* and Martha Joanna Reade Lamb's *The Homes of America* were published. Although serious in their efforts to educate Americans, these texts retain something of the anecdotal style of their day, a tone modern readers frequently misinterpret as feminine or domestic.

The first professional woman architectural critic and journalist, Mariana Griswold Van Rensselaer (1851–1934), flourished in the 1880s, when a handful of young women architects were receiving training in graduate schools and private offices. Unlike the aspiring architects, Van Rensselaer quickly rose to the top of her field, contributing perceptive articles to a wide range of popular and professional periodicals. She wrote a nine-part series on "Recent American Architecture" for *Century Magazine,* a historical sketch on the art

FIGURE 8. Volumes by Clara Erskine Clement [Waters]. Courtesy International Archive of Women in Architecture.

of gardening in *Garden and Forest,* and frequent essays for *American Architect and Building News.* The social mores barring women from construction sites did not hinder Van Rensselaer from writing about recent New York architecture. The extent of Van Rensselaer's acceptance in elite professional circles is best illustrated by her publication of *H. H. Richardson and His Works* (1888), the first biography of a major American architect and a volume written at the request of Richardson's close friend and colleague, Frederick Law Olmsted.

Although Van Rensselaer is best remembered for her biography, her popular articles about landscape and her book *Art Out-of-Doors* (1893), an introduction to landscape architecture, were more widely read in their day. Like Tuthill, Van Rensselaer intended to increase interest in architecture among women, but, since the 1840s, the field had become much more specialized and had grown to include landscape architecture. Van Rensselaer made the profession accessible to women just at the time when professional organizations began to offer programs in which they might pursue their ambitions as practitioners. And, as Van Rensselaer's articles became regular features of both popular and professional journals, many more women were accepted as commentators on American architecture, landscape architecture, and interior design, and their contributions reached a new level of professionalism. With a variety of educational opportunities to choose from, including women's colleges and coeducational institutions, women were no longer assumed to be ignorant, scribbling dilettantes. Among the emerging professional writers was Harriet Monroe, a contributor to the *Chicago Tribune* on art-related topics and a biographer of her brother-in-law, the architect John Wellborn Root. Three years before publishing the Root biography, Monroe had written part of a book for the 1893 World's Columbian Exposition, edited by Candace Wheeler, a powerful national advocate of the decorative arts movement.[24] Wheeler also edited and contributed to another publication produced "expressly" for the exposition, *Household Decoration,* which included an essay by Van Rensselaer entitled "The Development of American Homes." As such connections demonstrate, women were beginning to develop professional networks, not only with the common goal of furthering the arts and women's opportunities in artistic fields, but also with the ability to organize, publicize, and fund projects national in scope.[25]

Along with the increase in women's educational opportunities and social organizations came a growing insistence on achieving political equality, both inside and outside the home. The women's rights advocate Charlotte Perkins Gilman created new architectural spaces for women in her essays and fiction. In *Women and Economics* (1899), Gilman describes a kitchenless apartment house in New York City for women with families. Most concerned with consolidating housework and childcare duties, and thereby giving women the freedom for other activities, Gilman is hesitant to imagine the plan such an apartment might take. She writes, "No detailed prophecy can be made of the precise forms which would ultimately prove most useful and pleasant; but the growing social need is for the specializing of the industries practiced in the home and for the proper mechanical provision for them."[26] Little did Gilman know that, in another part of New York City, the architects Mary Gannon and Alice Hands were designing the first hotel for and by women.

It seems likely that Gilman's hopes for social reform were bolstered by time spent living at Hull-House, a Chicago settlement organization, during the 1890s. Hull-House was founded in 1889 by Jane Addams and Helen Gates Starr in an attempt to create better living conditions in Chicago slums. The complex of buildings provided unmarried women a place to live and work. Although ostensibly a refuge for poor women and their families, Hull-House offered training in the decorative arts that led to the establishment of the Chicago Society of Arts and Crafts, inspiring "cities and towns across the nation" to organize similar groups for the improvement of American industrial arts.[27] Addams and Starr focused on social reform, but, as they improved urban slum conditions, they also created a community of female professionals. Hull-House brought together the principles behind the decorative arts movement, domestic science, and Gilman's more radical ideas about the most beneficial architectural designs for communities of women.

Gilman's radical essays and Hull-House's society for women, although influential, were on the fringe of acceptable social practice. Such efforts were viewed as utopian, the work of a left-wing minority whose outspoken politics and humanitarian schemes had little effect on upper-class society. The writings of Edith Wharton (1862–1937) and a handful of other women provided the upper class with a more comfortable forum for considering architectural themes and the changing roles of nineteenth-century women. Whereas Gilman remained imprisoned by the stereotype of the female politician (and related in the public mind, as well as by family, to the stalwart spinster Catharine Beecher), Wharton was one of an elite social circle that included Henry James and the architect Charles F. McKim. Gilman and the Hull-House group could be written off as utopians, but Wharton was accepted as a lady of discernment. Her first book, *The Decoration of Houses* (1897), written with the architect Ogden Codman Jr., conveys a society woman's perception of good taste, appropriately devoted to architectural interiors. In 1902, Wharton put her principles to use in the design of her own house, The Mount, in Lenox, Massachusetts, and in its landscaping, which was a collaboration with her niece, the landscape architect Beatrix Farrand. Wharton's expertise in design was recognized by *Century Magazine,* which commissioned her to write a series of articles on Italian gardens, later published as *Italian Villas and Their Gardens* (1904). But it is in her novels that Wharton rivals Gilman in her sensitivity about the boundaries enclosing women's freedom. *The House of Mirth* (1905) chronicles the descent of a "fallen" woman, Lily Bart, through a succession of increasingly dilapidated accommodations. Wharton manages to describe the architecture of society in an acceptable manner, while exposing the bitter side to those perceptive enough to see it.

Practicing women architects first wrote for publication in the last decade of the nineteenth century and responded to public curiosity about their involvement in the profession as much as to the state of American architecture. Louise Bethune's article "Women and Architecture" (1891) and Minerva Nichols's comments on the Columbian Exposition's Woman's Building (1893) brought additional legitimacy to their claims as architects.[28] By writing and speaking to popular audiences about their experiences in the profession, Bethune and Nichols spread the word of a new career opportunity for women. In a series entitled "Talks by Successful Women," a writer for *Godey's Magazine* interviewed Mary Gannon and Alice Hands, who had recently established the nation's first firm of female architects.[29] Now others interested in such work might search for a way to emulate Nichols, Bethune, and the other "girl architects." For most, advancement would logically begin with an appropriate educational program, and several options were available.

IIIIIIIIIIIIIIIIIIIIIIIII
Educating American Women in the Design Professions
IIIIIIIIIIIIIIIIIIIIIIIII

The first women architectural designers, like the first male builders, did not consider themselves professional architects. They acquired knowledge from architectural histories, pattern books, and practical experience, but most had little technical training. One of the earliest accounts of a woman overseeing architectural design appears in an English journal, the *Foreign Quarterly Review,* in 1831. After speculating on reasons for the lack of women architects, the author footnotes an exception to his argument, "the example of a lady of rank, whose devoted application to, and proficiency in the study of architecture, form an exception to our rule." He goes on to praise the contribution of Lady Stafford, Francis Henrietta Jerningham, to the renovations of Costessey Hall in Windsor during the 1820s. Like other elite women of her day, Lady

Stafford probably achieved her "proficiency" through reading and observation, rather than any sort of professional training or apprenticeship. Her rank and wealth contributed to her unusual influence. Whatever her role in designing the building, Jerningham remains only a footnote and a reminder that similar work performed by less prestigious women will probably never be known.

In America, the earliest female designers had deep religious or ideological convictions that inspired them to take on traditional male roles. Mother Joseph (1823–1902), a Catholic missionary, is known as the designer of more than twenty-five religious structures throughout the Northwest (fig. 9). She became the one in a community of women to execute architectural designs and oversee building construction. There was no one else as capable to do the job. Martha McWhirter (1827–1904), a member of a self-supporting commonwealth founded in 1866, designed the group's Central Hotel in Belton, Texas. She and other members of the Woman's Commonwealth, which practiced feminism and celibacy, also designed their own homes in the early 1880s. A generation later, the visionary Alice Constance Austin put ideals before professional architectural aspirations in her effort to build a socialist city during World War I. Her "kitchenless houses" in Llano del Rio, California, were intended to make living easier for everybody. Many more women probably served as the architects for other social and religious groups, but such work is rarely known since the intention was to fulfill a community need rather than to serve a client. For example, an 1882 biographical dictionary makes brief mention of Harriet E. Warner, who designed Lake Geneva Seminary in Wisconsin for her mother, its president. Warner's opportunity may have been another case of a woman's taking on a typically masculine role by default.[30]

Women did not become actively involved in the architectural profession until the second half of the nineteenth century, in large part because there were few educational opportunities available to them before the 1870s. Literary women like Beecher and Tuthill were taught in female seminaries, often surrounded by intellectuals and books, but they were expected to be satisfied with a secure home life. Without access to a university education or the business network of architects' offices and clients, even the most gifted woman could not join the architectural profession. By the 1870s, this situation had begun to change. A woman interested in becoming an architect had several alternatives to pursue her chosen career: she could apprentice to an architect (if one would take her on); she could enroll in an architectural program at one of the land-grant colleges, the coeducational institutions established on federal land grants under the 1862 Morrill Act; or she could hope to obtain suitable training at a design or mechanical arts school. Many successful early

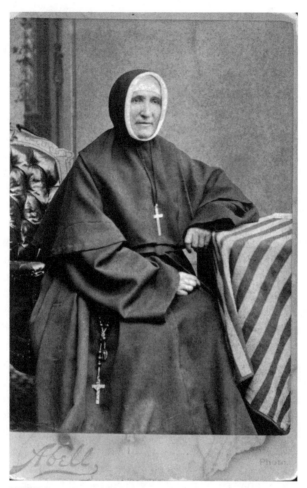

FIGURE 9. Mother Joseph of the Sacred Heart. Photograph by Frank G. Abell, ca. 1882. Courtesy Providence Archives, Seattle.

female architects received their education by combining several of these new possibilities, such as taking classes while working in an office or, if funds were available, paying for lessons from private tutors.

The development of the design school movement roughly paralleled the growth and organization of America's architectural profession and the educational system that groomed potential architects for its ranks. Future male architects were receiving training as apprentices in American architectural firms early in the nineteenth century, a time when such practical education was still primarily in the hands of carpenters and builders. During the late 1840s, Richard Morris Hunt went abroad to find suitable instruction at the famous Ecole des Beaux-Arts in Paris. The American Institute of Architects, the first professional organization for architects in the United States, was not founded until 1857. Even in the early 1860s, Henry Hobson Richardson had no choice but to finish his architectural education at the Ecole.

A profession so recently established by men was not eager to accept women. The system for training drafters was well in place, but it was a man's world, and the crucial network of professional contacts did not extend outside the office. Future women architects entered firms (and studios or ateliers) as apprentices only once land-grant colleges were open to them, although attending such institutions was not a prerequisite. After 1900, some women still chose the traditional apprenticeship over an academic degree in the field.

Since the 1850s, design schools had been an option for women interested in art-related careers, but such institutions did not prepare students to become architects until the late nineteenth century.[31] Sarah Worthington King Peter founded the Philadelphia School of Design for Women in 1848, and by 1860 similar schools had been established in Boston, New York, Pittsburgh, and Cincinnati. The patrons and administrators of the schools had different motives for training women to become industrial designers. The Philadelphia school was founded, in part, with the philanthropic intent of employing destitute women and bolstering American manufactures. In Boston, Ednah Cheney, cofounder of the New England School of Design for Women, stressed the importance of giving middle-class women a worthy means of supporting themselves. If the schools did not always emphasize individual creativity, the design school movement did provide new opportunities for women to interact in the public world of business and technology; many design school graduates were employed by publishers, carpet manufacturers, and textile factories. The schools also caused groups of upper-class women, both intellectuals and philanthropists, to organize and promote a movement intended to benefit their sex. Ednah Cheney became an officer of the New England Woman's Club, formed in 1868, and began a horticultural school for women in 1870. Although design schools flourishing at this time provided women with new skills and markets for their services, potential women architects found advancement difficult, and those in search of a career requiring drawing ability were often forced to satisfy themselves with traditional occupations—such as designing wallpaper patterns, etching, or decorating ceramics.

Despite the emphasis on craft and interior decoration, design schools offered some instruction to women over twenty years before universities first did so, and eventually this included better instruction in drawing and drafting, at least in Philadelphia and New York. The Franklin Institute Drawing School, which had sponsored the Philadelphia School of Design for Women from 1850 until it incorporated independently in 1853, began to accept female students in its previously all-male drawing classes in 1870. Elizabeth and Caroline Shreve, students at the Franklin Institute Drawing School in the winter of 1870, were followed by a steady enrollment of women, including that of Minerva Parker Nichols, who became Philadelphia's most accomplished nineteenth-century female architect. The design school movement's legacy included the opening of the New York School of Applied Design for Women in 1892. Like its predecessors, the school offered degrees in illustration, pattern making, painting, and other arts; however, the new school also provided instruction for women interested in becoming architectural drafters, a position "which at present men only perform."[32] The architectural course was taught by recognized local professionals, such as Austin W. Lord of McKim, Mead, and White, and jurors in competitions included Professor William Ware of Columbia College and Barr Ferree, an editor of *Engineering Magazine*. For the first time, women students had access to a network of experienced practitioners (fig. 10).

FIGURE 10. Drawing by M. Katherine Lines while a student at the New England School of Applied Design for Women, 1896. Courtesy Avery Architectural and Fine Arts Library, Columbia University.

During their two years of training at the New York School of Design for Women, Mary Gannon and Alice Hands received numerous awards for individual drawings, won a competition for a $40,000 hospital in San Francisco, and received second prize for their Woman's Building design at the Cotton States International Exposition in Atlanta.[33] Within just two years, the school could boast of educating the first women "in the country to have their work hung on the line with the men's at the Architectural League," as well as the first female members of the Sketch Club.[34] Upon Gannon's graduation, Austin Lord provided her with a recommendation attesting to her ability at producing measured drawings and drawings in pen and ink. The practical training received at the school proved sufficient preparation for launching women into professional architectural practice. In 1894, Gannon and Hands opened an office in the school building and became the first partnership of female architects in America. Three years later, the firm of Gannon and Hands would collaborate with the firm of Lord, Hewlett, and Hull.[35]

Gannon and Hands were not without female colleagues who had received academic degrees in the field of architectural design. During the 1870s the newly founded architecture schools of Cornell University (1871), Syracuse University (1871), and the University of Illinois (1873) were open to female students. Mary L. Page received a certificate in architecture from the University of Illinois in 1878 and a B.S. in architecture in 1879, becoming the first woman to graduate from architecture school; Margaret Hicks, who earned her A.B. at Cornell in 1878, graduated with a B.S. from the University in 1880. Despite this promising start, women did not begin graduating from architectural schools in numbers until the early twentieth century (fig. 11).

The country's oldest school of architecture, MIT, popularly known as "The Tech," was founded in 1865 but did not admit female architectural students until 1885. Anne Graham Rockfellow became the first woman to graduate from MIT's two-year architectural program in 1887. Lois Howe completed the same program three years later, and her classmate, Sophia Hayden, earned a four-year degree in architecture. Thesis records indicate that by 1900 twelve women had graduated with architectural degrees from the school. In fact, many more had gained their education as special students, who took a limited number of courses but did not submit a thesis. With its superb location in Back Bay Boston, MIT quickly became the most exciting educational option for aspiring female architects. By 1930, Louise Hall could reminisce on her experience in a class with fourteen women who found role models in Eliza Newkirk Rogers and Mary Almy, both MIT alumnae and respected local architects eager to hire students each summer.[36] No other

Students and Faculty of the Architectural Dept. U.of M. April 30-14

FIGURE 11. Architectural students at the University of Michigan, 1914. Courtesy Bentley Historical Library, University of Michigan.

university offered young women students the chance to share their experience with female peers and, more important, to find work after graduation.

The first school devoted exclusively to educating women architects and landscape architects—the Cambridge School of Domestic Architecture and Landscape Architecture—evolved from a persistent student's interest in the subject and the effort of dedicated Harvard professors. In 1915, Katherine Brooks, a Radcliffe College student, decided she wanted to become a "landscape gardener" and sought admission to the Harvard School of Landscape Architecture (fig. 12). When told it was closed to women, Brooks met with the head of the school, Professor James Sturgis Pray. He arranged for Henry Atherton Frost, a design professor, to tutor her in her home. The drafting course in Brooks's parents' living room lasted only a few months. By February 1916, Frost was teaching Brooks and four other female students from his offices in the Brattle Building at Harvard Square. Frost's partner, the landscape

FIGURE 12. Katherine Norcross, a Cambridge School student, ca. 1915. Courtesy Sophia Smith Collection, Smith College Archives.

architect Bremer Pond, also taught in the makeshift school for women. Word of the new program spread quickly, and by the 1916–17 academic year formal announcements were sent out advertising an official course of study.[37]

Cambridge School students benefited from the high standards set by its professors, who taught the same curriculum presented to Harvard graduate students (fig. 13). The Cambridge School women became acquainted with the real business of architecture at the offices of Frost and Pond; they received instruction and sometimes even contributed to the firm's design projects. The first recipients of the three-year degree certificate were the school's "founder," Katherine Brooks, and Rose Greely, who would have a distinguished career as an architect and landscape architect in Washington, D.C. Among the 1920 graduates were Mary P. Cunningham, a future professor of architecture at Smith, and Eleanor Raymond, a successful residential architect. After completing the school program, some graduates found work in local offices, usually through connections made at the Frost and Pond firm. One member of the 1920 graduating class, Laura Cox, became an associate in the office of Frost and Raymond and worked for the firm for at least five

FIGURE 13. Cambridge School students with a tripod. Courtesy Sophia Smith Collection, Smith College Archives.

years. During the early 1930s, she designed the Richard Lennihan house and an office building for the Hamilton Woolen Company, both in Southbridge, Massachusetts. Alumna records indicate that Cambridge School architects formed partnerships and actively sought and hired graduates of their school. Eleanor Raymond worked with Ethel Power, and Mary P. Cunningham, who had a private practice in Boston, took on Edith V. Cochran, a Cambridge

School graduate, as an associate. By 1930 two landscape architects, Margaret Henderson (Mrs. Earle Baillie) and Anne Baker, had found work in association with Beatrix Farrand. In the early 1930s, both Faith Bemis and Anita Rathbun were employed by the New York firm Cross and Cross, which was in the midst of designing the General Electric Tower (1931) and the City Bank Farmers Trust Building (1932).[38]

The Cambridge School of Architecture and Landscape Architecture, as it came to be known after many subtle name changes, was affiliated with Smith College in 1934 and became the college's Graduate School of Architecture and Landscape Architecture. Although Harvard faculty remained divided on the issue of coeducation, World War II forced the university to consolidate its resources, initially by combining the Graduate School of Design summer school with Smith College's graduate architectural program in 1940. Finally, in a further effort to cut costs during the summer of 1942, the Graduate School of Design was opened to female college graduates.[39]

||||||||||||||||||||||||||

Early Professional Opportunities for Women Architects

||||||||||||||||||||||||||

Beginning with the 1876 Centennial Exposition in Philadelphia, women discovered unusual design opportunities at expositions, where traditional boundaries were extended to include what might otherwise be considered of little value. These events became extraordinarily popular as a means of demonstrating national progress, and both contemporary accounts and recent historical studies mention the role women played in displaying native talent in these venues. A wide range of work was exhibited, from figures carved from butter to mechanical inventions. In such settings, the achievements of female artists and architects were deemed worthy of special recognition. For example, Mary Nolan of Missouri exhibited the Nolanum, a prototype house of interlocking bricks.[40] Students from the Women's Art School at Cooper Union, the Lowell School of Design at MIT, the Pittsburgh School of Design, and the Cincinnati School of Design all presented work at the Centennial Exposition.

The women's exhibits were originally supposed to appear in the Main Building but an unexpected deluge of entries from foreign countries filled the space. Elizabeth Duane Gillespie, the head of the Woman's Centennial Committee, was told that she would have to fund and build her own structure. With support from women throughout the country, Gillespie raised enough money to hire Hermann J. Schwarzmann, the architect of the Main Building. In her memoir, *A Book of Remembrance,* Gillespie expressed deep regret for the oversight, recalling that "we never thought of employing a woman architect! And thus made our first great mistake. . . . I left home, promising to return in early September, when the plans would be ready for inspection. I had not been gone many days before I heard the praises sung of a woman architect in Boston, and I wished I could annul the contract with Mr. Schwarzmann. To this hour I feel pained, because I fear we hindered this legitimate branch of women's work instead of helping it."[41] So troubled was Mrs. Gillespie that she mentioned the name of the architect, "Miss Kimball of Lowell," in her *Final Report of the Women's Centennial Executive Committee* in 1877. Emma F. Kimball earned her livelihood as a drafter during the 1870s in Lowell, Massachusetts, and was listed as a "draftist" from 1874 to 1876 in the Lowell City Directory.

During the late 1880s, excitement began to build at the prospect of a world's fair on American soil, and several cities—Philadelphia, New York, Chicago, St. Louis, and Washington, D.C., —sought support for hosting the celebration. After a year of hard lobbying, Chicago emerged the winner of a heated battle ultimately determined by Congress. The city would be the site of the World's Columbian Exposition, marking the four-hundredth anniversary of the arrival of Columbus in the New World. The elite women of Chicago were influential in obtaining the fair, and during the process they formed two groups representing very different perspectives of women in American society. The Woman's Department or Auxiliary Executive Committee (later the Board of Lady Managers) hoped to further the interests of women as philanthropists and educators. Many of its members were active in public service, and they planned to build a woman's building to exhibit the contributions of women and to have an assembly promoting charitable work. A second group, the Queen Isabella Society, formed in 1889 to further the political interests of women. The Isabellas, as they came to be known, included a majority of doctors, lawyers, and other professionals. They were suffragists who planned to use the fair as a way of promoting equal rights for women. According to the Isabellas, Queen Isabella of Castille was the figure responsible for Columbus's voyage and therefore an appropriate symbol of the fair and women's equality. The group planned to commission a statue of the queen and a woman's pavilion with a clubhouse for international conventions. The Woman's Department and the Isabella Society had united in fighting to have the fair in Chicago, but once they had won that battle, the two became rivals in choosing how to represent women at the exposition.[42]

In terms of architecture, the two groups had needs that required very different programs, and their conflict would manifest itself in architectural style as well as in their choice of architect. The members of the Woman's Department wanted a separate building devoted to women, an exhibition hall in which they could display all of the contributions women had made to the betterment of humanity. In contrast, the Isabellas imagined a statue erected in a prominent location on the fair grounds and a building that represented women's inclusion in society and the fight for equal rights. Both buildings would feature space for meetings—the former to host conferences on social reform and the latter to galvanize women fighting for suffrage. This split between the influential women of Chicago, a microcosm of that in American society, was reflected in the architectural commission. The Isabella Society was an independent group with private funds, and in 1891 it hired the professional architect Minerva Parker Nichols to design a pavilion in the Moorish style, in imitation of the Alhambra, the burial place of Queen Isabella. Harriet Hosmer, the country's foremost female sculptor, would design the statue of Queen Isabella.[43] Although the Isabellas fought persistently for their aims, they were no match for Bertha Palmer, chairman of the Board of Lady Managers. Palmer's fair committee was a well-established group with a tradition of philanthropic work dating back many generations; they considered it progressive for women to work for reform, and it was in this tradition that they began to garner support for a separate Woman's Building and a competition for the commission among women architects.

In March 1891, thirteen women who considered themselves trained in architecture submitted entries for the Woman's Building. Drawings were received from at least two practicing architects, Lois Lilley Howe of the Boston architectural firm Allen and Kenway, and Minerva Parker Nichols, whose entry was actually her design for the Isabella Pavilion submitted by a fellow club member. The list did not include the most prominent female architect of her day, Louise Blanchard Bethune. A successful professional in Buffalo and an AIA member, Bethune made a point of not joining the contest. In her 1891 article "Women and Architecture," written for the *Inland Architect and News Record,* she voiced her disgust at the competition for the Woman's Building and the pathetic remuneration offered. As Bethune explained, the male architects were not only appointed to their commissions but received ten times the monetary compensation. While other female architects jumped at any chance to design a building, Bethune saw that women would not be well served in the future by settling for less than the treatment accorded male professionals. In her words, it "is an unfortunate precedent to establish just now, and it may take years to live down its effects."[44] Although Bethune restrained herself from entering a political debate, she clearly favored equal rights for all involved.

The Woman's Building competition was won by Sophia Hayden, a recent MIT graduate, who submitted a finely rendered Renaissance design that blended perfectly with the classical architecture of the fair (figs. 14, 15). Throughout its conception, design, and construction, the Woman's Building was featured in national architectural magazines. For the first time, women architects were discussed in a lively public forum and the two most accom-

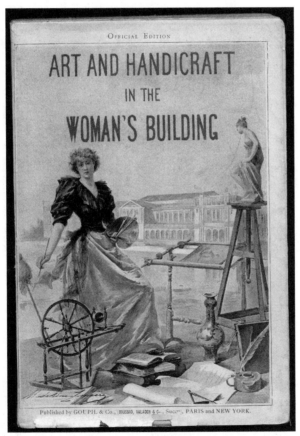

FIGURE 14. Title Page of *Art and Handicraft in the Woman's Building of the World's Columbian Exposition,* edited by Maud Howe Elliott (Chicago, 1894). Courtesy International Archive of Women in Architecture.

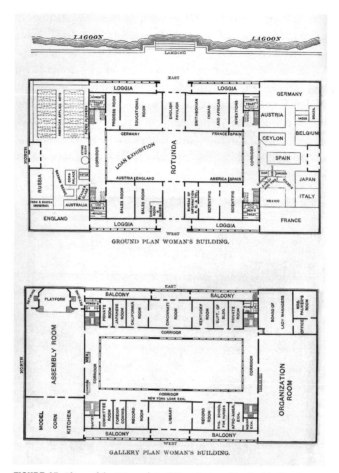

FIGURE 15. Plans of the Woman's Building, designed by Sophia Hayden. From *Art and Handicraft in the Woman's Building of the World's Columbian Exposition,* edited by Maud Howe Elliott (Chicago, 1894). Courtesy Sophia Smith Collection, Smith College.

plished, Louise Bethune and Minerva Nichols, both contributed their views to major periodicals. Even more attention was paid to the building and its architect after Hayden suffered a nervous breakdown during the construction process. Many of her peers questioned the ability of women to withstand the rigors of architectural design. Hayden's gender was the quality under examination, not the fact that she was the youngest, least experienced designer on the site or that she was continually harassed by the Board of Lady

Managers. Despite the doubt cast on women architects, *American Architect and Building News* defended Hayden by criticizing the managers for pressuring her to incorporate a motley assortment of state contributions, such as a carved door from Wisconsin and grillwork from Michigan, whether or not they enhanced the classical design. The magazine accused the managers of forgetting "what was due to the architect as an architect," a criticism that might well have been leveled against the competition as a whole.[45] There is no doubt that the fierce controversy between the Board of Lady Managers and the Isabella Society added to the pressures on Hayden and to Bertha Palmer's desire to emerge with a successful product.

All controversy aside, the Columbian Exposition set the precedent for a Woman's Building at the Cotton States and International Exposition held in Atlanta two years later. The Woman's Department of that exposition raised fifteen thousand dollars for the building and sponsored a national competition in search of a talented female designer. Elise Mecur, a Pittsburgh architect with over six years of experience, won the commission. The entry by the New York firm Gannon and Hands was one of that office's earliest efforts, for which it received second prize.

The Columbian Exposition and the politics surrounding its Woman's Building also paved the way for women to begin designing structures not exclusively devoted to their sex. After reading about the competition for a New England States Building at the upcoming Pan-American Exposition (1901) in Buffalo, Josephine Wright Chapman devised a strategy to win the commission. She developed drawings and plans of a colonial building and unveiled her design at a meeting of the New England Commission, which consisted of the six state governors who served as the jury for the competition. The governors were so impressed with her presentation that they awarded her the commission the next day.

If expositions gave women architects publicity, they were tainted by an aura of unreality. By the turn of the century, more and more women were finding that higher education gave them access to new opportunities. Now women without male relatives or friends in the profession could decide to become architects, assuming they could pay for the education. Julia Morgan was the only woman in the engineering department at the University of California, Berkeley, in 1894 and graduated from the Ecole des Beaux-Arts eight years later. Other women who had received training in Parisian ateliers by the early twentieth century include Katharine Cotheal Budd, Mary Rockwell Hook, Fay Kellogg, Anna Pendleton Schenck, and Verna Cook Shipway. Although these college-educated women were still virtually alone as females in the profession, a growing number had some experience with fellow female students and other networks of accomplished women. They sometimes found support through membership in women's clubs or business organizations, and occasionally through female patrons with the power to commission a new building.

There is evidence that more women architects were beginning to join others with their talents by the early twentieth century. Julia Morgan opened her own practice in 1904 and by 1927 her staff of fourteen included six women. Ida Annah Ryan and Florence Luscomb, classmates at the Tech (MIT), opened up shop in 1907. The office of Lois Howe and Eleanor Manning began in 1913 and added Mary Almy in 1926. Anna Pendleton Schenck and Marcia Mead enjoyed a brief partnership in New York, from 1912 until Schenck's death in 1915. As women began to form professional networks, they also made the first efforts to gather together in larger groups. The founding of the Association for Women in Architecture (AWA) dates to 1915, when a group of female students at Washington University in St. Louis founded the predecessor of Alpha Alpha Gamma, a sorority for students of architecture and landscape architecture that eventually had chapters in several states. One of its founders, Mae Steinmesch, became president of the national organization in 1928.[46] In 1920, the *Michigansian,* the yearbook of the University of Michigan, featured a photograph of the T-Square Society, a club for female engineering and architecture students established in 1915 (fig. 16). In the words of one member, Bertha Yerex Whitman, the T-Square Society was formed "to help make up for the lack of social relationships with the other women on campus, prevented by the nature of their work."[47] A new group for women architects in Chicago was begun by Elisabeth Martini in 1921. The Chicago Drafting Club appears to have been the core of a second organization launched seven years later, the Women's Architectural Club of Chicago. Two former T-Square Society members, Whitman and Juliet Peddle, were among its nine founding members. The Women's Architectural Club of Chicago was inspired by the 1927 Women's World's Fair, which featured architectural work and provided opportunities for networking among colleagues. In a memoir, Whitman recalls that the Woman's Architectural Club held exhibitions in the library and social hall of Perkins, Fellows, and Hamilton, the firm where both women were employed.[48] Members of the firm assisted the club in many other ways, including lecturing. The Women's Architectural Club remained active until the 1940s, when it became part of the Chicago chapter of the AIA and was reduced to an organization for members' wives.

FIGURE 16. T-Square Society, photo from the University of Michigan yearbook, the *Michigensian*, 1920. Top row, left to right, Isabel M. Wolfstein, Helen R. Pipp, Bertha Yerex, Delight Sweney, Ruth H. Perkins; bottom row, left to right, Lawrence Sims, Lalah E. Van Sickle, Helen A. Smith, Juliet A. Peddle. Courtesy Bentley Historical Library, University of Michigan.

|||||||||||||||||||||||||
Progress in the Profession after 1920
|||||||||||||||||||||||||

Women entering the architectural profession in 1920 faced a set of prospects and held attitudes that were very different from those of the women who preceded them, even those with graduate degrees. Following the pioneering work of architects like Louise Bethune, Minerva Nichols, and Josephine Wright Chapman, a new generation of women established themselves in offices and private practice. The firm of Howe and Manning in Boston had designed hundreds of buildings by 1920 and was receiving commissions throughout the region. Howe and Manning were mentors for MIT students like Florence Ward Stiles, a 1922 MIT graduate who worked in the office until 1931, when she became the librarian of MIT's architecture library and president of the institute's woman's association. Stiles continued her architectural practice and was involved in planning the expansion of the University of Massachusetts at Amherst from 1958 to 1967. Ida Annah Ryan also hired aspiring MIT architects for summer work in her Waltham firm, as did Eliza Newkirk Rogers, a Wellesley College graduate with a thriving regional practice. During the midtwenties, the Canadian architect Esther Marjorie Hill was able to find work in the offices of two New York architects, Marcia Mead (1923–24) and Katharine C. Budd (1925–28). In San Diego, Hazel Wood Waterman hired Lilian Rice as a drafter shortly after her graduation from Berkeley in 1910. Once Rice opened her own office, she hired another Berkeley graduate, Olive Chadeayne, who worked for her during the 1920s before going on to have her own successful practice.

In her 1977 article "A Distinguished Generation of Women Architects in California," Harriet Rochlin explains that the 1920s was an exceptional time for women architects in California for a variety of reasons, including enthusiasm for the women's rights movement, a coeducation system, plentiful work, and the development of a new, regional architecture.[49] At a national level, there is evidence that women architects were no longer considered extraordinary. In 1927, Ethel Bailey Furman, a designer with over ten years' experience, attended the Negro Contractors' Conference at the Hampton Institute (fig. 17). The 1928 publication "Women in Architecture and Landscape Architecture," written by one of the founders of the Cambridge School, was optimistic about women's prospects as architects and landscape architects, noting that "women are already busily engaged in doing good professional work and they are likely to continue in increasing numbers as years go by."[50] During the 1920s and 30s, work by women architects appeared in professional journals adjacent to that of their male peers without condescension or differentiation. A 1930 article in the *Architectural Record,* "The Place of the Apartment in the Modern Community," included buildings designed by Nelle Peters and Lilian Rice, alongside plans by Pleitsch and Price and apartments by Giulio Levy. In 1937, one *New York Times* reporter wrote that "for the last two decades the sight of a woman climbing the scaffolding of a half-completed house has been no novelty."[51] Of course, the presence of female architects varied by region. An architect working in Boston or New York might consider herself surrounded by role models, while her contemporary in the South or Midwest would most likely be singled out as the only woman in her field. However, one might expect that even Helen Butterfield in Michigan or Leila Ross Wilburn in Georgia would have heard of other successful women architects on the West Coast and in New England. Every reader of *American Architect and Building News* was exposed to the work of female practitioners.

By the early 1920s, aspiring female architects were also encouraged by other women professionals in fields that did not involve creating buildings but influenced design in other ways. For example, Theodora Kimball Hubbard (1897–1935), librarian of the Harvard School of Design, had a reputation as

FIGURE 17. Ethel Bailey Furman at the Negro Contractors' Conference, Hampton Institute, 1927. Photograph by Cheyne's Studio, Hampton. Courtesy Library of Virginia, Richmond.

one of the most prominent scholars of urban planning and landscape architecture history. Greta Gray (1880–1961) graduated from MIT in architecture in 1901 and worked as an architect for about nine years. She then embarked on a career in home economics and eventually chaired the Department of Home Economics at UCLA. The author of an important textbook, *House and Home* (1926), Gray emphasized the importance of high-quality housing and design at a national level. Edith Elmer Wood (1870–1945), a housing reformer, performed surveys of urban slum conditions, wrote *The Housing of the Unskilled Wage Earner* (1919), and served as head of a national housing committee. Wood's work to improve low-income housing helped to set national public-housing standards with the passage of the Wagner-Steagall Act in 1937. City planners like Elisabeth Herlihy (1880–1953), the secretary of the Boston City Planning Commission and a future member of the American

City Planning Institute, and Harlean James (1877–1969), executive secretary of the American Civic Association, played active roles in urban planning at the state and national levels.[52]

If the situation for women architects was looking brighter after 1920, finding employment in an office was still difficult. Bertha Yerex Whitman, the first female graduate in architecture from the University of Michigan, struggled to find her entry position as a drafter. Following the advice of Professor Emil Lorch, the dean of the school and an advisor who had been discouraging about her prospects, she moved to Chicago in the hope of landing a job. After looking for a couple of weeks, Whitman applied for work at a department store, and although she was hired, she left in frustration after just one day. Whitman recalled that some well-known Chicago architects "flatly refused" to grant her an interview. Once Whitman expanded her job search beyond the Chicago Loop, however, she eventually found the firm that hired her—Perkins, Fellows, and Hamilton. Whitman looked back on her experience with great fondness, beginning with the "magnificently staffed" office, which was "completely self-sufficient." During this early period, she was one of three women who worked in the office fulltime; the others appear to have been stenographers.[53]

Whitman flourished at Perkins, Fellows, and Hamilton, becoming "a really magnificent draftsman" and receiving a raise after Hamilton studied one of her completed sketches. Her experience could not have been better. "This office was like a large family. Everyone was friendly and we socialized even with the partners. I had the most intense education conceivable. I worked with every person. A two million dollar school involves a lot of engineering and I was permitted to work with every engineer." Her opportunities were the same as those of any male drafter, though she chose not to compare herself, declaring instead, simply, "there was nothing I wasn't allowed to do." Whitman's account of her life as a drafter confirms the experience shared by many women architects; once they were employed and allowed to prove themselves, they were accepted as professional equals.[54]

Professor Lorch appears to have been correct in assuming that Chicago could provide a suitable training ground for eager women architects. Alberta Pfeiffer, a talented graduate of the University of Illinois architectural program, found employment in the office of the Chicago firm Tallmadge and Watson in 1923 and immediately began proving herself. On her first day of work, Pfeiffer was sent to measure the basement of St. James Church, a "dusty, coal-furnace heated, dark place," as a test of her ability to perform any task for the firm. She "succeeded, with no lunch, to come back to the office with a sooty face, and hands, and a suit that had to be cleaned." Pfeiffer must have enjoyed her experience at Tallmadge and Watson because after a year with the firm she returned to the University of Illinois for graduate school. In 1925, she moved to New York to work for Harrie T. Lindeberg, a well-known residential architect. When she arrived, a place was made for her to work in the library, where she would be a safe distance from the rough atmosphere of the drafting room. Her isolation did not last long, however, and she soon became a full member of the office. Pfeiffer was responsible for drafting some of Lindeberg's most successful housing plans, which were later published in *Domestic Architecture of H. T. Lindeberg* (1940).[55]

Like Whitman and Pfeiffer, Mary Ann Crawford found herself accepted by her male peers after she had proven her dedication to the profession. Crawford began her studies at the University of Illinois in 1919, but an illness forced her to withdraw after a year, and she finally completed her education at MIT in the late 1920s. In a later interview, when questioned about the treatment she received as an architect, Crawford expressed few complaints. Her fellow students were friendly and the professors encouraging. One of her stories suggests that Crawford was ready for more difficulties than she encountered. In accordance with the Beaux-Arts method of instruction, MIT students were presented with an assignment—such as designing an entrance to an architectural school—and told to draw a small sketch by the end of the day. Sometimes these sketches would be expanded during the next week or two before a finished rendering was submitted. Whether they lasted one day or several weeks, these "problems" were usually judged by a group of professors, who gave criticism and determined who passed. During Crawford's first studio critique, one of the professors warned her not to "do too much on your drawing," because "people will think you know more than you should." Crawford "thought it was the way they talked" to her because of her sex and decided that it was the kind of treatment she was "going to have to contend with." It wasn't until much later that she was told by a fellow student that the professor thought she might have cheated by having an upperclassman help with the project. When questioned about whether her employers ever complained about her performance or restricted her in any way, Crawford denied any mistreatment. She worked for several architectural and engineering firms in Chicago and Arizona, as well as on her own, but could not recall having difficulties related to her gender.[56]

The professional experiences of Whitman, Pfeiffer, and Crawford were undoubtedly exceptional; the three were very talented women who succeeded among an unknown number who failed to advance in their chosen profession.

If unusual, however, their accounts indicate a growing acceptance of women architects during the 1920s. Architects of this decade had more educational options, professional role models, and career opportunities, but the biggest difference between female practitioners of the 1920s and their predecessors was that they finally received the right to vote. During the decades leading up to World War II, hundreds of women became architects, and several went on to have successful careers in modern architectural firms of the postwar era. One of the most impressive female architects of her generation, Olive Tjaden (1905?–1997), graduated from Cornell University in 1925 and designed more than two thousand buildings in her career as an architect in New York. Tjaden played a major role in the development of Garden City, Long Island, during the 1930s and early 40s, and then moved to Florida in 1945 to take advantage of intense residential growth in that region. Another extraordinary woman architect, Georgina Pope Yeatman (1902–82), graduated from MIT in 1925 and, beginning in May 1928, worked for the Philadelphia firm Bissell and Sinkler. Although the firm had established itself over twenty years earlier and had a successful history, it was struggling in 1933. Bissell and Sinkler decided to turn over the firm to Yeatman, who continued the office as her private practice. In January 1936, Yeatman began a four-year term as director of the Department of City Architecture for the City of Philadelphia. One of the greatest success stories belongs to Victorine Homsey (1900–1998), who went into partnership with her husband, Samuel, to start a major firm in 1935. Victorine and Samuel Homsey, Architects, specialized in domestic architecture, schools, and theaters in the 1940s and 50s. Homsey Architects, Inc., is still a thriving firm in Wilmington, Delaware.

The postwar years would prove to be productive for many of the architects established before the war, particularly in terms of residential design, but it was a difficult and discouraging time for aspiring female architects to enter the profession. The social pressure for women to remain home—the prejudice against their joining the work force—impeded their progress in the architectural field. Today, professors and architectural professionals continue to speculate about why women remain such a minority in the field, and what can be done to encourage their advancement. This book documents the presence and contributions of the first American women architects in the hope that knowledge of their past might inspire future achievement.

BIOGRAPHICAL ENTRIES

|||||||||||||||||||||||||||||
Adams, Ruth Maxon (1883–1970)
|||||||||||||||||||||||||||||

The only child of a Yale professor, Ruth Maxon Adams grew up in New Haven in the university's stimulating intellectual and architectural environment. During her youth and early adulthood, Adams traveled to England in the company of her father, the medieval historian George Burton Adams, and admired the work of William Morris, founder of the Arts and Crafts movement. When she graduated from Vassar in 1904, Adams had no plans for a career in architecture. Six years later, after enrolling in the New York School of Applied Design for Women, she imagined a future in interior decoration. Commissions for the remodeling of several Vassar College buildings in 1914 led to exciting opportunities for Adams. In 1915, she decided to open her own interior design firm in New York City.

During her first year of private practice, Adams received a commission to design a house for two Vassar professors, Edith Fahnestock and Rose Peebles. Over the next four decades she would design at least six Vassar residences in popular domestic styles, ranging from adaptations of medieval English and Tudor to neoclassical. A design consultant for Vassar until 1942, Adams compiled annual inventories of all the college buildings.

Beginning in 1921, Adams became the architect for the community of Yelping Hill in West Cornwall, Connecticut, a summer retreat in the Berkshires established by six families with ties to Yale and Vassar. Founding residents included Henry Noble MacCracken, president of Vassar, and Henry Seidel Canby, editor of the *Saturday Review*. Adams not only designed all the community residences at Yelping Hill, but also played a major role in planning the site and supervising construction. The houses were without kitchens—meals were taken in a communal dining room—and childcare was provided. Such domestic innovations have caused modern scholars to consider Adams's designs an expression of feminist ideology.

Despite her success as an architect, Adams did not promote herself as such. She is listed in the 1920–21 city directory of New York as an interior decorator and signed her house plans "designer," rather than architect.

Partial List of Buildings

1915	Edith Fahnestock and Rose Peebles House, 129 College Ave., Poughkeepsie, N.Y.
1920s	Yelping Hill Community, West Cornwall, Conn.; Henry Noble MacCracken House (1922); Mason Trowbridge House, "the Gingerbread House"; Henry S. Canby houses, "the Canby Cottages"; Ruth Maxon Adams House, "Cliffhouse"
1922	Violet Barbour House, 166 College Ave., Poughkeepsie
1936	Dean's House, Vassar College, 172 College Ave., Poughkeepsie
1950	Barbara Swain House, 39 Ferris Ln., Poughkeepsie
ca. 1968	Ruth Maxon Adams House, "the Roadhouse," West Cornwall, Conn.

Sources

Blake, Clarence. "Miss Ruth Adams." *Cornwall Journal,* March 19, 1970.
Halpern, Phyllis. "Ruth Adams '04: Architect Rediscovered." *Vassar Quarterly* 74 (Fall 1977): 17.

Hayden, Dolores. *The Grand Domestic Revolution.* Cambridge, Mass.: MIT Press, 1981. See esp. 261–63.

"Ruth Maxon Adams." Profile in Vassar College Encyclopedia, online at http://vcencyclopedia.vassar.edu/index.php/Ruth_Adams (accessed October 8, 2007).

LOCATION OF PAPERS. Correspondence and other materials relating to Adams's school years are in the Vassar College archives, Poughkeepsie, New York. Records of the founding of the Yelping Hill Community and its early buildings are in the Yelping Hill Association Archives, West Cornwall, Conn.

||||||||||||||||||||||||||
Almy, Mary (1883–1967)
||||||||||||||||||||||||||

Mary Almy grew up in Cambridge, Massachusetts, and graduated from Radcliffe College in 1905. A childhood victim of polio who walked with crutches, Almy taught at local private schools and developed an interest in architecture. Her family encouraged her to design and build a summer house for them on Cape Cod before she began formal architectural studies at MIT in 1917. Three years later, having submitted an office building design as her thesis, Almy graduated with a bachelor of science degree. After graduation, Almy spent two years working as a drafter for the London firm of Collcut and Hamp. During the early 1920s, she became a drafter for the firm of Lois Howe and Eleanor Manning, fellow MIT graduates who had an established architectural office in Boston. In 1926 she became a member of the AIA and a partner of Howe and Manning. The firm of Howe, Manning, and Almy survived much of the Depression, finally closing its doors in 1937 with the retirement of Lois Howe. Both Manning and Almy remained in private practice, the latter working with the landscape architect Henrietta Pope.

According to her biographers, Doris Cole and Karen Cord Taylor, Mary Almy was the firm's "generalist." She had natural drawing and mathematical abilities and was a perfectionist when it came to drafting. Almy's role in the firm included managing the business aspects as well as participating in architectural design and landscape planning.

List of Buildings

The biographical entry on Lois Howe includes a list of works by the firm of Howe, Manning, and Almy.

Sources

Cole, Doris, and Karen Cord Taylor. *The Lady Architects: Lois Lilley Howe, Eleanor Manning and Mary Almy, 1893–1937.* New York: Midmarch Press, 1990.

"Mary Almy." In *American Women, 1935–1940,* edited by Durwood Howes, 17. Detroit: Gale, 1981.

"Mary Almy's Membership to be Voted Upon, Boston Chapter." *AIA Journal* 14 (August 1926): 371.

Morse, Gail. "The Firm: A Study of the First Women's Architectural Firm in Boston: Howe, Manning, and Almy." B.A. thesis, Boston University, 1979.

LOCATION OF PAPERS. The Manuscript Collection, Institute Archives and Special Collections, MIT, holds the Howe, Manning, and Almy Papers, 1883–1973. The Almy family papers are in the Schlesinger Library, Radcliffe College.

|||||||||||||||||||||||||
Barney, Nora Stanton Blatch (1883–1971)
|||||||||||||||||||||||||

Nora Blatch Barney is remembered as the first female member of the American Society of Civil Engineers, but her career included architecture. Born Nora Stanton Blatch in Basingstoke, England, Barney was the daughter of an English brewer and, on her mother's side, granddaughter of Elizabeth Cady Stanton. The Blatch family moved to New York City in the 1890s and Nora was enrolled in the Horace Mann School. She entered Cornell in 1901 and graduated four years later as the first woman to earn a civil engineering degree. For the next two years she worked as a drafter for the American Bridge Company and the New York City Board of Water Supply.

After an unsuccessful marriage that ended before 1910, Nora Blatch worked for several years as assistant engineer and chief drafter for the Radley Steel Construction Company and as an assistant engineer for the New York Public Service Commission. In 1914 she became an architect and developer on Long Island. During this time, she was increasingly involved in the fight for woman suffrage and edited the *Woman's Political World,* the journal of the Women's Political Union.

Blatch married Morgan Barney, a naval architect, in 1919. After the birth of two children, she returned to a career in real estate development, this time in Greenwich, Connecticut. Although her contributions to civil engineering and woman suffrage seem to have overshadowed her architectural work, Barney is known to have designed dozens of residences on Long Island and in Greenwich, where she built her family's house in 1935. She remained an active developer until her death in 1971.

Writings by Barney

"Discussion on 'Works for the Purification of the Water Supply of Washington, D.C.'" *Transactions of the American Society of Civil Engineers* (December 1906): 400–408.
Life Sketch of Elizabeth Cady Stanton (1948). Pamphlet.
Women as Human Beings (1946). Pamphlet.

Sources

"Barney, Nora Stanton Blatch." In *Notable American Women: The Modern Period,* edited by Barbara Sicherman and Carol Hurd Green, 53–55. Cambridge, Mass.: Belknap Press of Harvard University Press, 1971.
Obituary. *Civil Engineering,* April 1971, 87.
Obituary. *New York Times,* January 20, 1971, 38.

|||||||||||||||||||||||
Bethune, Jennie Louise Blanchard (1856–1913)
|||||||||||||||||||||||

By the late 1880s, Louise Blanchard Bethune was not only a professional architect with a thriving practice, but the first female member of the American Institute of Architects. Born in 1856 in Waterloo, New York, Bethune was the only child of Dalson Wallace Blanchard and Emma Melona Blanchard, both educators. The family moved to Buffalo in 1866 and Jennie, as she was then known, enrolled in Buffalo High School, where she showed an early interest in architectural drawing. When she graduated in 1874, Bethune studied to enter the architecture program at Cornell, but ultimately chose apprenticeship, a more typical route into the profession. In 1876 she was lucky to find a position as apprentice drafter in the Buffalo office of Richard A. Waite (1848–1911) and F. W. Caulkings. Bethune worked long hours—from 8 A.M. to 6 P.M.—earning a small salary but gaining much in practical experience and benefiting from the use of her employers' architectural library. After five years as a drafter and Waite's assistant, Bethune felt prepared to open her own office. Her business expanded almost immediately when, in December 1881, she married a former coworker, Robert Armour Bethune and the office became R. A. and L. Bethune, Architects. The birth of the couple's only child, Charles W. Bethune, in 1883, appears to have had little impact on the firm's production. In 1890, William L. Fuchs was added to the firm, known in its later years as Bethune, Bethune, and Fuchs.

Bethune's office profited from a range of city building projects, including the expansion of the Buffalo school system, which brought in eighteen commissions alone (fig. 18). The firm was responsible for the Iroquois Door Company's plant on Exchange Street, the women's prison at the Erie County Penitentiary, grandstands for the Queen City Baseball and Amusement Company, and the transformer building for the first power line bringing electricity from Niagara Falls to the city trolley system. Bethune welcomed progressive building techniques and new materials, as illustrated by the firm's Denton, Cottier, and Daniels music store, one of the first structures built of steel frame construction with fire resistant concrete slabs. From 1898 to 1904, the

FIGURE 18. Public School no. 40, Buffalo, New York. Designed by the firm of R. A. and L. Bethune, Architects. Undated photo. Courtesy Buffalo and Erie County Historical Society.

firm worked on the Hotel Lafayette in Lafayette Square, Buffalo, a 225-room building in the French Renaissance style considered the cornerstone of her career (fig. 19). A million-dollar commission, the hotel was planned for the 1901 Pan-American Exposition but opened a few years too late. The majestic corniced block quickly became a local landmark worthy of picture postcards and is now on the National Register of Historic Places.

Bethune became a member of the Western Association of Architects in 1885 and immediately set to work organizing the Buffalo Society of Architects, a future AIA chapter. She was elected to the American Institute of Architects in 1888. The Western Association of Architects merged with the AIA in 1889, and Bethune became a Fellow of the AIA, along with the other Western Association members. Later in her career, she served as vice president of the Buffalo chapter of the AIA.

Insight into Bethune's thoughts about "women and architecture" can be gleaned from a talk she delivered on the subject to the Women's Educa-

FIGURE 19. Hotel Lafayette. Designed by Louise Bethune and constructed between 1898 and 1904 in preparation for the 1901 Pan-American Exposition, Buffalo, New York. Undated photo. Courtesy Buffalo and Erie County Historical Society.

tional and Industrial Union in Buffalo. Bethune considered herself a business woman, not a "professional agitator," and as such she demanded equal respect for her abilities and equal pay for her work. She wanted no special treatment. The architect demonstrated her philosophy in 1893, when she refused to participate in the country's most prominent opportunity for women architects, the design competition for the Woman's Building at the 1893 World's Columbian Exposition. Bethune declined because she felt that singling out the Woman's Building implied its inferiority and because the financial award for the winning female architect was a token $1,000 compared with the $10,000 awarded to male architects, all of whom were commissioned rather than forced to undergo the degradation of competition. As Bethune pointed out, the difference in remuneration was "an unfortunate precedent to establish."[1]

Bethune is remembered as the country's first professional woman architect and the first female member of the American Institute of Architects. The AIA has named a conference room in her honor and its Buffalo chapter placed a historic marker at her grave in the city's Forest Lawn Cemetery.

Partial List of Buildings

This list is based on a compilation of Bethune's works by Martin Wachadlo, "Louise Blanchard Bethune and Her Office, Partial List of Known Works, 1883–1897" (complete as of March 1996), ms. in the collection of the Buffalo and Erie County Public Library, Buffalo, N.Y. Unless noted otherwise, all buildings were in Buffalo.

1883	M. W. Tyler House, 39 Richmond Ave.
	R. K. Smither Store, 596 Niagara St.
	"Guard of Honor" Building, Washington St. near Chippewa St.
	Mrs. R. K. Noye House, "The Circle"
	G. W. Fields, stable, Delaware Pl.
	C. F. Bingham House, Seventh St.
1883–84	Public School No. 16, Utica and Masten Sts.
1884	Public School No. 17 (project competition)
1884–86	Public School No. 24, High St.
1885	Public School No. 8
	Spencer Kellogg House, 211 Summer St.
	Police Station, Broadway and Williamsville Rd.
	Police Station No. 11
	H. T. Koerner Factory, Lake View Ave.

H. G. Brooks House, alterations, Dunkirk, N.Y.

E. Webster and Son House and Stable, Prospect Ave.

G. N. Mitchell House, Prospect Ave.

A. A. Hickman House, 1268 Main St.

Dr. J. H. Potter House, Dearborn St.

Mrs. E. Baldauf House, Hodge Ave.

Mrs. John Pierce House, Hodge Ave.

Mrs. Davidson House, Ashland Ave.

George L. Thorn House, Elmwood Ave.

74th Regiment Armory and Drill Hall

Kellogg and McDaugall, factory building

Cossack and Co., factory building

Miss Reynolds House

Roger W. Graves House, 310 W. Utica St.

Michael Riley House, Prospect Ave.

John Druar House

1885–86   Public School No. 18, Vermont St.

George Waterman House, Albion, N.Y.

Police Station, Seneca and Babcock Sts.

1886   Homeopathic Hospital, additions, Twelfth St. and
Maryland St.

David S. Bennett, stable, Tracy St.

Mrs. M. B. Beemer stores, 145–149 Seneca St.

Plans and specifications for lightning rods, City of Buffalo

Public School No. 17, janitor's cottage, plans for graveling
yard

Buffalo Hammer Company, shops, Niagara St.

Odd Fellow's Hall, Victoria, Ontario, Canada

Peter Hoffman, millinery house, 197–201 Genesee St.

W. Guenther store, North St.

Mrs. Collignon House, Ellicott St.

Police Station No. 5, alterations, Niagara St.

Public School No. 31, Oneida St.

Police Station No. 8 and patrol barn, William and
Watson Sts.

White Brothers, livery stable, 13th St. between Pennsylvania
and Porter Sts.

William Lautz House, Dodge St.

George Bell House, Prospect Ave.

1886–87	Carl Lautz House, Dodge St.
	Abner Cutler House, Jewett Ave.
	Public School No. 40, Oneida St.
1887	Public Schools No. 38 and No. 40, ventilation work
	Public School No. 4, additions, Elk St. and Abbott Rd.
	Public School No. 20, additions
	Police patrol stables no. 6 and no. 7, alterations
1888	Volker and Felthausen Manufacturing Company, factory buildings, Black Rock, N.Y.
	Public School No. 33, additions, Elm St.
	Public School No. 26, Miller St.
1888–89	Kensington Episcopal Society, chapel, Shawnee St. and Marigold Ave., Kensington, N.Y.
1889	John C. Jewett Manufacturing, factory building, Black Rock, N.Y.
	Hamburg High School, Hamburg, N.Y. [unbuilt]
	John Robinson, six houses, 15th St.
	N. G. Benedict, apartment house, 319–321 14th St.
	C. R. Bard House, Allegheny, Pa.
	Miss Nisell House, alterations, 329 Porter Ave.
	C. J. Boehme House, Fargo Ave.
	M. J. Byrne, building, Connecticut St.
	L. B. Crocker House, Lake View, N.Y.
	W. J. Connors hotel
	Apartment house, Bridgeport, Conn.
	Philip Houck House, Genesee St.
	T. O'Brien, two houses, Genesee St.
	William Somerville Jr., veterinary stable, Franklin St.
	Michael Newell, block of stores, Broadway
	Miss Martin House, Bouck Ave.
	Mease and Snyder, storage building, Niagara St.
	Buffalo Baseball Club, grandstand and fence
1889–90	R. K. Smither, block of stores and flats, 590–592 Niagara St. at Jersey St.
	George W. Comstock House, 45 Lexington Ave.
	M. F. Warren House, 41 Lexington Ave.
	C. Lee Abell House, Lexington Ave.
	Mrs. Elizabeth Baldouf, block of stores and flats, Main St.
1890	Lockport Union High School, Lockport, N.Y.

East Aurora Bank, East Aurora, N.Y.

Mease and Snyder, Niagara storage warehouse enlargement,
Niagara St.

Ed Smith House and Store, Seneca and Exchange Sts.

Police Station No. 8, stable

1890–91   Erie County Penitentiary, extension, Pennsylvania Ave. at
5th

Livestock Exchange

1891   August Beck, business block, 186 Genesee St.

Joseph Leonard, stable, Elm St.

F. N. Trevor House, Lockport, N.Y.

Charles Whitmore House and Store, Lockport

Seven Sutherland Sisters House, Lockport

August Beck House, 330 Elm St.

Dr. Stockton House, 436 Franklin St.

Moore and Snyder, storage warehouse, adds., Maynard St.

Louise Bethune, remodeling of 5 houses, Huron St. between
Franklin and Pearl Sts. (future office)

1894–95   Samuel W. Wetmore House, 30 Woodlawn Ave.

1895   Fuchs Bros. theater, 515 Washington St.

Masten Park High School (competition project)

H. Messersmith House, 392 Summer St.

1897   Buffalo Savings Bank, Main, Huron and Genessee Sts.
(competition project)

1898   grandstands, Buffalo Baseball Association

J. A. Oaks Caterers, factory, Grote St. and Central

1899   Fred Jehle, grocery store and residence, 309 Bryant St.

1900   O. H. P. Champlin manufacturing, Ellicott St.

Stoddart Bros., druggists and surgical supplies, 86–88
Seneca St.

1901   Jacob Dold, wholesale meat packing, 145 E. Swan St.

1902   Buffalo Weaving Company, weaving mill, 234 Chandler St.

1902–4   Hotel Lafayette, 391–405 Washington St. (originally planned
for the Pan-American Exposition)

1903   Queen City Baseball and Amusement Company,
grandstands and additions, Offerman Stadium, East Ferry
and Michigan Sts.

1904   Iroquois Door Plant Company warehouse, 659 Exchange St.

1905   Wilson Building stores, 695–705 Main St.

Undated Buildings Attributed to Bethune

Springville High School [Old Griffith Institute], additions,
Springville, N.Y.

Morris Guske, merchant tailor manufactory, 192–196 Seneca
St., Buffalo

Cataract Power and Conduit Co., transformer building,
2280–2286 Niagara St., Buffalo

Bickford and Francis Building, leather belting and hose,
53–55 Exchange St., Buffalo

Hall and Sons, fire and common brick factory, 69
Tonawanda St., Black Rock, N.Y.

Bricka and Enos Building, house furnishers, 558–560
Genesee St., Buffalo

William H. Granger, grocery wholesale, 166–178 Michigan
Ave., Buffalo

Henry Bald, meat market and residence, 1762 Main St.,
Buffalo

Willman Estate, multiple dwellings and stores, 586–590
Washington and Chippewa Sts., Buffalo

Wile and Wile Bros. Company, wholesale clothing stores,
37–39 Pearl St., Buffalo

M. J. Byrne, Byrne and Bannister, contractors, 394 Fargo
Ave., Buffalo

Andrew Wieman, hats and caps store, 7 E. Genesee St.,
Buffalo

74th Regiment Armory (Elmwood Music Hall), Virginia St.
and Fremont Pl., Buffalo

Denton and Cottier Music Store, Court St., Buffalo

Police Station No. 2, 405 Seneca St., Buffalo

A. J. Meyer House, Buffalo

Buffalo Public Schools
  No. 9, 2060 Bailey Ave.
  No. 23, 891 East Delavan
  No. 30, South and Louisiana Sts.
  No. 39, 487 High St. at Johnson
  No. 48, 124 Edna Pl.
  No. 44, Miller St. and Broadway
  No. 52, Bird Ave. at Grant

Railroad Station, Black Rock, N.Y.

Writings by Bethune

"Influence of Women on Architecture." *American Architect and Building News* (January 1, 1893): 3–4.

"Women and Architecture." *Inland Architect and News Record* 17 (March 1891): 20–21; reprinted in *Inland Architect* 27 (July–August 1983): 46–47.

Sources

Barbasch, Adriana. "Louise Blanchard Bethune: The AIA Accepts Its First Woman Member." In *Architecture: A Place for Women,* edited by Ellen Perry Berkeley, 15–25. Washington, D.C.: Smithsonian Institution Press, 1989.

"The Lafayette, A Fireproof Hotel." *Illustrated Buffalo Express,* May 29, 1904, 11.

"Louise Bethune." *Architectural Era* (August 1888): 149; (November 1888): 214; (August 1889): xiv, 286; (February 1890): 47; (March 1890): 64; (June 1890): 138.

"Louise Bethune." *National Cyclopedia of American Biography,* vol. 12, 9. New York: James T. White, 1904.

Paine, Judith. "Pioneer Women Architects." In *Women in American Architecture,* edited by Susana Torre, 54–69. New York: Whitney Library of Design, 1977.

Willard, Frances E., and Mary A. Livermore, eds. *A Woman of the Century.* Buffalo: Charles Wells Moulton, 1893. See esp. 80–81. Reprinted by Detroit: Gale Research Company, 1967.

Withey, Henry F., and Elsie R. Withey. *Biographical Dictionary of American Architects.* Los Angeles: Hennessey and Ingalls, 1970. 55.

"Women in Architecture: One Who Has Been Successful in it Talks to Other Women." *Buffalo Morning Express,* March 7, 1881, 6.

LOCATION OF PAPERS. The American Institute of Architecture Archives in Washington, D.C., has a file of articles on Bethune. Extensive research has been done on Bethune's architectural career, and scholars believe that her drawings, correspondence, and other personal papers have been destroyed.

IIIIIIIIIIIIIIIIIIIIIIIII
Bridgman, Lilian (1866–1948)
IIIIIIIIIIIIIIIIIIIIIII

Architecture was a second career for Lilian Bridgman, a native of Kansas who graduated from Kansas State Agricultural College with a science degree in 1888. Bridgman continued to pursue her scientific interests at the University of California, Berkeley, and graduated with a master's degree in 1893. She immediately found employment as a physics and chemistry instructor, teaching at several schools from 1893 to 1912, including the California School of Mechanical Arts. A woman of many talents, Bridgman published short stories and poems in popular journals and, in 1899, designed her own home near Blackberry Canyon in Berkeley (fig. 20). Bridgman's friend the architect Bernard Maybeck offered encouragement on this project and suggestions for providing the home with natural light, a feeling of the outdoors, and an adventurous lack of symmetry. The house features barn shingles and clapboards on the exterior, local redwood paneling inside, and built-in window seats that also served as beds for visitors. Although Maybeck has been acknowledged as the architect of the house, Bridgman executed the drawings and should be given credit for collaboration.

Inspired by her first attempt at architectural design, Bridgman became an architecture student at the University of California in 1912 and joined the school's Architectural Association. After three years of study, she became a licensed architect in the state of California. Following World War I, Bridgman received a major commission for an Italianate villa overlooking the bay, the Bioletti House, which included the design of prominent pieces of furniture. In 1923 a major fire in north Berkeley created new opportunities for local architects, and Bridgman advertised herself as available to meet clients by appointment at the local Whitecotton Hotel. One of her post-disaster

FIGURE 20. Lilian Bridgman in her studio, n.d. Courtesy Bancroft Library, University of California at Berkeley.

commissions was the reconstruction of the Davidson House on its original foundations. Bridgman used a chair back, purchased at the San Francisco waterfront direct from China, as a decorative window screen set into the front door.

Bridgman is credited with the design of at least fifteen houses, including two that are undated, the Millicent Shinn House in Niles, California, and the Dort House in North Berkeley. The list of attributed buildings below was developed by Bridgman's niece, Lillian Bridgman Davies, based on evidence provided by photographs, drawings, and local testimonies. In addition, Bridgman created several drawings for projects that were never executed, including a residential development for Junction City, Kansas; a Berkeley apartment building; and a three-story residence called Rediviva House.

Partial List of Buildings

1899–1900	Lilian Bridgman House, 1715 La Loma Ave., Berkeley, Calif. (with Bernard Maybeck)
1908	Lilian Bridgman Studio, 1715A La Loma Ave., Berkeley
1920	Professor and Mrs. F. T. Bioletti House, 2440 Martinez Ave., Berkeley
ca. 1920	Gompertz House, 1236 Bonita Ave., Berkeley
1922	Cannon House, 2629 La Vereda Ave. at Hilgard, Berkeley
1922–23	House, 1020 Cragmont, Berkeley
1923	Davidson House, 1404 LeRoy Ave., Berkeley
	Gunthorpe House, 2511 Hill Court, Berkeley
1924	Rear studio, 3132 Eton Ave., Berkeley
1925	Stephens House, Los Altos, Calif.
1931	Barker House, Cerrito St., Oakland, Calif.
ca. 1935	Wills House, Lafayette, California
1939	Bioletti House (2nd), 2661–2663 Le Conte Ave., Berkeley

Writings by Bridgman

"Lost Prairie." *Harper's Magazine,* ca. 1910.
"Spirit and Flesh." *Century Magazine,* ca. 1899.
"To a Wayfarer." *Harper's Magazine,* February 1906.

Sources

Lillian Bridgman Davies. *Lilian Bridgman Architect.* Berkeley, Calif.: Berkeley Architectural Heritage Association, 1983.

LOCATION OF PAPERS. The Bancroft Library of the University of California at Berkeley holds the Lilian Bridgman Papers, 1881–1977. This collection includes some of Bridgman's correspondence, writings, and architectural plans and sketches. The Lilian Bridgman Photograph Collection, ca. 1881–1940, is part of the Bancroft Library's California Heritage Collection and can be accessed online at http://bancroft.berkeley.edu/collections/calheritage.html (accessed September 21, 2007). The Lilian Bridgman Papers, 1899–1983, at the Smithsonian Institution's Archives of American Art is a small collection of photographs, property tax records, and receipts relating to Bridgman's work.

||||||||||||||||||||||||||
Brunson, Emma F. (1887–1980)
||||||||||||||||||||||||||

Little is known of Emma F. Gruetzke Brunson, a Minnesota architect who worked for fifteen years as a drafter for Augustus F. Gauger before opening her own firm in 1920. Brunson became a registered architect in 1921 in response to a new state registration requirement. Her practice was primarily residential and she worked independently until her retirement in 1968. Brunson died in St. Paul in 1980.

Partial List of Buildings

1923–24	Hugo Koch House, Osceola Ave., St. Paul, Minn.
1925	Emma Brunson House, Maryland St., St. Paul
1926	Theodore Maier House, 616 Gotzian St., St. Paul
	C. E. Smith House, 673 Nebraska Ave., St. Paul
n.d.	Dr. W. B. Stone House, Morton and Delaware Sts., St. Paul
	Harry Walsh House, Portland Ave. and Pascal St., St. Paul

LOCATION OF PAPERS. The Emma F. Brunson Papers, 1923–26, are held at the Northwest Architectural Archives, University of Minnesota, Minneapolis. The collection contains specifications and plans for about fifteen residences. The finding aid for the papers includes a brief biography that can be accessed at the University of Minnesota Libraries Manuscript Division Web site, http://special.lib.umn.edu/findaid/xml/naa123.xml (accessed September 21, 2007).

IIIIIIIIIIIIIIIIIIIIIIIII
Budd, Katharine Cotheal (1860–1951)
IIIIIIIIIIIIIIIIIIIIIIIII

In her 1924 application to the AIA, Katharine Cotheal Budd revealed that she had been in practice for thirty years, but details of her family background and early career are vague. Budd received private instruction from William R. Ware, an accomplished architect and professor at Columbia University, and spent time in a studio in Paris. She worked for several important American architects in her formative years, including Grosvenor Atterbury, the designer of the model suburb Forest Hills Gardens in Queens, and the firm of Grenville T. Snelling and William Potter. A 1910 letter by Snelling reveals that Budd was in charge of his office at one time, and that she had later entered a partnership with Henry G. Emery and worked with him for several years. During these early years, Budd was a prolific contributor to contemporary journals, including *Architectural Record, Country Life,* and *American Homes and Gardens.* As early as 1899, Budd advertised "general work" from her office at 18–20 West Thirty-fourth Street, New York City.

In 1916, Budd became the first female member of the New York chapter of the AIA. During World War I, she was given the commission to design YWCA-sponsored Hostess Houses in the South and Midwest. Along with Julia Morgan, who was assigned to the Pacific Coast, and Fay Kellogg, Budd was responsible for developing what her contemporaries described as a new type of architecture. The National War Council of the YWCA commissioned Budd and Morgan to design accommodations for the female relatives and friends of troops stationed at army camps throughout the country. Budd's first design, the Great Lakes Hostess House, was modeled after a seventeenth-century timber-fronted house in Chester, England, known as "God's Providence House." She went on to design or alter seventy-two of the ninety-six Hostess Houses constructed for the war effort. Her inspirations for the buildings' styles included the American barn, with attached porches instead of lean-tos, and the American country house, a central cube with two gables and two piazzas.

Budd was registered as a professional architect in Georgia in 1920, probably as a result of her work for the military. From 1925 to 1928 she engaged Marjorie Hill, the first women to receive an architectural degree in Canada, to work in her New York office.

Partial List of Buildings

1908	H. J. Burchell House, alterations, 29 E. 63rd St., N.Y.
n.d.	Anna Winegar studio, "Old Masterton barn" alterations, Bronxville, N.Y.
1918	YWCA National War Work Council Colored Hostess House, Fort Jackson, Columbia, S.C., among others including: YWCA National War Work Council Hostess House, Spartanburg, S.C. YWCA Hostess House, Charlotte, N.C. YWCA Hostess House, Camp Hanock, Augusta, Ga. YWCA Hostess House, Camp Mills, N.Y.
1925	Harry C. Duncan House, Tavares, Fla. (National Register, 1997) M. G. Howey House, Lake County, Fla. (National Register, 1983)

Writings by Budd

"The American Pantry." *Architectural Record* 18 (September 1905): 225–33.
"Japanese Houses" *Architectural Record* 19 (January 1906): 1–26.
"The Kitchen and Its Dependent Services—I. With Sketches by the Author." *Architectural Record* 23 (June 1908): 463–76.
"Saragossa." *Architectural Record* 19 (May 1906): 327–43.

Sources

Manufacturer's Record, June 20, 1918; August 8, 1918; October 31, 1918.
Moulton, Robert. "Housing for Women War Workers." *Architectural Record* 19 (November 1918), 424.
Ward, Estelle Frances. "Bringing Home to the Army Camps." *House Beautiful,* February 1919, 76–77.

LOCATION OF PAPERS. The American Institute of Architects Archives in Washington, D.C., has uncataloged papers relating to Budd's membership in the AIA.

||||||||||||||||||||||||||

Butterfield, Emily Helen (1884–1958)

||||||||||||||||||||||||||

Michigan's first licensed female architect, Emily Helen Butterfield, was born in Algonac, Michigan, and began her studies of art and architecture as a child.

Butterfield entered Syracuse University in 1903. She was a founding member of the sorority Alpha Gamma Delta, as well as the designer of the Alpha and Chi chapter houses and summer camp lodges for underprivileged children sponsored by the group. Butterfield graduated with an architectural degree in 1907 and received her architect's license the same year.

In a Syracuse University alumni form, Butterfield described herself as an architect and her position as "self-conducting." From 1915 to 1935 she practiced in partnership with her father, Wells D. Butterfield. The firm of Butterfield and Butterfield was responsible for twenty-six churches throughout Michigan, as well as schools, factories, and stores. The firm had an office in Pontiac, but Butterfield also worked from a Detroit studio. She became a member of the AIA in 1927.

A woman of many interests, Butterfield exhibited her watercolors and sketches at the J. L. Hudson Gallery in Detroit and the Toledo Arts Club in Ohio. She wrote a book on heraldry, worked for a fraternity jewelry company, and banded birds. In 1912 Butterfield became a founding member of the Detroit Business and Professional Woman's Club, the oldest such organization in the state. Although few details have been found relating to her firm, Butterfield appears to have been the primary architect of a flourishing practice. Near the end of her career, she wrote *The Young People's History of Architecture* (1933) and illustrated the book with one hundred eighty drawings from her travels. During World War II, Butterfield served as postmaster of Neebish Island, part of Michigan's upper peninsula, where she retired.

Partial List of Buildings

n.d.   Christ Community Church, Methodist, Inkster, Michigan

Writings by Butterfield

College Fraternity Heraldry. Menasha, Wis.: George Banta, 1931.
The Young People's History of Architecture. New York: Dodd, Mead, 1933.

Sources

"Emily H. Butterfield." In *American Women, 1935–1940*, edited by Durwood Howes, 136. Detroit: Gale, 1981.
"Emily H. Butterfield: Obituary." *Michigan Society of Architects Monthly Bulletin* 32 (May 1958): 4.

LOCATION OF PAPERS. Syracuse University Archives has some school records, alumna forms completed by Butterfield, and various unidentified newspaper clippings.

||||||||||||||||||||||||
Chapman, Josephine Wright (1867–1943)
||||||||||||||||||||||||

Josephine Wright Chapman was one of the most extraordinary women architects of her day. Without formal education, male relatives in the profession, or
encouragement from her family, Chapman became an accomplished designer
in Boston and New York. After leaving her childhood home in Fitchburg,
Massachusetts, Chapman pawned jewelry and clothing to support herself.
In 1892, she convinced Clarence H. Blackall, a Boston architect known for
his theater designs, to take her on as an apprentice with his firm, Blackall,
Clapp, and Whittemore. Blackall had received his education at the University
of Illinois and at the Ecole des Beaux-Arts in Paris; he was the first recipient
of the Rotch Traveling Scholarship for the study of European architecture and
became a member of many professional organizations. During Chapman's
five years with the office, she benefited from Blackall's expertise, experience
in public building design, and willingness to experiment with new materials. In 1893, the firm designed the first steel-frame structure in Boston, the
Carter Building.

When Chapman set up her own Boston office in a "women's artist col-
lective" called Grundman Studios in 1897, she was almost immediately commissioned by Harvard University to design the Craigie Arms dormitory.
While this work was in progress, Chapman also designed St. Mark's Episcopal
Church in Fitchburg, Massachusetts, a commission financed by a prominent
Fitchburg resident, Minerva C. Crocker. By the turn of the century, Chapman
employed five or six drafters in her office, including at least one woman.

In 1901, Chapman won a highly competitive design competition for the
New England States Building at the Pan-American Exposition in Buffalo,
New York. Inspired by her success, Chapman submitted an application to the
American Institute of Architects. Both the AIA and the Boston Architectural
Club refused to admit her, however, and it was not until she settled in New
York during the recession of 1907 that she was accepted by a professional
organization, the New York Society of Architects. After relocating to New
York City and opening an office in Washington Square, Chapman decided
to focus exclusively on residential design.

Over the next two decades, Chapman would design a wide range of
houses, from cottages to mansions, in popular styles of the day. Unlike women
who were pressured into concentrating on domestic architecture, Chapman
seems to have chosen this area because it needed improvement; she felt that
women architects could contribute a sensitivity towards clients' needs that

was lacking in the profession. In a 1914 interview with the *Ladies Home Journal,* she spoke of the "psychological relation between architect and client that cannot readily be expressed in words. In that relation I am generally able to divine just the sort of house that we will accomplish in the end—the owner and I."[2] At the Douglas Manor development on Long Island, a series of eight houses she designed for a community of successful artists, Chapman was able to put her domestic theories into action. She collaborated with a female builder, Alice Foster, on five of the residences. Today, the development remains distinctive for its well-planned, unique houses, as well as its excellent state of preservation.

In 1921, Chapman traveled to Europe to study architecture. The trip clearly influenced her final work, "Hillandale," a grand residence in the Italian style. Designed in 1923 for a Standard Oil heir, Anne Archbold, Hillandale was based on the Italian villas Archbold knew as a child. The thirty-four-room mansion, sited on seventy acres in Washington, D.C., is now on the National Register of Historic Places. Considering Chapman's shift to a residential focus midway through her career, Hillandale was a fitting conclusion to an exciting and productive professional life. As construction on the project ended in 1925, Chapman retired and moved to Paris. She died in Bath, England, in 1943.

Partial List of Buildings

1897	Craigie Arms, dormitory for Harvard University (now Chapman Arms apartments), 112 Mount Auburn St., Cambridge, Mass. (National Register)
ca. 1897	St. Mark's Episcopal Church, Fitchburg, Mass.
1901	New England States Building, Pan-American Exposition, Buffalo, N.Y.
1901–2	Worchester Woman's Club (now Tuckerman Hall) 10 Tuckerman St., Worchester, Mass. (National Register)
1903	Hayes-Saul House, Arlington, Mass.
1908	Alice Foster House, Kenmore Rd., Douglas Manor, Douglaston, Queens, N.Y.
1909	Women's Club, Lynn, Mass.
1912	A. B. Holmes House, Ridge Rd., Douglas Manor, Douglaston, Queens
1913	Alice Foster House, garage addition, n.p.
1916	Alice Foster, three houses, Grosvenor Ave., Douglas Manor, Douglaston, Queens

| 1917 | Daniel Combs House, Hillcrest Ave., Douglas Manor, Douglaston, Queens |
| 1922–25 | Anne Archbold House, "Hillandale," 3905 and 3907 Mansion Dr., N.W, Washington D.C. (National Register) |

Sources

American Architect and Building News 64 (April 15, 1899): 23, plate 1216.

American Architect and Building News 78 (December 27, 1902): 103, plate 1409.

Mullett, Mary B. "Women and the Pan-American." *Harper's Weekly,* August 1901, 782.

"Novel Apartment House Planned by Woman Architect." *Architect and Engineer* 49 (April 1917): 92.

Wolfe, Kevin. "Josephine Wright Chapman." *Metropolis,* July/August 1992, 17–22.

"Woman Architect Plans Apartment." *Southern Architect and Building News* 37 (October 1916): 36–37.

"The Woman's Club-house, Worcester, Massachusetts." *American Architect and Building News* 78 (December 27, 1902): 103, plate.

"A Woman Who Builds Homes." *Ladies Home Journal,* October 1914, 3.

|||||||||||||||||||||||||
Coit, Elisabeth (1892–1987)
|||||||||||||||||||||||||

A native of Winchester, Massachusetts, Elisabeth Coit attended three prominent schools—Radcliffe College (1909–11), Boston's Museum of Fine Arts
School (1911–13), and MIT, where she graduated with a B.S. in architecture
in 1919. After graduation she worked in the office of the New York architect
Grosvenor Atterbury, FAIA, as well as for Robert Coit, a relative who was an
architect. Elisabeth Coit became a registered architect in New York in 1926,
the year she opened her own practice, and an AIA member in 1929. She was
also a registered architect in New Jersey and Virginia. In 1932, Coit received a
"special mention" in the Better Homes in America competition for her design
of a small house plan, the residence of Miss Anna B. Van Nort of Croton
Heights, New York. The judges noted that Coit's work showed "domesticity
and real charm and fits its rugged site very well."[3]

Although best known for her work in low-income housing, Coit designed a cafeteria (fig. 21) and offices, as well as renovations and alterations
of existing buildings. Her firm gained considerable publicity when she became the first female recipient of the AIA's Langley Award, a funded research

FIGURE 21. Consumer's Cooperative Service, Inc., New York. Designed by Elisabeth Coit. Gottscho-Schleisner, Inc., photographer, 1939. Courtesy Library of Congress, Prints and Photographs Division.

scholarship that she held from 1938 to 1940. In the two years after the award, Coit wrote important articles based on her research describing the design of low-income units and the realities of tenant life. From 1942 to 1947, Coit served as architect and technical standards editor of *Public Housing Design*, the Federal Public Housing Authority publication, and consulted with the New York architectural firm Mayer and Whittlesey. In 1955, Coit became only the third female Fellow of the AIA. She was the New York City Housing Authority's principal planner from 1948 until she retired from practice in 1962. After her retirement, Coit continued her design work as a consultant on housing for federal and private clients and in 1968 became editor of the newsletter of the New York metropolitan chapter of the National Association of Housing and Redevelopment Officials.

In addition to her design practice, Coit was a well-known writer on architectural topics and served for several years as the book review editor for *Architectural Record*. A complete inventory of her writings has not yet been made.

Partial List of Buildings

1932	Anna B. Van Nort House, Croton Heights, N.Y.
ca. 1939	Cafeteria, Consumer's Cooperative Service, Inc., 136 E. 44th St., New York City.

ca. 1940   Philip Maguire House, Shrub Oak, N.Y.
n.d.   Winslow Sommaripa House, Boyce, Va.

Writings by Coit

"Housing from the Tenant's Viewpoint." *Architectural Record* 91 (April 1942): 71–84.
"Notes on the Design and Construction of the Dwelling Units for the Lower Income Family." *The Octagon* (October 1941): 10–30, and (November 1941): 7–22.
"A Plea for More Space." *CHPC Housing News* 9, no. 3 (January 1951): 3.
Report on Family Living in High Apartment Buildings. Washington, D.C.: Government Printing Office, 1965.
"Terra Cotta in Mantua, 1444 A.D." *Atlantic Terra Cotta* 7, no. 4 (some photos and drawings by Coit).

Sources

"Prize-Winning Home Plans Stress Compact Layouts." *New York Times,* February 26, 1933, RE1.
"A Thousand Women in Architecture." *Architectural Record* 103 (March 1948): 105–13; part 2, 103 (June 1948): 108–15.
Wright, Gwendolyn. "On the Fringe of the Profession: Women in American Architecture." In *The Architect: Chapters in the History of the Profession,* edited by Spiro Kostof, 300, 308. New York: Oxford University Press, 1977.

LOCATION OF PAPERS. The Elisabeth Coit Papers are in the Schlesinger Library, Radcliffe College. The collection includes architectural drawings and photographs of Coit's designs from 1925 to 1976, writings on housing from 1935 to 1969, and various personal papers such as photographs, clippings, and correspondence. Her Langley Award papers are in the AIA Archives, Washington, D.C.

|||||||||||||||||||||||||||
Colter, Mary Jane Elizabeth (1869–1958)
|||||||||||||||||||||||||||

Mary Jane Elizabeth Colter's adventures in the West began in 1887, when the seventeen-year-old left home in St. Paul, Minnesota, to attend the California School of Design in San Francisco. During high school, Colter had expressed interest in pursuing an artistic career, and when the death of her father left the family without a means of support, her mother allowed her to enroll in the design school. Upon returning to St. Paul with her degree, Colter was able to find a position teaching drawing and architecture at a state school in Menomonie, Wisconsin. The next year she found a job in her hometown and for the next fifteen years she taught freehand and mechanical drawing at Mechanic Arts High School. She also lectured on architecture at the University Extension School and participated in the Century Club lecture series in Minnesota and Iowa.

Although Colter's education prepared her for teaching—a proper occupation for a woman—it indirectly laid the foundation for an unusual career in architecture. As a student, Colter had apprenticed in an architect's office, gaining necessary practical experience to pass on to her classes at Mechanic Arts. She also established a network of friends on the West Coast. According to one source, Colter took a trip to San Francisco and visited a friend who worked in a Fred Harvey gift shop. Because Colter expressed interest in the popular hotel chain, the shop manager later sent her a telegram regarding a job with the company. A more recent Colter biography suggests that Minnie Harvey Huckel, Fred Harvey's daughter, knew about Colter's artistic achievements, encouraged her husband to hire her, and ultimately became her mentor and benefactor.[4]

In 1902, Mary Colter left home for the West again, this time headed to Albuquerque, New Mexico. Fred Harvey had opened an Indian department the year before, and Colter's job would be to decorate the Indian Building adjacent to the recently constructed Alvarado Hotel. This was a temporary summer position, but Colter would continue working for the Fred Harvey Company for the next forty years, as both interior decorator and architect. Fred Harvey followed the rapidly expanding Atchison, Topeka, and Santa Fe Railroad with a network of Harvey Houses, exploiting the tourist trade in this remote but increasingly popular part of the National Park system. When the Santa Fe Railroad bought a line to the South Rim of the Grand Canyon, Fred Harvey employed Colter to design an Indian building across from its luxury hotel, El Tovar. In the end, Colter would decorate El Tovar's cocktail lounge and open her Hopi House before the hotel was finished.

Thus far, Colter had worked on contract with Fred Harvey and returned to her teaching career upon completion of each project. Beginning in 1910, Colter was offered a permanent position with the company as architect and designer based in the Kansas City office but traveling to various sites in the Southwest. Most of her work centered around the Grand Canyon, where she was given freedom to design buildings in a mixture of Native American, medieval, and rustic styles evocative of a more romantic America. Colter's Lookout, Hermit's Rest, Phantom Ranch, and Bright Angel Lodge (fig. 22) were designed to give visitors a sense of adventure and respect for the canyon's history, as well as picturesque views. As interior decorator and architect,

FIGURE 22. Mary Colter (right) showing Bright Angel Lodge plans to Anna Thompson Ickes, wife of Secretary of the Interior Harold L. Ickes, c. 1935. Courtesy Grand Canyon National Park Museum Collection.

Colter created buildings that relied on artistic sensibility and furnishings to create a theatrical sense of the past complementary to the country's natural wonders. Colter's biographer Arnold Berke points out that her work influenced the National Park Service architect Herbert Maier, who was an important figure in establishing the rustic style for park buildings. Maier's Yavapai Point Observation Building (1928), east of Grand Canyon village, is clearly influenced by Colter, as are buildings in Oregon, Texas, and Arizona that were under his design supervision. Her buildings along the South Rim of the Grand Canyon are still appreciated as some of the finest examples of rustic Park Service architecture.

Colter began work on her first hotel for Fred Harvey, the El Navajo in Gallup, New Mexico, in 1916, but the war delayed its design and construction. From its origins, the hotel was without precedent. Unlike all but one Fred Harvey hotel, it featured a Native American style achieved through the imitation of local Navajo buildings and crafts, the observation of contemporary native life, and the incorporation of authentic objects. The building included "sand paintings," which were considered sacred and required a special native American ritual before the building could be opened. Even more unusual, El Navajo was described as a modern building by the architectural historian

David Gebhard, who commented on its "vertical grouping of windows, 'cub-istic' handling of walls and projecting balconies, the three-tasseled pairs of lights attached to the main block of the building, all of which were design motifs which had become the vocabulary of the early modern movements in European and American architecture."[5]

At the height of her career, Colter designed two buildings that represent the range of her work, La Posada (hotel) in Winslow, Arizona, and the Watch-tower on the rim of the Grand Canyon. In his 1964 article, Gebhard praises a group of Fred Harvey hotels, including the El Navajo, which superseded any definable style. It is especially significant, then, that Gebhard, one of the nation's premier architectural historians and the author of a catalog on the California architect Lutah Maria Riggs, failed to mention Colter in the article. But Colter was virtually unknown by the early 1960s, in part because her work was signed off by the Santa Fe Railroad's chief architect, E. A. Harrison. In contemporary newspaper and magazine articles, Colter was consistently referred to as the Harvey designer. She signed her work and business cor-respondence "Harvey architect and designer."[6]

In recent years, Mary Elizabeth Jane Colter has been the subject of sev-eral biographies, at least one film, and a National Public Radio series. The popular appeal of this colorful figure is obvious. Although recent books on Colter rediscover the importance of her work, no complete study has been made of her buildings in the context of American architectural history.

Partial List of Buildings

1905	Hopi House, Grand Canyon National Park (National Historic Landmark)
1914	Lookout, Grand Canyon National Park (NHL)
	Hermit's Rest, Grand Canyon National Park (NHL)
1922	Phantom Ranch, Grand Canyon National Park
1923	El Navajo Hotel, Gallup, N.M.
1930	La Posada Hotel, Winslow, Ariz. (National Register)
1932	Watchtower, Grand Canyon National Park (NHL)
1935	Bright Angel Lodge, Grand Canyon National Park (NHL)
1936	Men's Dormitory, Grand Canyon National Park
1937	Women's Dormitory, Grand Canyon National Park

Writings by Colter

Manual for Drivers and Guides Descriptive of the Indian Watchtower at Desert View and Its Relations, Architecturally, to the Prehistoric Ruins of the Southwest. Grand Canyon, Ariz.: Fred Harvey, 1933.

Sources

Berke, Arnold. *Mary Colter: Architect of the Southwest.* New York: Princeton Architectural Press, 2002.

Chappell, Gordon. "Railroad at the Rim: The Origin and Growth of Grand Canyon Village." *Journal of Arizona History* 17, no. 1 (1976): 89–107.

"El Navajo Hotel Reflects the Painted Desert." *Hotel Monthly* (July 1923): 40.

Gebhard, David. "Architecture and the Fred Harvey Houses." *New Mexican Architect* (January/February 1964): 18–25, and (July/August 1964): 11–17.

Grattan, Virginia L. *Mary Colter: Builder upon the Red Earth.* Flagstaff, Ariz.: Northland Press, 1980.

"Impressions of El Ortiz." *Santa Fe Magazine,* October 1910, 55.

"La Fonda, Tripled in Size Becomes Spanish Fairyland." *New Mexican,* May 1929, 2.

"Mary Colter." *Macmillan Encyclopedia of Architects,* vol. 1, 441–42. New York: Free Press, 1982.

"Mary Colter Dies Here." *New Mexican,* January 8, 1958, 2.

Tweed, William C., Laura E. Soulliere, and Henry G. Law. *National Park Service Rustic Architecture: 1916–1942.* San Francisco: National Park Service, 1977.

LOCATION OF PAPERS. Records on Colter and her buildings can be found in the following collections: Atchison, Topeka, and Santa Fe Railway Collection, Bancroft Library, University of California at Berkeley; Fred Harvey Collection, Hayden Papers, Arizona State University, Tempe; Fred Harvey Collection, Special Collections Library, University of Arizona, Tucson; Fred Harvey files, Fred Harvey, Chicago; Grand Canyon files, Western Regional Office Library, National Park Service, San Francisco; Painted Desert files, Western Regional Office Library, National Park Service, San Francisco; National Park Service Library, Grand Canyon, Arizona; National Park Service Library, Mesa Verde, Colorado; Heard Museum, Phoenix, Arizona (biographical sketch by Colter).

||||||||||||||||||||||||
Connor, Rose (1892–1970)
||||||||||||||||||||||||

Rose Connor was born in Des Moines, Iowa, and attended local public schools through eleventh grade, before beginning an educational quest that would take her throughout Europe and the United States. In 1912 she attended a printing institute in Paris and then the Municipal School of Art in Birmingham, England. After a few years she moved back to the states and enrolled in the New York School of Fine and Applied Arts, where she probably began her architectural education. By 1923, she was living in Los Angeles and working as a drafter for T. Beverly Keim Jr. She studied at the Pasadena Atelier from 1925 to 1930, and throughout her studies supported herself as a drafter. After leaving Keim's firm in 1926, she worked for many offices from 1926 to 1936, including Allen and Collens (Boston), Soule and Murphy (Santa Barbara), and three Los Angeles firms: Reginald D. Johnson, W. L. Risley, and Allison and Allison.

Connor opened her own office in Pasadena in October 1936, the year she received her license to practice architecture in California. Her business was primarily residential, and, with the exception of three years during World War II, she worked for herself until the early 1950s. Her wartime experience included working for the U.S. Army Corps of Engineers in Los Angeles from 1942 to 1945. She became a member of the AIA in 1944. Connor described her firm in an "AIA Architect's Roster Questionnaire" in 1953:

> My work has been almost entirely residential, with the exception of some work on schools and public buildings in order to obtain my certificate and, during the past two years, as Associate Architect on the Fuller Theological Seminary. From 1936 to 1942 all my work consisted of private houses, mostly for professional women. From 1946 to 1950 I specialized in small Housing Projects, 16 to 74 houses, and kept from two to four draftsmen very busy. Since then I have been busy on residential work for individual clients. Since October 1951, I have run a "one-man" office, taking only enough work to keep myself busy because it has been increasingly difficult to find good draftsmen. However, I enjoy working as an Associate Architect on larger projects.[7]

On the Fuller Theological Seminary project in Pasadena, California, Connor worked with the firm of Orr, Strange, and Inslee. Connor often employed the landscape architects Florence Yoch and Lucile Council, Pasadena, as consultants. She became an AIA member emeritus in 1965.

Partial List of Buildings

This list of buildings, all of them in California, was compiled by Connor when she responded to a 1953 "Architect's Roster" questionnaire sent out by the AIA. Connor noted that she had also undertaken various smaller jobs, additions, and alterations to several of her prewar houses (also in California).

1937	Beardsley House, Eagle Rock
1938	Hickman House, Los Angeles
	Ransome Beach House, Three Arch Bay
1939	Marshall Triplex, Los Angeles
1940	Fuller, two houses, South Pasadena
	Fuller House, Palm Springs

1941–47	Fuller, three houses, South Pasadena
1942	Caldwell House, Hollywood
1946–47	Sixty-three houses (Yardley), Lakewood
1947	Sturtevant House, Balboa
	Forty-seven houses (Yardley), Lakewood
1948	Twenty houses (Yardley), Lakewood
	Brown House, Laguna
1949	Forty houses, (Yardley), Lakewood
	Twenty houses (Sturtevant), Lakewood
	Seventy-four houses (Yardley), Downey
1950	Twenty houses (Yardley), Anaheim
	Brown-Mountain House, Seven Oaks
	Fuller House, Newport Beach
1951	Nineteen houses (Yardley), Downey
1952	Nightingale Mountain Cabin, Sky Forest
	Fuller House, San Marino
1952–53	Four apartments (White), Pasadena
	Fuller Theological Seminary, Pasadena

Sources

AIA membership files. Record Group 803, box 33, folder 17. AIA Archives, Washington, D.C. Includes "Architect's Roster" questionnaire.

"A Thousand Women in Architecture." *Architectural Record* 103, part 2 (June 1948): 111.

LOCATION OF PAPERS. The University Art Museum, University of California at Santa Barbara, has a collection of drawings by Rose Connor. The Schlesinger Library, Radcliffe College, has papers of the Union International des Femmes Architectes donated by Rose Connor.

||||||||||||||||||||||||||
Craig, Mary (1889–1964)
||||||||||||||||||||||||||

A native of Deadwood, South Dakota, Mary Craig made a significant contribution to California architecture without any formal training in design. She married James Osborne Craig and between 1914 and 1915, the couple moved to Santa Barbara in search of a cure for his health problems. Although James Craig never earned an architectural degree, he was responsible for popularizing the Spanish colonial revival style in Santa Barbara, first with the Bernard

Hoffman House (1917) and then with El Paseo, an idealized Spanish village designed for retail purposes.

When Craig died of tuberculosis in 1922, Mary took over his practice and continued to employ one of his best drafters, Ralph Armitage. Craig designed the Anacapa Annex section of El Paseo in the 1920s, as well as the arcade of the W. C. Logan Building and a group of cottages below Mission Santa Barbara known as Plaza Rubio.

Mary Craig's designs were characteristic of the Spanish revival; they were often built around courtyards and featured slanting roofs, wide chimneys, arches, and porticoes. For much of her career, Craig worked with Armitage as supervising architect, and the two were responsible for many Santa Barbara residences. Mary Osborne Craig Skewes-Cox recalled that her mother received several awards for her work, including a commendation for the Montecito Water District building. Skewes-Cox also remembered a white brick house in Beverly Hills designed for Jesse Lasky and designs for residences in Virginia and Washington, D.C.

Partial List of Buildings

ca. 1923	Jefferson Estate cottages, Montecito, Calif.
1925–26	Mrs. J. A. Andrews houses, Plaza Rubio, Santa Barbara, Calif.
1927–30	Dietrich House, "Casa Bienvenida," garden pavilion, Montecito
1928	Miley House, "El Prado," Montecito
1929	First Slater House, "Casa Aleli," Montecito
1930	Second Slater House, Montecito
ca. 1930	"Bellogia," house, Montecito
1932	Amy E. Dupont estate, "Dauneport," Wilmington, Del.
ca. 1937	Stephen Gates House, Solvang, Calif.
1953	Hayes House, Montecito
n.d.	Craig House, Montecito
	W. C. Logan Building, arcade, Santa Barbara
	G. T. Thomsen House, Montecito
	Lloyd House, Santa Barbara
	Prud'Homme House, Santa Barbara
	Harvey beach house, Santa Barbara
	Anacapa Annex, El Paseo, Santa Barbara
	Montecito Water District building, Montecito

Writings by Craig

"The Heritage of All California." *California Southland* 33 (September 1922): 7–9.

Sources

Andree, Herb, et al. *Santa Barbara Architecture*. 3rd ed. Santa Barbara, Calif.: Capra Press, 1995.

LOCATION OF PAPERS. The prints and photographs department of the Library of Congress has several drawings of Craig buildings available for reproduction through its online service. The Santa Barbara Historical Society has a brief biographical sketch of Craig written by her daughter in 1982 and a photographed drawing of the architect.

||||||||||||||||||||||||
Darling-Parlin, Maude (1885–1979)
||||||||||||||||||||||||

Born into a family of architects in Fall River, Massachusetts, Maude Darling-Parlin inherited the firm established by her grandfather, Joseph M. Darling, and her father, George. An excellent math student, Maude enrolled in the architecture program at MIT and designed "a community dining hall" for her thesis. After graduation in 1907, Darling-Parlin studied at the Pratt Institute in New York City. She married a fellow MIT architecture student, Raymond W. Parlin, in 1910. Evidently, Darling-Parlin thought about a career in teaching, but she was encouraged by her father to focus exclusively on architecture. In 1921, she joined the family firm. Within the next few years, Darling-Parlin and her brother, George S. Darling, took over the business and changed its name to Darling and Parlin. In 1924, Darling-Parlin's husband died and she was left with three children to raise. She appears to have been financially independent at this time, and there is little doubt that by the 1930s she was able to support the family. A devastating fire in 1928 burned much of downtown Fall River, giving the firm the opportunity to design many important new buildings, including the elegant Durfee Theater, with its dramatic lobby based on the Alhambra.

According to the National Park Service, which featured Darling-Parlin's work in a travel itinerary celebrating women's history, she "left behind a legacy of impressive buildings, theaters, churches and more than one hundred Fall River homes."[8] In addition to the Durfee Theater, Darling and Parlin designed the Rialto, Capitol, Bijou, Strand, Park, and Empire theaters. The firm of

Darling and Parlin played a major role not only in shaping the urban fabric of Fall River, but also in preserving the architectural history of the region. Maude Darling-Parlin worked to preserve the Luther Store in Swansea, now the Swansea Historical Society Museum; the Brayton and Jerathmael Bowers houses in Somerset; the Barnaby House in Assonet; and the Waite-Potter House in Westport, all in Massachusetts. In the 1930s, she worked on Works Progress Administration surveys of historical buildings. During World War II, she was employed by the War Department in Newport, Rhode Island, and helped design the navy base officers' club.

Partial List of Buildings (including undated Fall River buildings)

1916	Buffington Building, Fall River, Mass.
ca. 1929	Durfee Theater, Fall River (demolished 1973)
n.d.	Eagle Restaurant
	Welcome Home Arch (World War I)
	Baptist Temple
	Mills Building (R. A. McWhirr Co.)
	Sullivan Building
	Mohican Hotel
	Peoples Cooperative Bank
	First Baptist Church, Sunday School addition
	Adams House, Highland Ave., north wing addition
	Bristol County Agricultural School, dormitory
	Hector L. Belisle Elementary School, Clarkson St.
	Woman's Club of Fall River, 1542 Walnut St. (National Register)
	Temple Beth El, High St.
	Fall River Cooperative Bank
	Fall River Trust Company

Source

Durand, Kathleen. "Maude Parlin: Early Architect." *Herald News* (Fall River), March 14, 2004.

LOCATION OF PAPERS. The National Register of Historic Places includes a brief biography of Darling-Parlin in one of its travel itineraries, "Places Where Women Made History," which can be found on its Web site, http://www.nps.gov/history/nr/travel/pwwmh/ma73.htm (accessed September 21, 2007).

|||||||||||||||||||||||||
Deakin, Edna (1871–1946)
|||||||||||||||||||||||||

A Bay Area native, Edna Deakin was the daughter of a painter, Edwin Deakin, and the niece of an architect-businessman, Frederick H. Dakin (the two brothers spelled their surnames differently). Edna was a mechanics major at the University of California at Berkeley when she and her cousin, Clarence Dakin, dropped out of school to study architecture with John Galen Howard, a Berkeley professor and the campus architect. After her "apprenticeship," Deakin worked as a drafter for prominent local firms such as Dickey and Reed, C. W. Dickey, and George T. Plowman. Deakin advertised herself as a "designer," using her home address, and also collaborated with Clarence. Both architects are mentioned as practicing during the construction of the Studio Building in Berkeley, a mansard-roofed tiled structure built by Frederick Dakin in 1905 for his investment and mining company. The design of the building may have been a family affair. In the wake of the 1906 earthquake, Frederick Dakin also commissioned a company warehouse, which was constructed using his own "Dakin White Hollow Building Blocks."

After a fire in 1923, Edna and Clarence collaborated on a redesign of the "Temple of Wings," the home of Charles C. and Florence Treadwell Boynton on Buena Vista Way. Originally designed by Bernard Maybeck and A. Randolph Monroe, the structure was based on the Boyntons' ideas of healthy outdoor living. The "cousin architects" enclosed the structure, providing two living areas with ground-floor dance studios on either side of an open courtyard. The building's original concrete Corinthian columns had survived the fire and were incorporated into the remodel. Further details of Edna and Clarence's collaborative work and the extent to which they contributed to their fathers' designs are unknown.

Design of the apartment house on the family property at Telegraph and Woolsey in Berkeley has been attributed to Edna Deakin.

Partial List of Buildings

1934   Charles C. Boynton House, "Temple of the Wings," remodel
             with Clarence Dakin, 2800 Buena Vista Way, Berkeley

Sources

Marvin, Betty. *The Residential Work in Berkeley of Five Women Architects*. Berkeley, Calif.: Berkeley Architectural Heritage Association, 1984.

|||||||||||||||||||||||||
Dozier, Henrietta Cuttino (1872–1947)
|||||||||||||||||||||||||

In an oral history interview recorded for the Federal Writers' Project, Henrietta Dozier recalled wanting to study architecture from childhood and actually drawing plans since the age of seven. She graduated from high school in Atlanta, Georgia, and spent a year as an apprentice in an architect's office before attending Pratt Institute in Brooklyn for two years. In 1895, while a student at Pratt, Dozier sent an architectural model to the Cotton States and International Exposition in Atlanta. After this substantial preparation, Dozier entered MIT, completing a four-year architectural degree in 1899 and submitting a thesis entitled "A Palace for Receptions." Shortly after her graduation, Dozier began practicing architecture in Atlanta. She worked briefly with Walter T. Downing and from 1903 to 1910 shared office space in the Peters Building with George W. Laine. During this time, Dozier designed several residences and churches that helped to build her reputation as a dependable professional. Throughout her career, Dozier used various names that disguised her gender, going by "Cousin Harry," "Harry," and "H. C. Dozier."

In 1905, Dozier became the third female member of the AIA. The next year, she was one of six founding members of the Atlanta chapter of the AIA and later served two terms as secretary of the chapter. A delegate to the Eighth International Congress of Architects in Vienna in 1908, Dozier was active as an AIA board member, working to establish a registration requirement for architects in Georgia. By 1916 she had moved her practice to Jacksonville, Florida, where she designed the Federal Reserve Bank of Atlanta (1924) in association with the Atlanta architect A. Ten Eyck Brown (fig. 23). During the 1930s, Dozier served as one of the first delineators for the Historic American Building Survey (HABS), documenting buildings in St. Augustine and Tallahassee, Florida.

When Rose Shepherd of the Federal Writers Project interviewed Dozier in 1939, the architect was in her late sixties, supervising a busy office in a practice that was primarily residential. After losing her home in the Depression, Dozier had reopened her firm inspired to provide better low-cost housing and trusting in the common belief that women had an affinity for efficient, well-organized interior design. But Dozier's idea of good residential design was far from ordinary. At the end of the interview, Dozier described her "earth-rammed house," which would "catch on like wildfire—durable, vermin-proof, termite-proof, insulated against cold and heat from the outside, with an average expenditure cost of around $500.00 a room, compared

New Federal Reserve Bank, Jacksonville, Fla.

FIGURE 23. Federal Reserve Bank of Atlanta, Jacksonville, Florida, branch, Hogan and Church streets, postcard view, late 1920s. Designed by Henrietta Dozier in association with A. Ten Eyck Brown, 1924. Courtesy State Library and Archives of Florida.

with the present government cost of around $1,000 a unit, it will be Florida's own house and home, good for the constant use of two or three generations."[9] Dozier was a dynamic, idealistic character and a mentor for at least twenty-four aspiring architects, many of whom went on to work for major firms.

In 2006, Henrietta Dozier was still remembered in a popular restaurant, Henrietta's, at Ninth and Main Streets in Jacksonville, and in "The Dozier elevation and floor plan," offered by a local developer, SRG Homes and Neighborhoods, as among its elegant residential options. She would have seen the irony in both, with her preference for "Harry" and low-income housing.

Partial List of Buildings

1898   G. W. Gignilliat House, Seneca, S.C.
1902   John C. Cooper, Sr., House, Market and Duval Sts., Jacksonville, Fla.
        C. P. Cooper, three houses, Monroe St., Jacksonville
1903   All Saints Episcopal Church, chapel, W. Peachtree and North Ave., Atlanta, Ga. (burned 1906)
        St. Philips Episcopal Church, 801 N. Pearl St., Jacksonville

1909	John Blackmar House, alterations, Columbus, Ga.
n.d.	Southern Ruralist Building, Hunter St. (now Martin Luther King, Jr., Dr.), Atlanta
n.d.	Atlanta Bible School, 88 Cooper St., Atlanta
1924	Federal Reserve Bank of Atlanta, Jacksonville branch building, Hogan and Church Sts., Jacksonville (associate architect with A. Ten Eyck Brown)
1925	Welshan-Palmer House, Riverside, Jacksonville

Sources

Coleman, Kenneth, and C. Stephen Gurr, eds. *Dictionary of Georgia Biography.* Athens: University of Georgia Press, 1983.

"Henrietta Dozier (1872–1947)." New Georgia Encyclopedia, http://www .georgiaencyclopedia.org (accessed September 25, 2005).

"Henrietta C. Dozier." In *The South Carolina Architects, 1885–1935,* edited by John E. Wells and Robert E. Dalton, 42. Richmond, Va.: New South Architectural Press, 1992.

"Miss Henrietta C. Dozier, Architect." Interview by Rose Shepherd, March 10, 1939. Transcript on file in Archive of Women in Architecture, American Institute of Architects, Washington, D.C. American Life Histories: Manuscripts from the Federal Writers' Project, 1936–1940, Library of Congress, http://lcweb2.loc.gov/ammem/wpaintro/ index.html (accessed September 21, 2007).

Smith, Susan Hunter. "Women Architects in Atlanta, 1895–1979." *Atlanta Historical Journal* 23 (Winter 1979–80): 85–108.

LOCATION OF PAPERS. The Henrietta C. Dozier Papers are in the collection of the Haydon Burns Library, Jacksonville, Florida.

IIIIIIIIIIIIIIIIIIIIIIII
French, Helen Douglass (b. 1900)
IIIIIIIIIIIIIIIIIIIIIIII

Born in Arlington, Massachusetts, in 1900, Helen Douglass was one of the first graduates of the Cambridge School of Architecture and Landscape Architecture. She received her architectural degree in 1921, the year her future husband, Prentiss French, completed his degree at Harvard. Douglass worked as a drafter for the Boston architect Charles Loring from 1921 to 1925 and then spent a year with William Delano and Chester Aldrich. Her European travel from 1926 to 1927 included study at the Ecole des Beaux-Arts. Upon her return to the states in 1927, Douglass married French, a landscape architect, and the two may have collaborated on projects in Boston and Stockbridge. By the early 1930s, the Frenches were both working for the architect Clarence Martin in Sarasota, Florida. They moved to the Bay Area in 1946 and soon established themselves in a San Francisco office, where they would practice from 1947 to the 1960s. Although they collaborated on many residential projects, with Helen designing the buildings and Prentiss the landscape plans, they also worked independently on commissions throughout Northern California.

Helen French was a member of the Northern California chapter of the AIA and took an active role in civic affairs.

Partial List of Buildings (undated)

Proctor Place (Orelton Farm), Stockbridge, Mass.
Daniel Chester French Studio, remodel, Stockbridge
William S. Rosecrans House, "Hacienda del Gato," Indio, Calif.

Sources

"Helen Douglass French." In *Who Is Who on the Pacific Coast.* Chicago: A. N. Marquis 1949.

LOCATION OF PAPERS. The French (Helen D. and Prentiss) Collection, 1932–78, is part of the Environmental Design Archives at the University of California, Berkeley. The collection includes the couple's professional papers and project records, as well as Helen D. French's personal project records from 1936 to 1959.

||||||||||||||||||||||||||
Fritsch, Margaret Goodin (1899–1993)
||||||||||||||||||||||||||

The first licensed female architect in Oregon, Margaret Goodin Fritsch has been erroneously identified as the first woman architecture student to graduate from the University of Oregon. Born in Salem, Oregon, Goodin attended Willamett University for one year before enrolling in the university's pre-med program to please her father, who favored the profession of nursing for women. Fritsch struggled with chemistry and was encouraged by friends in the School of Architecture to change majors. Dean Ellis F. Lawrence repeatedly attempted to convince Fritsch to change to the fine arts department but eventually accepted her decision to remain in architecture. In an oral history on deposit at the Oregon Historical Society, Fritsch recalls a school of about forty "fellows," who were good friends, and she did not recollect any major problems as a female student. She received special dispensation to be out of her sorority house after hours, a requirement for completing Beaux-Arts studio projects in a timely fashion. Although university records show that two other women, Phoebe Elisabeth Gage Hayslip and Helene Kuykendall Deadman, belonged to the architecture class ahead of Fritsch, Fritsch makes no mention of female colleagues.

After graduation from the School of Architecture in 1923, Fritsch joined the firm of Houghtaling and Dougan as a drafter in 1924. The next year, she worked for Van Etten and Company, General Contractors, and then later that year found a position in the office of Morris H. Whitehouse and Associates. After this required three-year apprenticeship in the field, in 1926 Fritsch earned her license to practice architecture and immediately received her first commission, the Delta Delta Delta (Tri-Delt) sorority house at the University of Oregon. She described the building as a modified French design with "long" windows in the central block and with wings extending from the main house. Fritsch was elected the first female secretary of the State Board of Architectural Examiners in 1926 and served in this capacity until 1956.

Margaret met her future husband, Frederick Fritsch, at an AIA meeting in 1925. The two were married three years later. The couple traveled to Philadelphia in 1929 to seek medical advice for Frederick, who would later be diagnosed with an incurable illness. During this time, the Fritsches completed their only collaboration, the Tri-Delt House at the University of Pennsylvania. Margaret found additional employment with the architects Horace W. Castor and Georgina Pope Yeatman (1902–82). When the Fritsches returned to Portland in 1930, Margaret supported her husband, working for Jamieson Parker from 1932 to 1935 and opening her own office. Frederick committed suicide in 1934. Suffering from loneliness after the death of her husband, Margaret adopted an eleven-year-old girl in 1935. The next year, she was elected a member of the AIA.

Fritsch ran her own firm in Portland until 1956. She described her practice as residential, stating that her education had not prepared her for the design of large structures. Despite this comment, Fritsch never mentioned gender as a factor limiting her practice in any way. During World War II, she worked for the Portland Housing Authority, an experience that contributed to her interest in city planning. According to Fritsch, architecture was not fun after the war because everything was "stock," and custom work became impossibly expensive; without craftsmen and fine materials, she could no longer express herself through architecture. In 1957, Fritsch worked on a three-year project for the Alaska Housing Authority in Juneau and fell in love with the city. She became planning director of Juneau in 1963, retiring from the position in 1974. Fritsch described her Alaska years as devoted exclusively to zoning and city planning.

Partial List of Buildings

1926   Tri-Delt House, University of Oregon, Portland
1929–30   Tri-Delt House, University of Pennsylvania, Philadelphia
              (with Frederick Fritsch)

Sources

Margaret Goodin Fritsch, oral history by Linda Brody, March 29, 1982. Tape recording. "Voices Recorded for Posterity" Collection. Research Library, Oregon Historical Society, Portland.

Ritz, Richard Ellison. *Architects of Oregon; A Biographical Dictionary of Architects Deceased—Nineteenth and Twentieth Centuries.* Portland, Ore.: Lair Hill Publishing, 2002.

LOCATION OF PAPERS. The University of Oregon has very limited records on Fritsch's student years and a brief alumni notice marking her ninety-second birthday. The university's Special Collections division has one of her architectural renderings depicting the National Youth Agency Recreation Building (1940) in Salem, Oregon.

|||||||||||||||||||||||||
Furman, Ethel Madison Bailey (1893–1976)
|||||||||||||||||||||||||

Ethel Bailey Furman (fig. 24) had been practicing architecture for decades before the first reference to her professional achievements appeared, in the January 23, 1937, *Pittsburgh Courier.* Even at that late date, she is considered the first African American architect in Virginia. A native of Richmond and the daughter of Madison J. Furman, a prominent contractor, Ethel Furman attended a local high school before moving to Philadelphia and graduating from Germantown High School in 1910. Her first architectural training took place in New York City, where she received private tutoring. Once Furman moved back to Richmond, her knowledge of drafting was supplemented by practical experience in her father's company. Her architectural practice was operated from a home built by her father at 3024 Q Street. By 1927, Furman was an acknowledged professional in the field, as demonstrated by her participation in the Negro Contractors' Conference at the Hampton Institute in Hampton, Virginia.

FIGURE 24. Ethel Madison Bailey Furman, n.d. Courtesy Library of
Virginia, Richmond.

Although Furman designed about two hundred buildings during her career, including many churches, she seldom signed her drawings. Because local
administrators would not accept her as an architect, Furman was forced to ask
male contractors to sign the finished plans and submit them for approval.

Between 1944 and 1946, Furman attended Chicago Technical College for
further architectural training. An active member of civic and religious groups,
she donated two of her church designs to the Lott Carey Missionary League,
which constructed the buildings in Liberia. In the year of her death, Furman completed designs for Springfield Baptist Church in Hanover County,
Virginia, and Rising Mount Zion Baptist Church in Sandston, Virginia. Ethel

Bailey Furman died in February 1976, in the midst of a still flourishing architectural career. The city of Richmond created Ethel Bailey Furman Park in her honor.

Partial List of Buildings

The following list of buildings is based on the drawings in the Ethel Bailey Furman Papers and Architectural Drawings, 1928–2003, at the Library of Virginia. Many of Furman's earlier drawings have been destroyed, and a more complete list of her built work may not be possible. All of her buildings except the two erected in Liberia are in Virginia.

1939	St. James Holiness Church, Richmond
ca. 1950	Isaac Dickerson House, Goochland Co.
	Thomas N. Edwards House, Chesterfield Co.
	Nathan Pleasant House, Powhattan
1955	Mt. Carmel Church, Noel
1956	St. James Holiness Church (remodel?), Richmond
1961	Fourth Baptist Church, Richmond
1965	Junius Snead House, Glen Allen
1968	Edward Snead House, Goochland
	James Snead House, Richmond
	Mack Snead House, Goochland
	Samuel Snead House, Goochland
	Thomas M. Snead House, Goochland
ca. 1973	Mr. and Mrs. Edward Snead House, Goochland Co.
1974	Mt. Olive Baptist Church, Henrico
1976	Rising Mt. Zion Baptist Church, Sandston
	Springfield Baptist Church, Hanover Co.

Drawings for the following buildings are undated:

Apostolic Faith Church, Richmond
Cedar Street Memorial Baptist Church, Goochland
Fair Oak Baptist Church, Richmond
John J. Bazemore House, n.p.
Leland S. Cauthorne House, Goochland
Mt. Nebo Baptist Church, n.p.
Mt. Pleasant Baptist Church, Bermuda Hundred,
    Chesterfield Co.
Robert J. Wilder House, 933 N. 28th St., Richmond
St. James Baptist Church, Beaverdam
St. James Baptist Church, Goochland Co.

Union Baptist Church, Quinton
Union Hope Baptist Church, King William

Sources

"Records of Pioneering Architect Donated to Library of Virginia." *Library of Virginia* 62 (March/April 2004): 5.

LOCATION OF PAPERS. The Library of Virginia, Richmond, holds the Ethel Bailey Furman Papers, 1928–2003. The collection includes about one hundred architectural drawings, a few photographs, and various personal papers. No other materials from Furman's architectural practice are known to have survived.

|||||||||||||||||||||||||||
Gannon, Mary Nevan (b. 1867)
|||||||||||||||||||||||||||

Mary Nevan Gannon, a New York architect, was cofounder and partner in the firm of Gannon and Hands, the first firm of female architects in America. Established in 1894, the Gannon and Hands firm got off to a promising start that year, when it won the design competition for Florence Hospital in San Francisco. Although this building remains unidentified, Frances Willard extolled its virtues in 1897, noting that the hospital was "pronounced by physicians a model of sanitation, convenience and architectural beauty."[10]

Born in Bethlehem, Pennsylvania, in 1867, Gannon was the eldest child of Irish immigrants. Little is known of her childhood, but she eventually found work in an architect's office in Bedford, Pennsylvania. During her employment she decided to seek further architectural education and learned of a new institution for women founded by Ellen Dunlap Hopkins in 1892. Gannon and her future business partner, Alice Hands, entered the first graduating class of the New York School of Applied Design for Women (NYSAD). The school offered an unusual two-year architectural program directed by practicing architects from prominent firms, many of whom employed NYSAD pupils in subsequent years. Among the school's most accomplished students, Gannon and Hands frequently received awards for individual drawings and commissions for work from the public. Immediately after graduation, the two young architects opened an office in the school building.

During their first winter in private practice, Gannon and Hands inspected housing conditions in the city's Tenth Ward as members of a Sanitary Investigation Committee. In order to experience urban poverty firsthand, they spent an entire winter in a New York tenement. The firm of Gannon and Hands soon became known for its innovative, low-cost apartment houses. A February 1895 article in the *New York Times* announced the young architects' commission for fifteen model tenements in New York and Jersey City. One of their drawings for a model tenement plan and elevation appeared in the March 1899 *Municipal Affairs,* along with designs by Ernest Flagg and James E. Ware. In his book on housing reform, *A Ten Years' War* (1900), Jacob Riis praised the architects' tenements for letting "in an amount of light and air not dreamed of in the conventional type of double-decker, while providing detached stairs in a central court." The lasting influence of the work of Gannon and Hands is illustrated by the reprint of their model tenement for a twenty-five-foot lot in *Slums and Housing* (1936), a history of American housing by James Ford.[11]

An 1896 interview in *Godey's Magazine* suggests that, like their predecessor Louise Bethune, Gannon and Hands wanted nothing more than to be accepted as successful architects. Earning pay and recognition equivalent to that of male colleagues was a primary concern. The architects made a point of supervising the construction of their buildings. Unlike the nameless female drafters Bethune criticized for not participating in the "brick-and-mortar-rubber-boot-and-ladder-climbing" aspect of architecture,[12] Gannon and Hands challenged women to study advanced mathematics and gain practical knowledge of building technology.

Gannon and Hands demonstrated their architectural skill in a range of work, mostly in the New York area. They designed a women's hotel, a women's club building, student apartment houses, and numerous cottages by the seashore and in the mountains. According to the *New York Times,* they were the first women to have work recognized by the Architectural League. In 1897 the firm moved its office from the school building at 200 West Twenty-third Street to 16 East Twenty-third Street. This was also the year of Gannon's marriage to John Walp Doutrich, a tailor. Another move by the firm to a more fashionable neighborhood in 1900—a handsome five-story office building at 13 West Eighteenth Street—indicates a successful partnership at the turn of the century, but little is known about the firm's later years. The business may have dissolved about this time, when the Doutrichs and their young son (born 1899) moved to Spokane, Washington.

Partial List of Buildings

1894	Florence Hospital, San Francisco
	Competition for Woman's Building, Cotton States and International Exposition, Atlanta, Ga. (2nd prize)
1895	Model tenement, 71st and Avenue A, N.Y.

Hotel for Women, 7th and 37th, N.Y.

Student Apartment House, 20th St., N.Y.

Misses McWilliams, cottage in the Catskills, Twilight Park, N.Y.

J. H. Lange, House, alterations and additions, Twilight Park, N.Y.

ca. 1896 Gretchen Cottage, Asbury Park, N.J.

New Era Building, offices and club rooms, N.Y.

1897 Women's Hotel, Broadway and 37th, N.Y.

Sources

Ford, James. *Slums and Housing: With Special Reference to New York City.* Westport, Conn.: Negro Universities Press, 1936. See esp. 681, 885, plates.

Gould, E. R. L. "The Housing Problem." *Municipal Affairs* 3, no. 1 (March 1899): 138–39 (plates).

"Model Hotel for Women." *New York Times,* May 12, 1895, sec. 16, 5.

Riis, Jacob A. *A Ten Years' War.* 1900. Reprint. Freeport, N.Y.: Books for Libraries Press, 1969, 96.

Severance, Alice. "Talks By Successful Women IX.—Miss Gannon and Miss Hands on Architecture." *Godey's Magazine* 83, no. 795 (September 1896): 314–16.

"Successful Women Architects: Sixteen Tenements to be Built on Their Plans—Also a Woman's Hotel." *New York Times,* February 25, 1895, sec. 6, 8.

Willard, Frances E. *Occupations for Women.* Cooper Union, N.Y.: Success Company, 1897. 366–370.

"Women as Architects." *New York Times—Saturday Review of Books and Art,* June 5, 1897, 13–14.

"Working Girls' Home, Plans for an Apartment House to Have All Comforts." *New York Times,* December 15, 1895, sec. 19, 6.

||||||||||||||||||||||||
Greely, Rose Ishbel (1887–1969)
||||||||||||||||||||||||

Born in Washington, D.C., Rose Greely received her early education at the National Cathedral School for Girls in the District; Abbott Academy in Andover, Massachusetts; and the Finch School in New York. After graduating from high school in 1905, Greely pursued a variety of interests, studying interior decorating at the Art Institute of Chicago; various types of metalwork in Washington and Florence, Italy; and farming at the University of Maryland. In 1920, Greely was among the first graduates of the Cambridge

School for Domestic Architecture and Landscape Architecture, receiving certificates in both disciplines. She soon found work as a drafter in the office of the Boston landscape architect Fletcher Steele. When Greely returned to Washington, D.C., in 1923, she worked for Horace W. Peaslee, and two years later she became the first licensed female architect in the District.

Greely opened her own landscape architecture firm in 1925, employing a secretary, an assistant, and two drafters in an office in downtown Washington. One of her associates in the 1930s was Dorothy Butler Graves, a Cornell graduate who became the first female landscape architect practicing in North Carolina. Although Greely focused on residential landscape design, she emphasized the integral relationship between buildings and their surroundings. During her forty-year practice, Greely designed gardens for wealthy East Coast clients, many of whom later hired her to work on their second and third homes in the South and West. Her nonresidential projects included the grounds of military facilities, schools, embassies, and museums.

In 1936, Greely became a fellow of the American Society of Landscape Architects' advisory committee for the Williamsburg restoration project. Beginning in the 1920s, she published articles in popular journals such as *House Beautiful, House and Garden, Country Life,* and *Landscape Architecture,* as well as in a variety of newspapers. Today, Greely's work is sometimes remembered in histories of American landscape architecture, but the architectural component of her practice is yet to be carefully examined.

Partial List of Buildings

1936–37	Mr. and Mrs. William H. Taylor House, 28th and Q Sts., Washington, D.C.
1937–38	Mr. and Mrs. Morris Cafritz House, Washington, D.C.
n.d.	Rose Greely House, Georgetown, Washington, D.C.
	Mrs. William Hurd Hill House, Washington, D.C.
	Miss Frances A. Sortwell House, Georgetown

Writings by Greely

"An Architect's Garden in the City." *House Beautiful,* November 1926, 557.
"Belgian Square into Memorial." *Landscape Architecture* 36, no. 2: 64–65.
"A Child's Own Garden." *House Beautiful,* November 1935, 55+.
"A House that Combines Beauty and Comfort." *House Beautiful,* March 1922, 202–3.
"A Small House of Distinction." *House Beautiful,* November 1922.
"Why Should the Garden Have Design? I: Some of the Factors, Both Practical and Aesthetic, the Influence of the Design of the Grounds." *House Beautiful,* November 1932,

100–103. First in a series of four articles; for parts 2–4, see *House Beautiful*, December 1932, 75–78; January 1933, 59–61+; February 1933, 128–29+.

Sources

Alumnae Bulletin of the Cambridge School of Domestic and Landscape Architecture. Vols. 1–8, May 1929–November 1935. Sophia Smith Collection, Smith College.

Birnbaum, Charles A., and Lisa E. Crowder, eds. *Pioneers of Landscape Design: An Annotated Bibliography*. Washington, D.C.: U.S. Department of the Interior, 1993. See esp. 54–56.

Palache, Mary. "A Little House in Old Georgetown; Remodeled by Rose Greely." *House Beautiful*, August 1928, 35–37.

Smith, Susan. "One from Several: The House and Garden of Miss Frances A. Sortwell, in Georgetown." *House Beautiful*, December 1933, 251–54.

Tankard, Judith B. "Women Pioneers in Landscape Design." *Radcliffe Quarterly*, March 1993, 8–11.

Wilson, Joanne Seale. "The Philosophy of Rose Greely, Landscape Architect." *APT Bulletin* 32, no.2/3 (2001): 39–46.

LOCATION OF PAPERS. The Rose Greely Architectural Drawings and Papers, 1909–1985, are in Special Collections, Alderman Library, University of Virginia, Charlottesville. The collection includes more than six hundred fifty architectural drawings, client files, correspondence, photographs, and many unpublished manuscripts.

||||||||||||||||||||||||||||
Griffin, Marion Mahony (1871–1961)
||||||||||||||||||||||||||||

Born in Chicago, Marion Mahony Griffin helped to raise four siblings after her father's death in 1882. The financial assistance of a local civic leader, Mary Wilmarth, helped her to enter MIT in 1890. Four years later, Griffin submitted her thesis, "The House and Studios of a Painter" and became the second woman to graduate from MIT with a bachelor of science degree in architecture. Immediately after graduation, Griffin was able to find employment as a drafter in the office of her cousin Dwight Perkins. After only a year, she began working in the studio of Frank Lloyd Wright, the most famous architect in the nation, but also continued to accept jobs with other architects as well as independent commissions. She was the first woman licensed to practice architecture in Illinois (fig. 25).

Griffin's earliest undisputed commission was for All Souls Church in Evanston, Illinois, constructed in 1902–3. Her first drawings for the building showed

FIGURE 25. Marion Mahony Griffin, n.d. Courtesy MIT Museum.

considerable originality, but the client preferred something more conservative. In line with the Wrightian philosophy, Griffin produced fine designs for Arts and Crafts furniture, stained glass windows, and other architectural embellishments that contributed to the built environment as a total work of art.

Griffin shared Wright's love of drama, and in particular of dressing up in period costumes and performing theatricals. Fellow drafters remember her rare wit and ability to stand up to Wright's ego, which was considered no mean feat. They also recalled her homely appearance, and while this opinion appears related to the sexism of the time, it was usually tempered by recognition of the fact that her work exuded unusual beauty.

In 1909 Wright asked Griffin to take over the office while he was abroad, and when she refused, he settled for the architect H. V. von Holst as his substitute. Von Holst agreed to this role only after Griffin promised to serve as lead designer. Two residential designs have been attributed to Griffin during this period—the Adolph Mueller House (1910) in Decatur, Illinois, and the David M. Amberg House (1909–11) in Grand Rapids, Michigan. During her fifteen years in Wright's studio, Griffin also designed several unexecuted buildings, including the Childe Harold Wills House (1910–12) in Detroit; the

Doyle House (1912) in Rogers Park, Illinois; and the Henry Ford House in Dearborn, Michigan (1912). In retrospect, Griffin's greatest contribution to architectural history may have been her drawings for the famous Wasmuth Portfolio, the publication that would ultimately spread Wright's influence around the world.[13]

Marion Mahony formed a new collaboration in 1911 when she married a fellow architect from the studio, Walter Burley Griffin. The two won the international competition for the design of a new Australian capital at Canberra in 1912 and moved their practice to Australia. Although Griffin made it clear that her husband was principal designer for Canberra, many historians believe her drawings secured the commission. Throughout her marriage, Griffin declined to take credit for more than the traditional duties of helpful spouse. Nevertheless, several buildings have been attributed to her during the couple's time in Australia, including Castlecrag (1921), a community on the banks of Sydney Harbor, and the Capitol Theater (1924) in Melbourne. The Griffins moved to India in the 1930s and after Walter died there in 1937, Marion completed much of his work. Pioneer Press (1937) in Lucknow may have been hers alone. Upon her return to the United States, Griffin remained active in the field, completing several major projects. She wrote a lengthy autobiography, "The Magic of America," between 1938 and 1949. A complex, incomplete manuscript, "The Magic of America" has never been published in its entirety (see Writings by Mahony, below).

Marion Mahony Griffin stands alone among early women architects as the only one of her gender included in the canonical architectural histories. Although she has been considered worthy of biographical accounts since the 1960s, Griffin is most often described as an artist or delineator of exceptional ability. Historians of Frank Lloyd Wright and the Prairie School found it impossible to ignore her contribution as a drafter, but they have given her less credit for her design work. Opinions of what Griffin achieved in Wright's office vary widely, but no one disputes that she was amazingly talented. The studio was a collaborative effort, but Griffin had a unique touch and historians have agonized over which projects bear her stamp and how much credit she might be given for various projects. The extent of her role in Wright's office has been the subject of several studies but remains undefined. Although early scholarship on Marion Mahony Griffin emphasized her role as an artist and collaborator, more recent work has described her as an architect whose gender kept her from being recognized as a major figure of the Prairie School.

Partial List of Buildings

1902–3	Church of All Souls, Evanston, Ill. (demolished)
1909–11	David Amberg House, Grand Rapids, Mich.
1910	Adolph Mueller House, Decatur, Ill.
1942	World Fellowship Center, Conway, N.H. (project)
1943	Town Plan for Hill Crystals and Rosary Crystals, Boerne, Tex.

Writings by Mahony

"The Bungalow Indoors." In *One Hundred Bungalows,* edited by the Building Brick Association of America, 115–20. Boston: Rogers and Manson, 1912.

"The Magic of America." Manuscript, 1938–49. Three copies exist; one is at the New-York Historical Society and two are at the Burnham Library, Art Institute of Chicago. It is accessible in an electronic format: The Magic of America Electronic Edition, www .artic.edu/magicofamerica (accessed September 21, 2007).

Sources

Art Institute of Chicago. *Walter Burley Griffin, Marion Mahony Griffin: Architectural Drawings in the Burnham Library of Architecture.* Edited by John Zukowsky. Exh. cat. Chicago: Art Institute of Chicago, 1982.

Brooks, H. Allen. "Frank Lloyd Wright and the Wasmuth Drawings." *Art Bulletin* 48 (1966): 193–202.

"Church of All Souls, Evanston, Illinois." *Western Architecture* 18 (September 1912): plate and plans.

"Marion Mahony Griffin." *Macmillan Encyclopedia of Architects,* vol 2, 248. New York: Free Press, 1982.

"Marion Mahony Griffin." *Western Architect* 19 (April 1913): 38; (May 1913): 33; (October 1913): 88.

Peisch, Mark L. *The Chicago School of Architecture: Early Followers of Sullivan and Wright.* New York: Random House, 1964. See esp. 33–35, 43–46, 48–51, 57–58.

Van Zanten, David. "The Early Work of Marion Mahony Griffin." *Prairie School Review* 3, no. 2 (1966): 5–24.

von Holst, Hermann. "A Small Stone Church of Unusual Merit." *Modern American Homes,* plate 108. Chicago: American School of Correspondence, 1912.

Wells, Judy. "Representations of Marion Mahony Griffin." *Architectural Theory Review* 32 (1998): 123–25.

"The Woman Architect." *Southern Architect and Building News* 27 (April 1912): 27–28.

"The Woman Architect and Low-Cost Homes." *Architect and Engineer of California* 28 (February 1912): 103.

Wood, Debra, ed. *Marion Mahony Griffin: Drawing the Form of Nature.* Evanston, Ill.: Northwestern University Press, 2005. Published in conjunction with the exhibition "Marion Mahony Griffin: Drawing the Form of Nature," Block Museum, Northwestern University, Evanston, Illinois, September 23–December 4, 2005.

LOCATION OF PAPERS. Drawings by Marion Mahony Griffin are on deposit at the Northwestern University Art Department, the New-York Historical Society, the Avery Library at Columbia University, and the Burnham Library at the Art Institute of Chicago. The MIT Archives owns her thesis drawings and papers. Copies of her unpublished autobiography are in the collection of the New-York Historical Society Library and the Burnham Library of the Art Institute of Chicago.

|||||||||||||||||||||||||
Hall, Leola (1881–1930)
|||||||||||||||||||||||||

After the 1906 earthquake in San Francisco, Leola Hall became an entrepreneurial "girl architect" and developer of Craftsman-style homes. A painter, furniture designer, and suffragist, Hall was described by a *San Francisco Call* reporter in 1907 as "a girl who selects prospective bargains in real estate, who plans and builds her own houses and who sells them . . . quickly."[14] Hall was not an architect by training, but beginning in 1906 she designed groups of homes in Berkeley's Elmwood district and the surrounding area.

Upon her decision to marry Herbert Coggins in 1912, Hall designed a stuccoed house with elegant interior paneling for herself and her new husband. The house at 2929 Piedmont Avenue in Berkeley became a model of her mature architectural style, with a broad veranda, second-story balcony, central dormer window, stepped chimney, and cantilevered corner bay window. These intimate Craftsman-style details contrast with the spacious double-height living room, with its elaborate ceiling beams.

Like Julia Morgan and other Bay Area architects, Hall took advantage of the post-earthquake building opportunities. She maximized profits as a speculative builder by fitting four houses on lots typically planned for two and by using standardized features in most of her homes. Despite such efforts at cost cutting, Hall became known for her rendition of the Craftsman style and high-quality design. She was featured not only in the 1907 *Call* article about her unusual profession, but also in a newspaper account of her activities as a suffragist. Evidently Hall chauffeured a fellow suffragist, Margaret Haley, to various rallies in the Bay Area and was arrested for speeding in a vehicle decorated with banners. More than two hundred women attended Hall's court hearing, in which she claimed her arrest was a police setup, and she was eventually allowed to leave. Although some specific addresses of her buildings have been located by the Berkeley Heritage Association, the speculative nature of her houses adds to the difficulty of identifying her work.

Partial List of Buildings

All of the following buildings are located in Berkeley, California.

1906–7	Houses, 3004, 3006, 3008, 3012, 3026, 3030, 3032, 3036, 3040, 3042, 3046, and 3048 College Ave.
1908	Nellie and Emily Pitchford, flats, 2639 Regent
	Houses, 2618, 2620, 2624, 2628, and 2634 College Ave.
1909	Houses, 2730, 2732, 2747, 2804, and 2806 Stuart St.
	House, 2800 Kelsey St.
	Houses, 2752, 2754, 2758, and 2800 Piedmont Ave.
	House, 2709 Parker St.
1912	Houses, 2806 and 2808 Ashby Ave.
	House, 2929 Piedmont Ave.
1915	House, 2848 Russell St.
	Houses, 2904 and 2906 Pine Ave.

Sources

The Residential Work of Five Women Architects. Berkeley, Calif.: Berkeley Architectural Heritage Association, 1984.

Weinstein, Dave. "Signature Style, Leola Hall on Spec." *San Francisco Chronicle,* August 2, 2003, E-1.

|||||||||||||||||||||||||
Hands, Alice J.
|||||||||||||||||||||||||

Little is known of Alice J. Hands, who established the first firm of women architects with her business partner, Mary Nevan Gannon, in 1894. Hands studied for two years at the YWCA in New York City before enrolling in the New York School of Applied Design for Women, where she met Gannon. In 1896, a *Godey's Magazine* journalist reported that the friends "are so inseparable that they are indiscriminately called Gannon or Hands by their fellow-students."[15] For more information about the Gannon and Hands firm, see the entry on Mary Nevan Gannon.

|||||||||||||||||||||||
Hayden, Florence Kenyon (1882–1973)
|||||||||||||||||||||||

Although she never received a degree, Florence Kenyon Hayden is remembered as the first female architecture student at Ohio State University, as well as a successful architect in her own right. Born in St. Louis in 1882, Hayden moved to Columbus after the death of her father ten years later. She entered Ohio State in 1901 and completed at least two years of study. As a student, Hayden was influenced by Thomas French, a professor of engineering known for his innovative teaching methods. Perhaps modeling herself after her mentor, Hayden taught architecture at the university between 1905 and 1907.

At the age of twenty-five, Hayden began a very ambitious commission, the design of a new women's dormitory on the Ohio State University campus. Designed in 1907 and constructed in 1908, Oxley Hall is an imposing three-story brick building with a multitude of gables and an octagonal tower. The work was officially a collaboration with the Columbus architect Wilbur T. Mills, but Hayden is often given full credit for the design and was clearly the principal architect. During the construction of Oxley Hall, Hayden designed a substantial Arts and Crafts-style house on East Broad Street in Columbus.

In 1910, Hayden married James M. Rector. An active suffragist, she served as financial chairwoman of the National Women's Party in 1921. Despite her marriage and active political life, records indicate that Hayden maintained her architectural practice through the 1930s.

Partial List of Buildings

1908	Oxley Hall (Women's Dormitory), 1712 Neil Ave., Ohio State University, Columbus
	House, East Broad St., Columbus
1926	Florence Kenyon Hayden Rector House, Columbus

Writings by Kenyon Hayden

"Women Awake!" Manuscript, 24 pp., ca. 1920. Kenyon Hayden Rector Papers, Ohio Historical Society, Columbus.

Sources

Gordon, Steve. "Ohio's First Women Architects: Breaking Down the Walls." *Echoes Magazine,* March 27, 2000. Available online at the Web site of the Ohio Historical Society, Columbus, http://www.ohiohistory.org/intheknow/ink_archives/archive.cfm?te (accessed September 26, 2007).

LOCATION OF PAPERS. The Ohio Historical Society, Columbus, holds the Kenyon Hayden Rector Papers, 1893–1934. The International Archive of Women in Architecture, Blacksburg, Virginia, has a collection of Hayden's papers (1905–7) that includes a lecture notebook with teaching outline, photographs of Oxley Hall, and an advertising postcard addressed to Hayden. Information about Oxley Hall can be found at the Web site of the John H. Herrick Archives, Ohio State University, http://herrick.knowlton.ohio-state/edu/building. asp?building=34 (accessed September 26, 2007).

||||||||||||||||||||||||
Hayden, Sophia Gregoria (1868–1953)
||||||||||||||||||||||||

The first female graduate of the four-year program in architecture at MIT, Sophia Hayden was a good candidate to win the nation's most prominent design competition for women, the Woman's Building at the 1893 Columbian Exposition in Chicago. Hayden's design, based on her "Renaissance Museum of Fine Arts" thesis project, won first prize out of a field of thirteen entries, all submitted by women who considered themselves either specially trained in architecture or "in the profession of architecture." Ironically, Hayden's failure to supervise completion of the building made her the most famous woman architect of her day (fig. 26). Her "nervous collapse" at the exposition site proved to many observers what they had always believed: women had no place in the profession.

Born in Chile in 1868, Hayden moved to the Boston suburb of Jamaica Plain at age six. When she graduated from West Roxbury High School, the family moved to Virginia, but Hayden returned to the Boston area for college. After receiving her bachelor of science in architecture at MIT in 1890, Hayden taught mechanical drawing in Jamaica Plain.

Before the Woman's Building competition, the Board of Lady Managers had kept its rival group, the Isabella Society, from executing a Moorish pavilion designed by Minerva Parker Nichols, a professional architect in Philadelphia. The conflict between the female fair organizers created a tense atmosphere, and, as winner of the competition, Hayden felt great pressure to prove the worth of the Lady Managers' decision. In addition, the famous woman architect from Buffalo, Louise Bethune, refused to compete in the competition on principle. Bethune noted that her male peers were chosen to design particular exposition buildings, not required to prove themselves through competition, and that they received much more money for the

FIGURE 26. Sophia Hayden [Bennett], n.d. Courtesy MIT Museum.

privilege. Despite such controversy, Hayden produced a dignified exposition building that satisfied all requirements. Although she did not go on to pursue a career in architecture, Hayden and her Columbian Exposition experience is the most widely recorded historical account of a late nineteenth-century woman architect. Even today, Hayden's fair experience lives on in the national bestseller *The Devil in the White City* (2003). The author, Erik Larson, describes the challenges confronting Hayden in the competition and subsequent construction process, but he dwells on her failure, the mental breakdown that resulted in her being "driven from the park in one of the fair's innovative English ambulances with quiet rubber tires and placed in a sanitarium for a period of enforced rest."[16] Larson neglects to mention that professional architectural journals rushed to Hayden's defense or that she returned a few months later for the building's dedication ceremony.

Writings by Hayden

"Abstract of Thesis: Sophia G. Hayden, 1890." *Technology Architectural Review* 3 (September 31, 1890): 28, 30.
"The Woman's Building." In *Rand McNally and Company's A Week at the Fair,* 180. Chicago: Rand McNally, 1893.

Sources

Darney, Virginia G. "Women and World's Fairs: American International Expositions, 1876–1904." Ph.D. diss., Emory University, 1982.
"Designs for Woman's Building, World's Columbian Exposition." *Inland Architect and News Record* 18 (September 1891): plates.
"Hayden, Sophia Gregoria." In *Notable American Women: The Modern Period,* edited by Barbara Sicherman and Carol Hurd Green, 322–24. Cambridge, Mass.: Belknap Press of Harvard University Press, 1980.
Millet, F. D. "The Designers of the Fair." *Harper's New Monthly Magazine,* November 1892, 872–83.
Paine, Judith. "Pioneer Women Architect." In *Women in American Architecture,* edited by Susana Torre, 54–69. New York: Whitney Library of Design, 1977.
"An Unusual Opportunity for Women Architects." *Woman's Journal* 22 (February 21, 1891): 63.
Van Brunt, Henry. "Architecture at the World's Columbian Exposition, IV." *Century Magazine,* September 1892, 729.
Weiman, Jeanne M. *The Fair Women.* Chicago: Academy, 1981.
"Woman's Building." *American Architect and Building News* 32 (April 18, 1891): 45.
"The Woman's Building." *American Architect and Building News* 38 (November 26, 1892): 134.

IIIIIIIIIIIIIIIIIIIIIIIIIII
Henley, Frances Evelyn (d. 1955)
IIIIIIIIIIIIIIIIIIIIIIIII

A native of Crompton (Warwick), Rhode Island, Frances Evelyn Henley attended high school in Providence. She was the first woman admitted to the Rhode Island School of Design's architectural program and graduated with honors in 1897. Henley attended RISD on a state scholarship. As an undergraduate, Henley received several awards for her architectural designs, and her drawings appeared in school catalogs from 1894 to 1897. According to an undated newspaper article, a group of RISD students banded together to prevent Henley from working as a professional architect. She persevered, however, and was hired as a drafter in a local firm. When the owner of the firm died, Henley became the only woman architect in the state practicing under her own name, an achievement the newspaper article erroneously applied to the entire nation. Although Henley primarily designed residences, she has been cited as the designer of the main building at the Mary Wheeler School in Providence and for lavish summer camps at Rangeley Lakes in Maine.

LOCATION OF PAPERS. The Frances Evelyn Henley Papers are held by the Manuscripts Division, Rhode Island Historical Society, Providence. They consist of Henley's diaries written from 1922 to 1954, correspondence, clippings, manuscripts, speeches, and project specifications for Trinity Episcopal Church in Pawtucket. Catalogs from RISD from 1894 to 1897 include examples of her work.

IIIIIIIIIIIIIIIIIIIIIIIIII
Hicks, Margaret (1858–83)
IIIIIIIIIIIIIIIIIIIIIIIIII

Margaret Hicks is remembered as the first woman architect to publish her work in a professional architectural journal. Her student project, a "workman's cottage," appeared in *American Architect and Building News* in 1878. Hicks is also often identified as the first woman to obtain an architecture degree from an accredited university, although that honor actually goes to Mary Page, who preceded Hicks by one year in earning her B.A. from the University of Illinois in 1879. Hicks received a B.A. from Cornell University in 1878 and went on to earn her bachelor of architecture degree at Cornell in 1880.

The nineteenth-century historian Phebe Hanaford was impressed by Hicks's commencement essay on the tenement house, noting that "she seemed—unlike many of the architects who have sent plans to New York for which premiums are offered—to have remembered that houses must have light and air, closets and bed-rooms." Almost a hundred years later, the architectural historian Gwendolyn Wright commented on the social and political aspects of Hicks's choice to design housing for the poor while her peers were catering to the elite: "Hicks believed that her professional training should not be the private property of a single class and went on to do 'tenement architecture' for the growing numbers of immigrants in New York City."[17]

In 1880 Hicks married a fellow Cornell architecture student, Arthur Karl Volkmann. Whether Hicks would have continued her promising career in architecture will never be known. She died in Cambridge, Massachusetts, at the age of twenty-five.

Sources

"Design for a Workman's Cottage." *American Architect and Building News* 3 (April 13, 1878): 129.

Hanaford, Phebe A. *Daughters of America; or Women of the Century.* Augusta, Me.: E. E. Knowles, 1882.

"Some Professional Roles." In *Women in American Architecture,* edited by Susana Torre, 69. New York: Whitney Library of Design, 1977.

Wright, Gwendolyn. "On the Fringe of the Profession: Women in American Architecture." In *The Architect,* edited by Spiro Kostof, 292–93. New York: Oxford University Press, 1977.

LOCATION OF PAPERS. Cornell University Archives has a file with biographical information on Hicks that includes a photograph and sketch.

||||||||||||||||||||||||
Hill, Esther Marjorie (1895–1985)
||||||||||||||||||||||||

The first Canadian woman to receive an architectural degree, Esther Marjorie Hill graduated from the University of Toronto in June 1920. Her graduation attracted the attention of the Canadian press, and the chairman of architecture at the university, C. H. C. Wright, refused to attend the ceremony. Hill grew up in Edmonton and began her effort to gain an architectural education at the University of Alberta in 1916. When her program was cancelled two years later, she entered the University of Toronto, joining her classmate Mary Anne Kentner as the first women accepted to an architectural program in Canada.

Despite the publicity surrounding her graduation, Hill could not find employment as an architect. In 1921 she applied for registration with the Alberta Association of Architects. Although Hill met all requirements, she was turned down for lack of experience, and the association quickly altered its bylaws to include one year of postgraduate work in an office as a membership qualification. Finally, in 1922, Hill found brief employment with a well-known Edmonton firm, [George Heath] MacDonald and [Herbert Alton] Magoon Architects, and worked on designs for a new Edmonton Public Library, where her father would serve as chief librarian.

In the fall of 1922, Hill pursued postgraduate work in town planning at the University of Toronto and that summer she took courses at Columbia University in New York City. For the next few years, Hill would move between Canada and the United States, seeking employment. She worked for Marcia Mead from 1923 to 1924 and for Katharine C. Budd from 1925 to 1928. With this documented experience, she applied for registration once again and, in 1925 she became the first female registered architect in Canada.

Three years later, Hill was living in Edmonton and had returned to the firm of MacDonald and Magoon. During the Depression years she found herself without architectural employment and supported herself by making gloves, designing greeting cards, and weaving. After World War II, Hill established her own practice, primarily designing residences for veterans, and in 1945 became the first woman on the Victoria Town Planning Commission. She became a registered architect with the Architectural Institute of British Columbia eight years later.

By the 1950s, Hill had finally become known for functional, efficient buildings and began to receive more important commissions in Victoria. These included an addition to the Emmanuel Baptist Church, an apartment building on Ford Street, the main building in Lincoln Cemetery, and one of the first retirement homes in Canada, the Glenn Warren Lodge.

Hill's deteriorating health forced her to retire from architectural design in 1963, but she was able to continue weaving and teaching until her death at age eighty-nine. Hill is remembered as Canada's pioneer woman architect and celebrated not only for breaking down educational and professional barriers, but for persevering in a field notorious for its discrimination against female practitioners.

Writings by Hill

"Common Faults in House Design: Paving the Way to Better Building Methods." *Agricultural Alberta* (February 1921): 29.

Sources

Adams, Annmarie, and Peta Tancred. "Designing Women: Then and Now." *Canadian Architect* 45, no. 11 (November 2000): 16–17.

Contreras, Monica, et al. "Breaking In: Four Early Female Architects." *Canadian Architect* 38, no. 11 (November 1993): 18–20.

Women in Architecture Exhibits Committee. *Constructing Careers: Profiles of Five Early Women Architects in British Columbia.* Vancouver, B.C.: Women in Architecture Exhibits Committee, 1996. See esp. 18–25.

LOCATION OF PAPERS. Archives and Records Management, University of Toronto, Ontario, has a collection of Hill's architectural drawings, papers, and her unpublished thesis.

||||||||||||||||||||||||||
Holman, Emily Elizabeth (fl. 1892–1915)
||||||||||||||||||||||||||

Emily Elizabeth Holman appears in Philadelphia city directories as an architect from 1893 to 1914. Her office was at 1020 Chestnut Street from 1893 until 1913. The next year she seems to have expanded her business and moved to 1509 Arch Street as E. E. Holman Co., Architects. Although details of her career are scarce, the six plan books she published between 1884 and 1908 indicate a flourishing practice.

Partial List of Buildings

1895	L. P. Havaland House, Camden, N.J.
	House, alterations and additions, Hatboro, N.J.
	House, Woodbridge, N.J.
1898	I. W. C. Rylund House, Friendsville, Pa.
1901	Thomas C. Cairns House, Demopolis, Ala.
	Cottage, Coronado, Calif.
	J. Goodlow House and Office, Demopolis, Ala.
	W. S. Morse House, Seaford, Del.
	National Park Seminary, alterations and additions to theater and library, Forest Glen, Md.
	House, Garden City, Long Island, N.Y.
	A. P. Turner House, Cooper City, Ontario, Canada
	H. K. Wick House, Youngstown, Ohio
1908	N. R. Davidyan House and Stable, Moorestown, N.J.
1915	C. E. Cox House, Pennington, N.J.

Writings by Holman

A Book of Bungalows: Containing 30 New and Original Designs. Philadelphia: E. E. Holman, 1906.

New Picturesque Cottages: 30 Designs from $2,800 to $6,000. Philadelphia: E. E. Holman, 1904.

Picturesque Camps, Cabins and Shacks: Containing 40 New and Original Designs. Philadelphia: E. E. Holman, 1908.

Picturesque Cottages: 32 New and Original Designs. Philadelphia: E. E. Holman, 1894.

Picturesque Suburban Homes: 30 Designs from $3,000 to $10,000. Philadelphia: E. E. Holman, 1907.

Picturesque Summer Cottages: Containing 35 New and Original Designs. 3 vols. Philadelphia: E. E. Holman, 1900–1903.

Sources

Tatman, Sandra L., and Roger W. Moss. *Biographical Dictionary of Philadelphia Architects: 1700–1930.* Boston: G. K. Hall, 1985. See esp. 393.

||||||||||||||||||||||
Hook, Mary Rockwell (1877–1978)
||||||||||||||||||||||

Although Mary Rockwell Hook never became an official member of the American Institute of Architects, the AIA presented her with an award for architectural achievement on her hundredth birthday, in 1977. A native of Junction City, Kansas, Hook graduated from Wellesley in 1900 and in 1903 became the only woman in her class at the Art Institute of Chicago. Her parents and four sisters must have been surprised when she graduated and moved to Paris to study for an additional year in an Ecole des Beaux-Arts atelier. Hook completed her examinations under Marcel Auburtin in 1906.

After completing her European studies, Hook returned to her family in Kansas City and secured a position as an apprentice in the firm of Howe, Hoit, and Cutler. This was the successor firm to Van Brunt and Howe, which originated as a partnership between William Ware and Henry Van Brunt in 1865. In 1907, the year she began work, Hook may have witnessed the construction of Howe, Hoit, and Cutler's R. A. Long office building, the first steel-frame office building in Kansas City.

Despite Hook's obvious independence, her father refused to allow his twenty-nine-year-old daughter to accept a salary. At the same time, and perhaps as some sort of bargain with his daughter, Bertrand Hook purchased lots throughout the city and encouraged Mary to design residences on these properties. With the freedom to design as she pleased, Hook was able to experiment with new ideas, such as solar heating and earthen insulation, and a variety of materials, including recycled parts of demolished buildings. She designed the first house in Kansas City with an attached garage, the first with a private swimming pool, and the first employing cast-in-place concrete walls.

In 1913, Katherine Pettit and Ethel de Long chose Hook to design the Pine Mountain Settlement School in the southeastern mountains of Kentucky. The idea for Pine Mountain evolved out of the progressive urban settlement house movement, but in this case the school was intended to provide education and health care for children in a remote rural area. The commission gave Hook the opportunity to design an entire campus, as well as individual buildings, in the rugged, sparsely populated southern Appalachians. Her buildings, with names like the Big Log House and Laurel House, were constructed of native boulders and wood milled on the site. The Pine Mountain Settlement School, a National Historic Landmark since 1991, is now an environmental education center.

Mary Hook's life must have changed considerably when she married Inghram Hook in 1921, but this personal milestone does not seem to have slowed down her professional life. In fact, she opened a firm of her own—Hook and Remington—just two years later. Her partner, Eric Douglas Macwilliam Remington (1893–1975), was a graduate of the University of Illinois and a former student at the Ecole des Beaux-Arts. During the 1920, Mary Hook designed houses said to have an Italianate flavor that were notable for incorporating timber, stone, frescoes, and tile. A group of her residences in Kansas City's Sunset Hill neighborhood were designated as part of a National Register district bearing her name in 1983. The details of Remington's role in the firm are unclear, and by 1932 he had moved to San Francisco.

One of Hook's most impressive commissions came in 1935 when she began designing vacation homes along fifty-five acres of beachfront on Siesta Key, an island off Sarasota, Florida. This development, known at Whispering Sands, includes several extant properties on Sandy Hook Road. In addition, she is credited for early use of a solar panel to provide hot water for a Siesta Key resort hotel. Mary Rockwell Hook continued working well into her seventies, designing the Florence R. DeWalt House in Sarasota around 1950. She died on her one hundred first birthday at her Siesta Key home.

Partial List of Buildings

1908	Capt. and Mrs. Bertrand Rockwell House, 54 East Fifty-third Terrace, Kansas City, Mo. (National Register)
1913	Pine Mountain Settlement School, 36 Highway 510, Bledsoe, Ky. (National Historic Landmark)
1925–27	Four Gates Farm (Oak Hill Farm), 13001 Little Blue Rd., Raytown, Mo.
1927	House, 4940 Summit St., Kansas City (National Register)
ca. 1950	Florence R. DeWalt House, 679 Avenida N., Sarasota, Fla.
n.d.	Mrs. Bertrand Rockwell House, 5011 Sunset Dr., Kansas City (National Register)
	"The Pink House," 5012 Summit St., Kansas City
	Emily Rockwell Love House, 5029 Sunset Dr., Kansas City (National Register)
	Floyd Jacobs House, 5050 Sunset Dr., Kansas City
	Malcolm Lowry House, 6435 Indian Lane, Kansas City
	R. A. Ostertag House, 5030 Summit St., Kansas City (National Register)
	Mary Rockwell Hook House, 4940 Summit St., Kansas City
	Mrs. Inghram D Hook House, Fiftieth and Summit St., Kansas City
	Bertrand Rockwell House, 1004 W. Fifty-second St., Kansas City (National Register)
	Betty Strawbridge House, 172 Sandy Hook Rd., Siesta Key, Sarasota, Fla.
	Chapel for St. Boniface Church, Sandy Hook, Fla.

Writings by Hook

This and That. Booklet, May 1970. Deposited in the Mary Rockwell Hook Papers, Western Historical Manuscript Collection, University of Missouri, Kansas City, and the Kansas City Public Library.

Sources

Conrads, David. "Ahead of Her Time: Mary Rockwell Hook." *Kansas City Live!* 2, no. 7 (April 1991): 46–51. Collection of the Kansas City Public Library.

"IAWA Spotlight: Mary Rockwell Hook." International Archive of Women in Architecture Newsletter 3 (Fall 1991), online at http://spec.lib.vt.edu/IAWA/news/news3.html (accessed September 21, 2007).

Jones, Betty. "A Woman Ahead of Her Time." *City* 1, no. 4 (May 1978): 31–32. Collection of the Kansas City Public Library.

LOCATION OF PAPERS. The Mary Rockwell Hook Papers at the Western Historical Manuscript Collection, University of Missouri, Kansas City, contains correspondence, clippings, drawings, and personal papers. The International Archive of Women in Architecture, Blacksburg, Virginia, has biographical material on the life and work of Mary Rockwell Hook, 1929–99. The Kansas City (Missouri) Public Library has a typed interview in its vertical files special collection, as well as many magazine and newspaper articles in its general collection.

|||||||||||||||||||||||||
Howe, Lois Lilley (1864–1964)
|||||||||||||||||||||||||

A native of Cambridge, Massachusetts, Lois Lilley Howe was one of C. Howard Walker's first students at the School of the Museum of Fine Arts, Boston. After spending four years at the school, she enrolled as a special student in a two-year architectural program at MIT, where she was a classmate of Sophia Hayden. When Howe graduated in 1890, she continued work at MIT, serving as a drafter, artist, and librarian in the Department of Architecture and working for herself on the side. In 1893, Howe wrote to the building committee of the World's Columbian Exposition in Chicago, offering herself as designer of the Woman's Building. Her letter was written on the letterhead of Allen and Kenway, the Boston architectural firm on Devonshire Street where she had recently begun work, and included a recommendation from the distinguished architect Robert Swain Peabody. Although her design for the building placed second to that of Sophia Hayden, Howe went on to enjoy a much more distinguished architectural career than her former college classmate. She used the five-hundred-dollar second-place prize to finance a tour of European architecture with her mother and sisters (fig. 27).

Howe began working in an office on Tremont Street in downtown Boston in 1894, the year she received her first commission to build a house. She continued in private practice and in collaborations with others until 1900, when she established a firm. In 1901, she became the second woman elected to the AIA. According to C. H. Blackall, "Miss Howe came in to the Institute . . . because most of the members who voted on her thought Lois was a man's name."[18] Blackall may have believed her election to the professional organization a mistake, but Howe had all the necessary credentials, including the

FIGURE 27. Lois Lilley Howe, n.d. Photograph by Florence Maynard of Waban, Mass. Courtesy MIT Museum.

sponsorship of Robert Peabody. She was also one of the first women elected to the Boston Society of Architects. Howe's merits were validated by the AIA as a body in 1931, when she became a Fellow.

Never at a loss for work, Howe became known for her fine renovations of older homes; her ability to create simple, efficient floor plans; and her effort to minimize expense. One contemporary remembered that Howe "used to see a house being torn down and would run quickly and take the mantels and doors." As early as 1905, Howe's house for Miss Burrage in Brookline, Massachusetts, was pictured in an article entitled "Boston Suburban Architecture" in the *Architectural Record*. Howe performed two renovations on the Griswold residence, in 1901 and 1904. The Griswold House was purchased in the 1960s by the architect Graham Gund, who expressed his admiration for the house, stating that it "has a certain gutsy Thomas Jefferson quality about it," and "a grandness of texture, a sense of simple and free-flowing spaces," that influenced his own work. Howe favored the popular colonial revival and Georgian revival styles for her residences and took pains in her research of authentic architectural details, consulting measured drawings, postcards, photographs, and published accounts in her remodeling efforts.[19]

In 1913, Howe published *Details of Old New England Houses* with Constance Fuller and expanded her practice by forming a partnership with a fellow MIT graduate, Eleanor Manning. The new firm became known for its precise remodeling and restoration work, and in 1916 it created the first seventeenth-century-revival house in Cambridge, the Louis C. Cornish House. Howe's training in the arts at the museum school, her associations with local artists, and her membership in the Copley Society of Boston and the Council of the School of the Museum of Fine Arts all played a significant role in her methodology of architectural restoration. She had an artist's eye for detail and an art historian's fascination with architectural tradition. From 1916 to 1919, Howe was director of the Boston Society of Arts and Crafts.

Her new partner, Eleanor Manning, took the firm in a different direction by giving priority to projects related to public housing and urban renewal. In the early 1920s the firm was invited to participate in the design of Mariemont, Ohio, a planned community outside of Cincinnati based on the principles of John Nolan and the English garden city model. Twenty-five other firms were involved in the 420-acre development, which was originally planned to house nine thousand residents. Howe and Manning were responsible for designing Denny Place, seven single-family and two two-family houses, near the center of the development. The cottages, considered "English" by their designers, featured steeply pitched roofs, casement windows, arched doorways, and prominent chimneys.

In addition to its selection for public housing designs, the firm was singled out for its individual commissions. *McCall's* magazine asked Howe and Manning to provide a design for its small house series, and a *McCall's* book edited by the architect Marcia Mead also published the plan. In 1926, the year Mary Almy joined the office, the firm won first prize in the Cape

Cod home competition for its design of a residence in Hyannis, Massachusetts, for Almy's parents. The Charles Almy House was chosen as one of ten houses in the small house competition sponsored by *House Beautiful;* the plans were published in the May 1929 issue and then became part of a national exhibition. Periodicals directed at a more strictly professional audience also published Howe, Manning, and Almy designs. *Architecture* included the Frothingham House, Cambridge, in its article "One Hundred Small Houses" (October 1935), and the May 1937 issue of *American Architect and Architecture* published James Morgan's home in Lynn. In addition to residential work, the firm received commissions during wartime for an army and navy canteen, a cafeteria at Fort Devens, and a Liberty Bond booth, as well as private commissions for factory alterations, barns and stables, a chain of shoe stores, and the Fitchburg Art Center.

In 1931, Howe received her highest honor when she was voted a Fellow of the AIA, following in the footsteps of Louise Blanchard Bethune, who had become a Fellow along with all members of the Western Association of Architects when that body joined the AIA in 1889, and Theodate Pope Riddle, who had also been elected by a jury of Fellows. Six years later, Howe retired and the firm disbanded. Howe worked with Eleanor Manning O'Connor on a few projects and served as treasurer of the Old Cambridge Shakespeare Association, president of the Cambridge Plant Club, and vice president of the Cambridge Historical Society. Howe lived to be almost one hundred, missing that benchmark by only twelve days. Howe is remembered today as a pioneering alumna of MIT, and several of her homes have been featured on a National Park Service tour of "Places Where Women Made History."

Building Lists

Doris Cole and Karen Cord Taylor have identified four hundred twenty-six projects by Howe; Howe and Manning; and Howe, Manning, and Almy. The complete list can be found in their book *The Lady Architects: Lois Lilley Howe, Eleanor Manning, and Mary Almy, 1893–1937* (New York: Midmarch Press, 1990). The lists below include only those projects that have been identified and qualify as either a renovation, a new building, or a series of buildings.

Partial List of Buildings and Renovations by Howe

1894	Alfred C. Potter House, renovation, 1 Kennedy Rd., Cambridge, Mass.
1895	Mrs. E. Burnett House, addition and stable, Elmwood Ave., Cambridge

1897	Mrs. Norton Folsom House, renovation, n.p.
	Richard W. Hale House, renovation, Schoonerhead, Bar Harbor, Me.
1898	Henshaw House, Traill St., Cambridge
1899	A. A. Vaughan House, renovation, Berkeley St., Cambridge
	F. W. Hallowell House, renovation, Chestnut Hill, Mass.
1900	F. J. Garrison House, Pelham Rd., Lexington, Mass.
	G. B. Nayadier House, renovation, Hawthorne St., Cambridge
1901	A. M. Griswold House, addition, Craigie St., Cambridge
1902	Eliot House, alteration, Reservoir St., Cambridge
1903	White House, alteration, Reservoir St., Cambridge
1904	Gibbins House, addition, Irving St., Cambridge
	Burrage House, Beech St., Brookline, Mass.
1906	Stetson House, addition and alteration, Brattle St., Cambridge
1907	Edith Heath House, Heath Hill, Brookline
	Mrs. Edward A. Handy House, renovation, Barnstable, Mass.
1908	Newman House, addition, Moore St., Cambridge
	Runkle House, Willard St., Cambridge
1909	Edward C. Streeter House, renovation, Topsfield, Mass.
1910	Katherine Harsford House, veranda, Craigie St., Cambridge
	Spelman residence, addition, Brewster St., Cambridge
	Lucy Coburn House, Ipswich, Mass.
	Charles Henry Davis, studio, South Yarmouth, Mass.
1910–12	Mrs. Samuel Batchelder House, addition, Hilliard St., Cambridge
1910–13	Augustus H. Fiske House, addition, Buckingham Palace, Cambridge
1911	Theodore L. Frothingham House, renovation, n.p.
	Thomas H. Collins House, renovation, n.p.
1912	Anne M. Paul House, Newburyport, Mass.
	Bradford House, addition, Craigie St., Cambridge
	J. Murray Howe House, renovation, Fairmont Ave., Milton
	Business Women's Club, renovation, Bowdoin St., Boston

Undated Projects Attributed to Howe before 1900

R. Alcott Pratt House, renovation, Marblehead, Mass.
Upton House, renovation, Concord, Mass.

Mrs. G. S. Hale House, renovation, Bay State Rd., Boston
H. S. White House, renovation, Cambridge
F. Apthorpe Foster House, Waquoit, Mass.
Thomas Mott Osborne House, Lake Owasco, N.Y.
Charles T. Carruth, barn, Badeck, Nova Scotia
Mrs. James T. Storrow House, renovation, n.p.
Charles Newell House, renovation, Cambridge
Dr. H. S. McIntyre House, renovation, Garden St.,
    Cambridge
Mrs. William T. Piper House, renovation, Cambridge
Mrs. George W. C. Noble House, renovation, Cambridge
Miss M. H. Whitwell House, renovation, Chestnut Street,
    Boston

List of Buildings and Renovations by Howe and Manning

1913	A. E. Kennedy House, addition, Kennedy Rd., Cambridge
	Thayer House, addition, Berkeley St., Cambridge
	Walnut Hill School, exterior renovation, Natick, Mass.
	Charles T. Kimball House, renovation, Bedford
	Mrs. John Cotter House, renovation, Harwood St., Lynn, Mass.
	James Phelan Estate, store, Munroe St., Lynn
	Mrs. Charles H. Pinkham House, renovation, Western Ave., Lynn
1914	Scudder House, alteration, Buckingham St., Cambridge
	Charles B. Gleason House, Annisquam, Mass.
	C. B. Burnham, greenhouse, Everett Ave., Winchester, Mass.
	Mrs. James H. Carle House, Landers Rd., Wollaston, Mass.
	Oxford Club, renovation, Lynn
	Thomas H. Collins House, Princeton, Mass.
1915	James E. Manning House, renovation, Beacon Hill Ave., Lynn
	Edna B. Lewis House, renovation, Randolph, N.H.
1916	Cornish House, Fayerweather St., Cambridge
	Mrs. James H. Carle House, exterior renovation, Landers Rd., Wollaston
	John Allyn House and garage, Magnolia, Mass.
	John C. Runkle House, renovation, Willard St., Cambridge
	John H. Sturgis House, renovation, Brattle St., Cambridge

Pope Yeatman, garage and stable, East Jaffrey, N.H.

Sweezy House, Wilton, N.H.

1917   Mrs. James H. Carle House, renovation, Wollaston Parkway, Mass.

Mrs. H. K. Estabrook cottage, Chocorua, N.H.

Mrs. A. W. Locke House, Roundhill, Northampton, N.H.

Mrs. Charles H. Pinkham House, Brookfield, N.H.

Dr. J. F. Gardiner House, renovation, Hubbard Park, Cambridge

MIT, renovation, Cambridge

Suffrage Coffee House, renovation

Anna Biddle Frishmuth, apartment, Mt. Vernon St., Boston

1918   Mrs. Robert Gould Shaw House, Dover St., Wellesley

Thomas H. Logan, garage, Kimball Rd., Lynn

Lucy Stone Hospital, Boutwell St., Dorchester

Business Women's Club, renovation, Bowdoin St., Boston

Boston Army and Navy Canteen, Boston Common

East Boston Canteen, Federal Docks, Boston

Liberty Bond Booth, Lynn

Bay State Allied Bazaar, Copley Plaza Hotel, Boston

1919   Columbus Avenue Canteen, Boston

Carey, Fayerweather House, renovation, Cambridge

Mrs. C. W. Townsend House, renovation, Pinckney St., Boston

T. H. Logan and Co., alterations to factory, Hudson, Mass.

Mrs. L. J. Bracket, garage, Perley Vale, Jamaica Plain

Mrs. A. H. Goell House, renovation, Edgartown, Mass.

J. E. Manning House, Lynn

1920   John Gallishaw, Caribou Ridge Farm, Plymouth, N.H.

Mary Reed House, renovation, Burlington, Vt.

Mrs. T. H. Logan House, renovation, 12 Kimball Rd., Lynn

Mrs. F. Walker Johnson, candy shop, Beach Bluff, Mass.

Community Service of Boston, Army and Navy Club, 10 Park St., Boston

Mrs. Sydney Shuman House, renovation, Beverly, Mass.

Barbara Howe House, renovation, Beacon St., Boston

Mrs. Charles E. Abbott House, renovation, Commonwealth Ave., Boston

Mrs. George Dexter House, renovation, Sparks St., Cambridge

1921   John R. Donovan House, renovation, Kings Beach Rd., Lynn
        Major F. K. Knowlton House, renovation, Pittsford, N.Y.
        Richard W. Hale House, renovation, Exeter St., Boston
        Mrs. James H. Kimball House, renovation, Currier Rd., Lynn
        Martin E. Welch House, Grosvenor Park, Lynn
        Mrs. Luther Hitchings House, renovation, Hovey Terrace,
            Lynn
1922   Concord Art Center, renovation, Concord
        Emily Williston House, renovation, Cambridge
        Miss A. B. Chapman House, Gray Gardens East, Cambridge
        Oxford Club, renovation, Lynn
        Grace P. Colby House, Landseer St., West Roxbury
        Mrs. George C. Bradford House, renovation, Craigie St.,
            Cambridge
        J. Lennox Hannon House, Clifton Ave., Marblehead, Mass.
        Eugenia Frothingham House, Cambridge
        Mrs. Myrtie M. Eastman House, Puritan Rd., Swampscott,
            Mass.
        Mrs. Godfrey L. Cabot, garage, Highland Avenue,
            Cambridge
        Richard W. Hale House, renovation, Bay State Rd., Boston
        Mrs. A. M. Howe House, renovation, Fayerweather St.,
            Cambridge
        Mrs. O'Keefe House, renovation, Broad St., Lynn
1923   Mrs. James H. Carle House, East Elm Ave., Wollaston
        Mariemont, housing development, Denny Pl., Cincinnati,
            Ohio
        Mrs. Lawrence Lennox House, Bradlee Rd., Phillips Beach,
            Mass.
        Mrs. John E. Crowley House, renovation, Pinckney St.,
            Boston
        Mrs. Charles H. Merrill House, renovation into two-family
            house, Lynn
        Marguerite Stone, barber shop, 141 Milk St., Boston
        Chec-R-Shoe Stores, shoe stores in Boston, Lynn, and New
            Bedford
        John Nolen House, renovation, Cornhill Ln., North
            Marshfield, Mass.
        McCall's magazine, house plans
        George M. Flint House, renovation, Joy St., Boston

Harriet Peet House, renovation, Willard St., Cambridge
Mary W. Allen House, renovation, Traill St., Cambridge
Mrs. John R. McLane House, Chestnut St., Manchester, N.H.

1924   Dr. Harold Walker House, Carlton St., Brookline
Mrs. Augustus H. Eustis, renovation, Canton Ave., Milton
Frederick P. Bagley House, renovation, Fox Hill and High
    Sts., Westwood
Mrs. Arthur Dewing House, Willard St., Cambridge
Elizabeth Leonard Strang House, Leominster, Mass.
Mrs. F. Walker Johnson, candy store, Phillips Beach, Mass.
Reba Paeff House, renovation, Mt. Vernon St., Boston
Women's Republican Club, renovation, Beacon St., Boston
John G. Hart House, Gray Garden West, Cambridge
Mrs. Edward Scott O'Keefe House, renovation, Broad St.,
    Lynn
Richard W. Hale House, renovation, Bay State Rd., Boston
Mrs. P. Henry Lyons House, Beach Bluff, Swampscott
George R. Nutter House, renovation, 9 Cilson Ct., Boston

1925   Louis F. Bachrach, renovation, Highland, West Newton,
    Mass.
Mrs. W. Barclay Parsons House, Wareham, Mass.
Winston R. Hindle House, Dartmouth St., South
    Dartmouth, Mass.
Mrs. P. Henry Lyons, cottage, Beach Bluff, Swampscott,
    Mass.
J. L. Moore House, renovation, Brattle St., Cambridge
Richard W. Hale House, renovation, Bay State Rd., Boston
William Taylor House, Reservoir Rd., Chestnut Hill
Mrs. C. M. Eaton House, renovation, Banks Road,
    Swampscott
Simmons College, renovation of dormitory, Pilgrim Rd.,
    Boston
Johnson O'Connor House, renovation, Beacon St., Boston
Mrs. Joseph B. Williams House, Tuckahoe, N.Y.

List of Buildings and Renovations by Howe, Manning, and Almy

1926   Lynn Gas and Electric Co., renovation, Lynn
Mrs. Edgar Greene House, renovation, Loring, Newton
Fitchburg Art Center, renovation, Fitchburg, Mass.

Cape Cod Competition, house design winner, Hyannis,
Mass.

Agnes Balch House, renovation, Traill St., Cambridge

Simmons College, renovation, Allston St., Boston

George R. Nutter House, renovation, West Cedar, Boston

R. W. Hale House, renovation, Bay State Rd., Boston

C. H. Prichard House, Middleton, Mass.

Mrs. William B. Scarborough House, renovation,
Kennebunkport, Me.

Charles Almy Jr. House, Coolidge Hill, Cambridge

Sarah B. Fay House, renovation, Mt. Vernon St., Boston

Dr. and Mrs. Edward Scott O'Keefe House, renovation,
Ocean St., Lynn

Mrs. Thomas H. Logan House, renovation, Kimbell Rd.,
Lynn

David Dunbar House, renovation, Nahant St., Lynn

Mrs. C. V. H. Eaton House, renovation, Banks Rd.,
Swampscott

College Club, renovation, Memorial Library, Boston

Josephine Shaw House, renovation, Duxbury

1927   Pine Manor Junior College, renovation, Wellesley

Mrs. Daniel Brown House, renovation, Marshfield Hills,
Mass.

Bethesda Society, renovation, Watertown

F. R. Wulsin House, Coolidge Hill, Cambridge

Dr. George H. Powers House, renovation, Beacon St., Boston

Anne M. Paul House, addition, Newburyport

Grace Treadwell House, renovation, Kittery Point, Me.

Mrs. Andrew J. George, barn renovation into cottage, Jaffrey,
N.H.

College Club, renovation, Commonwealth Ave., Boston

George R. Nutter, renovation, West Cedar St., Boston

Mrs. Wyman Richardson House, Cohasset

Mrs. Stephen Rose House, Clifton, Mass.

Charles Magrane House, Little Point, Swampscott

Warren Manning, weekend cottages, Ala.

1928   William C. Codman House, High St., Brookline

Johnson, Dutch candy shop, Beach Bluff, Mass.

Radcliffe College, Trowbridge Barn addition to Athletic
Building, Cambridge

Gilchrist Company, store renovation, Boston

Dr. Frank Fremont-Smith House, renovation, Willard St., Cambridge

Mrs. Paul Reed House, renovation, Brimmer St., Boston

Mrs. Charles R. Sanger House, renovation, Appleton St., Cambridge

Mrs. C. J. Enebuske House, renovation, Garden St., Cambridge

Henry B. Cabot House, renovation, Heath St., Brookline

Mrs. Robert R. Bass House, renovation, Peterboro, N.H.

Wellesley Inn, renovation, Wellesley

Mrs. M. J. Simmons House, Gray Gardens West, Cambridge

Isabel Hyams House, renovation, New Port Richey, Fla.

1929   Mrs. James H. Carle House, renovation, Wollaston

Mrs. William Taylor House, renovation, Beacon St., Boston

Mrs. G. H. McGiffert House, Bayberry Point, West Falmouth, Mass.

Mrs. Frederick C. Shattuck House, renovation, Warren St., Brookline

Alfred Baker Lewis House, renovation, Gray Gardens East, Cambridge

Mrs. Elliot Perkins House, Southborough, Mass.

1930   Dr. Bronson Crothers, cottage, Sorrente, Me.

John C. Hurd House, Prospect Park, Belmont, Mass.

Mrs. Martin Glynn House, renovation, Swampscott, Mass.

George C. Lee Jr., renovation, Foxhill St., Westwood, Mass.

Arthur Manning farmhouse, Bolton, Mass.

Charles R. Prichard Jr., House, Marblehead, Mass.

George R. Nutter House, renovation, West Cedar St., Boston

Mrs. A. E. Hall House, Sorrento, Me.

Mrs. A. E. Hall House, renovation, Babcock St., Brookline

Mrs. Frederick Pevear House, renovation, Brattle St., Cambridge

Charles Putnam House, renovation, Crow Point, Hingham, Mass.

1931   T. N. Perkins House, renovation, Clapboard St., Westwood, Mass.

Mrs. Calvin Gates Page House, renovation, Marlborough St., Boston

Mrs. E. S. Holbrook House, renovation, South Sherborne, Mass.

James B. Greason, Jr., cottage, Whitefield, N.H.

1932   Stevens Institute of Technology, faculty housing, Hoboken, N.J.

James Morgan House, Prescott Rd., Lynn

Annie B. Chapman House, renovation, Cambridge

Mrs. Henry Colt House, addition, Brattle St., Cambridge

Dr. Harold F. Brown, office addition, Newton, Mass.

1933   Margaret Perry House, renovation, Marlborough St., Boston

Juliana B. Merryweather House, renovation, Commonwealth Ave., Boston

Magrane, apartment buildings, renovation, Elm, Baker, and Church Sts., Lynn

Edward Ballantine House, renovation, Traill St., Cambridge

James L. Hannan House, renovation, Marblehead

Lynn Slum Clearance Project, Bond, Church, and Pleasant Sts., Lynn

Fleur-de-Lis Camp, cabins, Fitzwilliam, N.H.

Subsistence Homesteads, U.S. Department of the Interior project

Paine Webber Company, office renovation, Gurney St., Lynn

1934   Lynn Boy Scout Camp, North Saugus, Mass.

Robert F. Kimball, renovation, Humphreys St., Phillips Beach, Mass.

National City Bank, various houses, Lynn

Pinkham, Smith Burnham, office renovation, Western Ave., Lynn

1935   Radcliffe College, Atkinson Room, Fay House, Cambridge

Cambridge Social Union, Brattle St., Cambridge

Fleur-de-Lis Camp, cabins, Fitzwilliam, N.H.

Kinsley Draper House, Canton, Mass.

Helen Durgin House, renovation, Bradford, Mass.

1936   Frances E. Wood House, Harvard, Mass.

Corinne Loomis, renovation, Louisburg Square, Boston

McLane, Davis, and Carleton, renovation of law offices, Manchester, N.H.

Radcliffe College, stage arrangement, Cambridge

Mrs. Buckmaster House, renovation, Woburn, Mass.

McLane Guest House, Three Acre, Manchester, N.H.
Josephine Perkins House, Southborough
Mrs. Francis J. Moors, parsonage, Wilton, N.H.
Mrs. Everett B. Sweezy House, addition, Memorial Dr., Cambridge
1937   James B. Greason, Jr., garage, Mountain View Rd., Whitefield, N.H.
Garland School, kitchen, Boston
Old Harbor Village, housing project, South Boston (seventeen associated architects)

Writings by Howe

"An Alumna's Architectural Career." *Technology Review* 66, no. 2 (December 1963): 21, 38.
An Architectural Monograph: The Colonel Robert Means House at Amherst, New Hampshire. White Pine Series of Architectural Monographs 13. New York: R. F. Whitehead, 1927.
"Serving Pantries in Small Houses." *Architectural Review* 14 (March 1907): 31–33.
Various articles in the *Cambridge Historical Society Publications, Proceedings.*
With Constance Fuller. *Details from Old New England Houses.* New York: Architectural Book Publishing Co., 1913.

Sources

Brown, Frank Chouteau. "Boston Suburban Architecture." *Architectural Record* 21 (April 1907): 245–80.
Cole, Doris, and Karen Cord Taylor. *The Lady Architects: Lois Lilley Howe, Eleanor Manning, and Mary Almy, 1893–1937.* New York: Midmarch Press, 1990.
"House of Mrs. A. A. Burrage, Beach Road, Brookline, Mass." *American Architect and Building News* 88 (July 15, 1905): 24, plate.
"Lois Howe: Portrait." *Architectural Forum* 101 (July 1954): 116.
"Lois Lilley Howe." In *American Women, 1935–1940,* edited by Durwood Howes, 430. Detroit: Gale, 1981.
"Lois Lilley Howe: Obituary." *Progressive Architecture* 45 (October 1964): 118.
McCavitt, Mary Jane. "Notes from Finding Aid to Hope, Manning, and Almy papers, 1883–1973." Manuscript Collection MC-9, Institute Archives and Special Collections, MIT.
Morse, Gail. "The Firm: A Study of the First Women's Architectural Firm in Boston: Howe, Manning, and Almy." B.A. thesis, Boston University, 1976.
Paine, Judith. "Pioneer Women Architects." In *Women in American Architecture,* edited by Susan Torre, 66–68. New York: Whitney Library of Design, 1977.
Reinhardt, Elizabeth W. "Lois Lilley Howe, FAIA, 1864–1964." *Cambridge Historical Society Publications* 43 (1980): 153–72.

LOCATION OF PAPERS. The Howe, Manning, and Almy Papers are part of the Manuscript Collection, Institute Archives and Special Collections, MIT, Cambridge. The MIT Museum and Historical Collections has a file on Lois Lilley Howe, as does the Schlesinger Library, Radcliffe College. The Daniel H. Burnham Papers at the Art Institute of Chicago contain information on Howe's participation in the World's Columbian Exposition.

|||||||||||||||||||||||||
Irwin, Harriet Morrison (1828–97)
|||||||||||||||||||||||||

A self-taught designer, Harriet Morrison Irwin was the first American woman to patent an architectural design. Descriptions of Irwin's family focus on her father's achievements as president of Davidson College and the fact that her sister, Mary Ann, was married to Stonewall Jackson. Born in Mecklenburg County, North Carolina, in 1818, Harriet Morrison Irwin was one of ten children in a family famous for its support of the Confederacy. Her formal education took place at the Institution for Female Education in Salem, North Carolina. After graduation, Morrison spent some time in Europe before marrying James Patton Irwin in Alabama. The family settled in Charlotte, North Carolina, and included nine children.

Morrison's experiments in architecture appear to have begun when she was in her fifties. In 1869, she received patent number 94,116 for "improvement in the construction of houses." Irwin's design, a hexagonal building, was built on West Fifth Street in Charlotte, North Carolina. One source of inspiration may have been *A Home for All* (1850), Orson Fowler's popular book on the social and economic benefits of hexagonal structures. Irwin's plan was intended to make better use of space for growing families and to reduce housekeeping chores by decreasing the number of corners to clean. According to Madeleine B. Stern, Irwin produced "at least two other dwellings which she designed along more conventional lines and angles."[20]

Writings by Irwin
The Hermit of Petraea. Charlotte, N.C., 1871.

Sources
Adams, Marie. "Harriet Morrison Irwin, Architect." *Charlotte News,* December 7, 1962, 2B.
Annual Report of the Commissioner of Patents, 1869. Washington, D.C.: Government Printing Office, 1871. See esp. 165, 474.

Fowler, Orson S. *The Octagon House: A Home for All.* New York: Dover, 1973. Reprint of the 1854 edition entitled *A Home for All.*

"Harriet Morrison Irwin." *Macmillan Encyclopedia of Architects,* vol. 2, 466–67. New York: Free Press, 1982

Heisner, Beverly. "Harriet Morrison Irwin's Hexagonal House: An Invention to Improve Domestic Dwellings." *North Carolina Historical Review* 58, no. 2 (1981): 105–23.

Lancaster, Clay. *Architectural Follies in America.* Rutland, Vt.: Tuttle, 1960. See esp. 130, 141.

Stern, Madeleine B. *We the Women: Career Firsts of Nineteenth Century America.* New York: Artemis, 1962. See esp. 55–61.

||||||||||||||||||||||||
Johnson, Alice E. (1862–1936)
||||||||||||||||||||||||

Like many male architects of her day, Alice E. Johnson received her architectural training in an office. Her apprenticeship was under her father, the architect John Carlton Johnson. The family firm in Fremont, Ohio, had many public buildings to its credit, including infirmaries, schools, jails, churches, city halls, and county courthouses. In 1889, Alice Johnson was listed in the Fremont city directory as a practicing architect. The family firm completed a major commission in 1890, the Sandusky County Jail and Sheriff House in Fremont, now on the National Register of Historic Places.

Trinity United Methodist Church, a Gothic building described in the *Art Work of Seneca and Sandusky Counties,* was designed by Johnson and built in 1895. After the death of her father in 1901, Johnson worked on her own, designing residences and business buildings in the Midwest. In 1903, *Ohio Architect and Engineer* took note of two houses she designed in Fremont: a wood frame house for David B. Love and a brick and stone residence for W. B. Kridler.

Partial List of Buildings

1895	Trinity United Methodist Church, Fremont, Ohio
ca. 1903	David B. Love House, Fremont
	W. B. Kridler House, Fremont

Writings by Johnson

"Architecture as a Woman Sees It." *Interstate Architect and Builder* 3 (April 13, 1901): 8.

LOCATION OF PAPERS. The Rutherford B. Hayes Presidential Center in Fremont, Ohio, holds manuscripts relating to the life and work of Alice Johnson. A portrait (ca. 1906) of Johnson is in the Reinhard Grob Collection at the Hayes Center.

IIIIIIIIIIIIIIIIIIIIIIIII
Keichline, Anna Wagner (1889–1943)
IIIIIIIIIIIIIIIIIIIIIIIII

Anna Keichline began her career as a designer at the age of fourteen, when she won first prize at the Centre County (Pennsylvania) Fair for a handmade oak table and walnut chest. The photograph of Keichline that appeared in the *Philadelphia Inquirer* after her achievement has been widely published. Keichline grew up in Bellefonte, Pennsylvania, and was taught carpentry skills by her father. She studied mechanical engineering at Pennsylvania State College for a year before graduating from Cornell University's architectural program in 1911. The next year, Keichline filed her first patent for a new type of combined sink and washtub. In 1920, she became the first female registered architect in the state of Pennsylvania, and, although her career as an industrial designer overshadowed her work as an architect, she is said to have designed buildings in Pennsylvania, Ohio, and Washington, D.C.

As an industrial designer, Keichline patented a total of seven inventions, including a portable partition design, a fold-away bed for apartments, and an economical, efficient form of kitchen construction. In engineering circles she is acknowledged for inventing and patenting the K-brick (1927), an inexpensive, lightweight clay brick designed for hollow wall construction that could be filled with insulation or soundproofing material (figs. 28 and 29). According to the MIT School of Engineering Web site (January 2005), the K-brick led to the development of today's concrete block. The American Ceramic Society honored Keichline for her invention in 1931.

Keichline was active in social causes, including suffrage and low-income housing. During World War II, she served as a special agent for United States military intelligence.

Partial List of Buildings

1912	Schoolhouse, Milesburg (Central City), Pa.
1915	Bald Eagle and Nittany Valley Presbyterian Church, Mill Hall, Pa.

FIGURE 28. K-brick, designed by Anna Keichline. Courtesy International Archive of Women in Architecture.

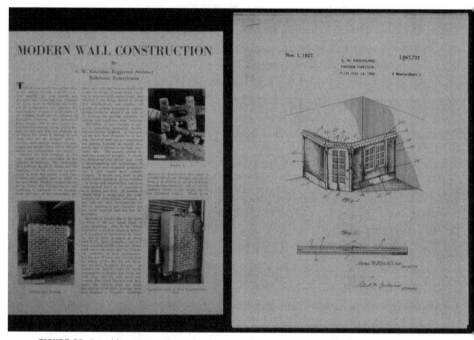

FIGURE 29. Portable partition design by Anna Keichline. Courtesy International Archive of Women in Architecture.

1916	Cadillac Garage and Apartments (County Chevrolet Garage), Bellefonte, Pa.
	George P. Bible House, Bellefonte
1925	Plaza Theater, Bellefonte
1927	Juniata Colony Country Clubhouse, Mt. Union, Pa.
1931	Decker House, Bellefonte
1935	B. O. Harvey Apartments, Bellefonte
1936	Model Home designs, Bellefonte
1939	Harvey House, Bellefonte
1940	Orthner Home and Office, Huntingdon, Pa.

Writings by Keichline

"Modern Wall Construction." *Clay Worker,* June 1, 1932.

Sources

Howard, Ella, and Eric Setliff. "'In a Man's World': Women Industrial Designers." In *Women Designers in the USA, 1900–2000,* edited by Pat Kirkham, 269–70. New Haven: Yale University Press, 2000.

LOCATION OF PAPERS. The International Archive of Women in Architecture in Blacksburg, Virginia, has a collection of Keichline's papers (1900–1940) that include photocopies of her patents, photographs, and biographical information.

IIIIIIIIIIIIIIIIIIIIIIIIII
Kellogg, Fay (1871–1918)
IIIIIIIIIIIIIIIIIIIIIIIIII

A Brooklyn native, Fay Kellogg attended Columbian University (now George Washington University) in Washington, D.C., with plans to become a doctor. Although she enjoyed studying medicine, her father encouraged her to give up the profession by offering to pay for architectural drawing instruction. Kellogg studied design under a German tutor for two years and then spent a year at the Pratt Institute in Brooklyn. She found employment with the architect R. L. Davis, working as a drafter on Davis's major projects, including the Thirteenth Regiment Armory and the Monastery of the Precious Blood. She also spent a year with the renowned New York firm Carrère and Hastings. Despite this intensive study and practical experience, Kellogg took the unusual step of attempting to gain admission to the Ecole des Beaux-Arts. Although she was not officially admitted to the school, she studied in the atelier of Marcel de Monclos, a young French architect with an American wife. According to the *New York Times,* Kellogg's efforts on behalf of women played a significant role in opening up the school to female students. In fact, Kellogg may have helped to pave the way for the first official woman graduate of the Ecole, Julia Morgan, who entered the school in 1898 and received a certificate in 1902.

When Kellogg returned to New York in 1900, she was employed by the architect John R. Thomas until his death three years later. Kellogg then opened her own practice. One of her first commissions involved remodeling seven buildings on Park Place to accommodate the American News Company. After the completion of this high-profile project, Kellogg was hired to draft blueprints for the company's buildings throughout the country, including a new office in San Francisco. In a 1907 *New York Times* article, "Woman Invades Field of Modern Architecture," Kellogg stated that she was often asked about her experience as a woman in the profession. Her response was that it had been "most happy" because she did "not permit sentiment to enter into it whatever," but met men "on equal lines."[21] And, as the *New York Times* reported, she was allowed to carry out her ambition and to influence modern architecture.

Later in her career, Kellogg designed Hostess Houses for World War I military camps in the southeastern United States. She died at the age of forty-eight in the midst of an exciting career. In an interview the year before her death, Kellogg encouraged women who were taking on men's work for the war effort not to limit their own professional aspirations.

Partial List of Buildings

1917	YWCA National War Council Hostess House ("country-club bungalow type"), Camp Sevier, Greenville, S.C.
	YWCA National War Council Hostess House, Charlotte, N.C.
	YWCA Hostess House, Camp Warden McLean, Chattanooga, Tenn.
1918	YWCA Building, Navy Yard, Charleston, S.C.

Writings by Kellogg

"Women as Builders of Homes." *Southern Architect and Building News* 29 (June 1912): 18–20.

Sources

Manufacturer's Record. September 13, 1917; September 27, 1917; October 25, 1917; November 1, 1917; January 24, 1918.

McQuaid, Matilda. "Educating for the Future: A Growing Archive on Women and Architecture." In *Architecture: A Place for Women,* edited by Ellen Perry Berkeley and Matilda McQuaid, 255. Washington, D.C.: Smithsonian Institution Press, 1989.

"Miss Fay Kellogg Passes." *Southern Architect and Building News* 41 (September 1918): 51.

"Miss Fay Kellogg, Woman Architect." *Pearson's Magazine,* February 1911, 227.

"Miss Kellogg Visits Atlanta, Talks." *Southern Architect and Building News* 40 (November 1917): 33–34.

"New York's Real Lure for Women—Opportunity." *New York Times,* November 12, 1911, SM7.

"Woman Invades Field of Modern Architecture." *New York Times,* November 17, 1907, SM11.

||||||||||||||||||||||||||
Luscomb, Florence Hope (1887–1985)
||||||||||||||||||||||||||

Florence Luscomb is better known for her work in the woman suffrage movement and as a civil rights activist than for her early architectural practice. Luscomb graduated from MIT in 1909, submitting a thesis entitled "A Country Estate at the Sea-shore," and immediately began work as a drafter for Ida Annah Ryan in Waltham. Ryan, the first woman to graduate from MIT with a master's degree in architecture, received several class awards and a traveling fellowship. She shared Luscomb's political views and encouraged her interest in woman suffrage, giving Luscomb freedom to participate in the cause as necessary (fig. 30). When the Cambridge School of Architecture and Landscape Architecture officially opened in 1916, Luscomb continued her education there, studying in the offices of Henry Frost and Bremer Pond. Her work in the Waltham firm ended when World War I put a stop to new building and the issuing of building permits.

In an oral history interview Luscomb described the difficulties women students encountered finding work in the architectural profession. At the end of sophomore year at MIT, architecture students customarily worked for architects to gain practical experience, usually receiving no pay for a full summer's work. When Luscomb attempted to follow this practice, she was turned down

FIGURE 30. Florence Luscomb distributing copies of the *Woman's Journal,* a weekly periodical of the American Woman Suffrage Association, n.d. Courtesy MIT Museum.

by eleven architects before one finally took her on. After the second week, her employer placed two dollars on her desk to cover carfare and lunches.

During the 1920s, Luscomb put aside her architectural aspirations and began a career as a social activist. She worked for prison and labor reform, supervised political campaigns, and was an organizer for the civil rights, antiwar, and women's movements.

Sources

Cantarow, Ellen. *Moving the Mountain: Women Working for Social Change*. Old Westbury, N.Y.: Feminist Press, 1980.

Koenigsberg, Lisa M. "Professionalizing Domesticity: A Tradition of American Women Writers on Architecture." Ph.D. diss., Yale University, 1987. See esp. 95.

"The 20th Century Trade Woman: Vehicle for Social Change." Interview by Brigid O'Farrell. Oral History Project, Ann Arbor, Michigan, 1978.

LOCATION OF PAPERS. Florence Hope Luscomb Papers, 1856–1979 Manuscript Collection, Schlesinger Library, Radcliffe College.

|||||||||||||||||||||||||||
Manley, Marion Isadore (1893–1984)
|||||||||||||||||||||||||||

Born in 1893, the youngest of nine children, Marion Isadore Manley grew up on a homestead known as "Cherrycroft," in western Kansas. After graduating from a local high school in 1911, Manley spent three years at Kansas State before transferring to the University of Illinois. One of only three universities open to women architectural students in the early 1870s, the university had granted architectural degrees to at least seven women before Manley, and two went on to earn master's degrees. However, when Manley graduated from the university with a bachelor of science degree in architecture in 1917, she was the only woman in her class.

Manley began her architectural career in Miami, Florida, where she was soon employed by the architect Walter DeGarmo, primarily in designing residences. During World War I, Manley worked on a project to remodel a convent in Key West into military barracks, and she helped design ships for the Emergency Fleet Corporation in Philadelphia. In 1918 Manley became the second woman licensed to practice architecture in Florida. She worked briefly as senior drafter for James J. Baldwin, an architect in Anderson, South Carolina, before settling in Florida for the remainder of her career. One early work attributed to Manley is a Spanish-style residence in a neighborhood called Miami Shores established north of Miami by the Shoreland Development Company. Manley became a member of the AIA in 1926.

In 1929, Manley was lucky to find an important position as a senior drafter for the architect Phineas Paist and to work on a United States Post Office and Courthouse in downtown Miami. Although the commission occupied Manley for about three years, she was barely able to make ends meet.

In fact, she could not even afford to pay her AIA dues. By the late 1930s, however, Manley had rejoined the AIA and maintained her own successful practice, primarily designing residences throughout south Florida. She gained considerable recognition for her ability to design stylish domestic spaces suited to the climate.

Although involved in civic affairs since 1920, when she served as treasurer of the Florida Business and Professional Women's Club, Manley eventually became frustrated with the state bureaucracy. From 1938 to 1945 she was a member of the Coral Gables Board of Supervising Architects, and from 1942 to 1945 she served on Miami's planning board. In both cases, Manley resigned after struggling to change what she viewed as a political situation that prevented the design of sound architecture. She continued her very active local efforts, however, serving as vice president of the Florida Association of Architects in 1945 and 1946. As president of the Florida South chapter of the AIA, Manley must have found her position less frustrating. In 1941, she attended the organization's seventy-third convention, at Yosemite National Park. While at the meeting, she met the Santa Barbara architect Lutah Maria Riggs. She later wrote to Riggs, "They [the members at the meeting] actually thought, before you turned up at Yosemite, that I was the first and only woman Chapter President."[22] In 1947, Manley was the AIA representative at the Pan American Congress of Architects in Lima, Peru. Three years later, she played the same role in Havana, and in 1952, at the Mexico City conference.

In 1943, Manley was hired to work on a master plan for the University of Miami, a brand-new campus with an anticipated enrollment of ten thousand (fig. 31). The architect Robert Law Weed became part of the planning team on her recommendation, and they collaborated on the Memorial Classroom Building in 1946 and a Veterans' Housing Project in 1948, the largest financed by the Federal Housing Administration in its day. She designed the Baptist Student Center (1949), Canterbury House (Episcopal) (1951), and the university's Ring Theater (1951, with the Miami architect Robert Little). According to several accounts, Manley's efforts at the university were overshadowed by those of the famous architect she had chosen as collaborator. It should be noted, however, that the Web site of the University of Miami School of Architecture states that Manley "designed the six buildings of the school in 1947 as part of a compound built to house the returning veterans of World War II." Weed is not mentioned.[23]

Manley did not give up on her efforts to influence regional zoning, particularly in reference to African Americans. Beginning in 1946 she worked on a Coral Gables zoning committee, and from 1948 to 1949, she was a mem-

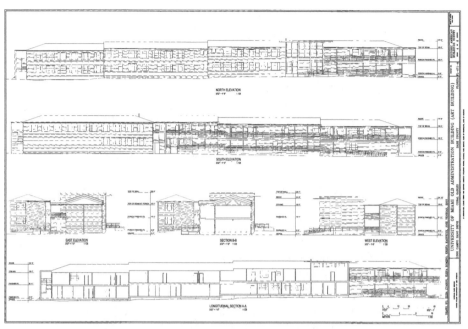

FIGURE 31. University of Miami, Old Administration Building, Coral Gables, Florida. Robert Law Weed and Marion Manley, architects. Drawings by HABS. Courtesy Library of Congress, Prints and Photographs Division.

ber of the Coconut Grove slum clearance committee and the committee for rezoning. One of her contributions was the donation of plans for the Negro Community Center and the St. Alban's Day Nursery for Negro Children, both in Coconut Grove.

In 1956, Manley became a Fellow of the AIA, a nomination supported with more than eighty letters of recommendation, including six from women architects, not to mention those from established practitioners such as William W. Wurster, Ralph Walker, and Eero Saarinen. The Florida AIA presented her with its gold medal award in 1973 and the Florida South chapter of the AIA gave her its silver medal in 1975. Despite many honors, numerous publications mentioning her work, and her obvious contribution to Florida's architecture, Manley has not been included in contemporary research on women architects. As Emily Adams Perry notes, "even in literature which deals specifically with women as architects, the name of Marion Isadore Manley is not included. The reason for this omission is not known."[24]

Partial List of Buildings

1926	Paul Scott House, 598 N.E. 56th St., Miami, Fla.
1935	Leo Terletzky House, Ye Little Wood, Coconut Grove, Fla.
1940	H. Bert Albury, store, Commodore Plaza, Coconut Grove
1948	Federal Housing Administration Veterans' Housing Project, Miami (with Robert Law Weed)
	Sarepta B. Terletzky House, Sunshine Villas, Douglas Rd., Miami
	Mr. and Mrs. Philip Wylie House, Erwin Rd., Dade County, Fla.
1949	Baptist Student Center, University of Miami, Coral Gables, Fla.
	Mr. and Mrs. Samuel Bell IV House, University Pl., S.W. 47th Ct., Dade County
1950	Peyton Wilson House, Dade County
	Mr. and Mrs. Gaines Wilson House, addition, 3853 Little Ave., Coconut Grove
1951	Mr. and Mrs. Samuel Bell III House, Coconut Grove
	Canterbury House (first portion), University of Miami, Coral Gables
	Mr. and Mrs. Stanley M. Rinehart Jr. House, Palm Vista subdivision, Dade County
	Koubek 27th Avenue Center, University of Miami, Coral Gables
	Ring Theater, 1312 Miller Dr., University of Miami, Coral Gables (with Robert Little)
1954	John and Mabel Ringling Museum of Art, addition, Sarasota, Fla. (with Guy C. Fulton)
	Mr. and Mrs. John Moulthrop House, addition, 4161 Battersea, Coconut Grove
1955	Marion I. Manley House, Coconut Grove
	Mr. and Mrs. Louis Olson House, Galleons Reach, Manasota Key (Sarasota County), Fla.
1956	Mr. and Mrs. Philip R. Anderson House, 4050 Battersea Rd., Coconut Grove
	Wirth Munroe, store addition, Coconut Grove
	Mr. and Mrs. Paul J. Sullivan House, Old Cutler Rd. at S.W. 129th Terrace, Pinecrest, Fla.

1957	Ray Sadeler, cottage, Northeast Miami
	Robert H. Thayer Jr. House, St. Gaudens Grove, Coconut Grove
	Mr and Mrs. Robert C. Hector House, South Miami
1959	Mr. and Mrs. Horace Brown, cottage, Penn Key Club, Islamorada, Fla.
	Canterbury House (Chapel of the Veneral Bede), University of Miami, Coral Gables
1960	Johnson, Lane, Space, and Co., Inc., brokerage office remodel, Lejeune Rd., Coral Gables
	Quaker Meeting House, Coral Gables
1961	Mr. and Mrs. Stanley M. Rinehart Jr. House, addition, Dade County
1962	Mrs. Forbes Hawkes House, addition, Coconut Grove
	Sengra-Graham office building, Miami Lakes, Fla.
1963	Lake Patricia Shopping Center, shops, Miami Lakes
	J. Wilson Smith and Laurence Cardwell House, Redlands, Fla.
	Mrs. and Mrs. Herbert S. Zim House, Plantation Key, Fla.
1964	Mr. and Mrs. Altmayer Jr. House, Dade County
	Professional Building, Lake Patricia Shopping Center, Miami Lakes
1966	Mr. and Mrs. Harold Graves, cottage, Plantation Key
	Mr. and Mrs. William H. MacTye House, renovations, Miami Beach, Fla.
1967	Mr. and Mrs. E. L. Ford House, addition and remodel, Pinecrest, Dade County
	Eugene and Gwladys Scott House, Dade County
	Herbert Zim cottage, Plantation Key
1968	Mr. and Mrs. Robert Altemus House, remodel and additions, Crawford Ave., Coconut Grove
	Mr. and Mrs. Robert W. Barker House, Plantation Key
	The Doctors Branning, cottage, Plantation Key
	Eleanor H. Hogg House, remodel, Coconut Grove
	Mr. and Mrs. Joseph M. Jones House, remodel, Coconut Grove
1970	Dr. Melville Bell Grosvenor House, renovation, Coconut Grove

1971   The Doctors Branning House, Plantation Key
     Mrs. Walter K. Myers House, remodel, Coconut Grove

Sources

"Architect Spells Profession, Nickname, for Marion Manley; It's Her Hobby Too." *Miami Herald,* May 11, 1952.

Bayer, William. "Architect Sees Politics Blocking the Way." *Miami Herald,* October 7, 1951.

"Miami University Adds Two More Building Groups to Its Brand-new and Growing Campus. *Architectural Forum* 90 (June 1949): 70–75.

"Modern College: Miami's New Buildings Set New Campus Style." *Life,* December 27, 1948, 72–73.

"A New Architecture for Tropical Florida." *Architectural Forum* 94 (February 1951): 131.

Perry, Emily Adams. "Marion Isadore Manley: Pioneer Woman Architect." In *Florida Pathfinders,* edited by Lewis N. Wynne and James J. Horgan. Saint Leo, Fla.: Saint Leo College Press, 1994.

"Ring Theater, Miami Florida." *Progressive Architecture* 34 (August 1953): 114–17.

"Second Story on Stilts (House in Coconut Grove, Fla.)." *House and Home,* August 1953, 86–91.

"University of Miami." *Architectural Forum* 89 (July 1948): 76–82.

LOCATION OF PAPERS. The Research Center of the Historical Museum of Southern Florida has the Marion Manley Architectural Drawings and Papers, 1935–71. Records of Manley's AIA membership and election to fellowship are in the AIA membership files, Record Group 803, American Institute of Architects Archives, Washington, D.C.

||||||||||||||||||||||||
Manning, Eleanor (1884–1973)
||||||||||||||||||||||||

Eleanor Manning grew up in Lynn, Massachusetts, the daughter of Irish immigrants. In 1906, she graduated from MIT with a bachelor of science degree in architecture, having produced a thesis entitled "Design for a Country Residence." Shortly after graduation, Manning embarked on a European tour and then worked privately for a year with assistance from the architect Eliza Newkirk Rogers (see her entry). In 1907, Manning became a drafter for Lois Lilley Howe. Six years later, she was made partner in Howe's firm, which became Howe and Manning, the country's fourth firm of female architects.

Manning coined the term "renovising" to describe how the firm renovated and revised outdated structures, a practice that became central to its livelihood and an essential part of its philosophy. The firm's large number of renovations—nearly two hundred—illustrates that such work was in high demand, and the fact that commissions often clustered in close proximity suggests that word of its success traveled through neighborhoods. The firm capitalized on this desire to renovate residences by focusing on the value of saving houses, reusing materials, and creating efficient, practical living spaces without wasting space.

In 1921, Manning applied for membership in the AIA, stating that she had spent one year practicing alone, five years as a drafter with Lois L. Howe, and nine years with the firm. She became an AIA member in 1923. Manning married Johnson O'Connor, founder of the Johnson O'Connor Research Foundation and the Human Engineering Laboratories, when she was forty-five, and some of her subsequent projects involved his work.

According to the biographer Doris Cole, Manning was the partner most concerned with social issues. Passionate about creating decent housing for all, Manning was involved in housing at the local, state, and national levels. She also believed in spreading her ideals through teaching; she taught at Simmons College for fifty years and lectured at other schools. The firm's commission for a major Boston public housing project provided an opportunity for Manning to experiment with some of her ideas. Along with seventeen associated architects, Manning designed low-cost housing in Old Harbor Village, a WPA housing project in an Irish neighborhood of South Boston (now called Mary Ellen McCormack Housing Development) constructed from 1933 to 1938. Old Harbor Village was one of the first public housing developments in the nation and has more than a thousand units. Despite the number of architects involved, Cole finds evidence of Manning's influence in the overall design, including the classical detailing, the choice of materials, and the attention to proportion, all of which contribute to a sense of home. Unlike typical public housing, the units are three-story apartment buildings and two-story townhouses grouped together around courtyards and entries, giving the eight hundred walk-up and two hundred row houses a residential feeling. The Mary Ellen McCormack Housing Development was considered the best designed and best functioning housing project in Boston during the early 1990s, and when state funds were finally available, basic maintenance was done to keep it running smoothly.[25]

During the 1940s, Manning served on several national housing committees, and, while working for the Massachusetts Civic League, she created and implemented one of the country's first housing management courses for specialists in the field. When the firm of Howe, Manning, and Almy dissolved in 1937, Manning continued in private practice until 1959. She died in Mexico in 1973, at the age of eighty-nine, while doing research on Indian cultures.

List of Buildings

See entry on Lois Howe for works by the firm of Howe, Manning, and Almy

Writings by Manning, as E. M. O'Connor

"Architecture as a Profession for Women." *Simmons Review,* Simmons College (April 1934): 71–75.
"Building for National Welfare." *National Altrusan,* March 1935.

Sources

AIA and Architectural League, New York. *Architectural and Allied Arts Exposition.* New York: AIA and Architectural League, 1925. See esp. 34.
Cole, Doris, and Karen Cord Taylor. *The Lady Architects: Lois Lilley Howe, Eleanor Manning, and Mary Almy, 1893–1937.* New York: Midmarch Press, 1990.
"Eleanor Manning." *Macmillan Encyclopedia of Architects,* vol. 3, 91–92. New York: Free Press, 1982.
"O'Connor, Eleanor Manning." In *American Women, 1935–1940,* edited by Durwood Howes, 669. Detroit: Gale, 1981.
"One Hundred Small Houses." *Architecture,* October 1935.

LOCATION OF PAPERS. The Howe, Manning, and Almy Papers, 1883–1973, are held by the Manuscript Collection, Institute Archives and Special Collections, MIT. An inventory of the collection has been published.

||||||||||||||||||||||||
Martini, Elisabeth A. (b. 1886)
||||||||||||||||||||||||

Little is known of the architect Elisabeth Martini other than the information she supplied on an AIA application in 1943. A native of Brooklyn, Martini attended high school in Fitchburg, Massachusetts, before entering Pratt Institute in Brooklyn and pursuing special studies at Columbia University. In 1913, she traveled in Holland and Germany. Before 1914, she had worked as a drafter for William A. Otis, William Pryon, John Sutcliffe, and Spencer and Powers, all firms in Chicago. After 1914, she maintained her own office but continued to assist others in what she called their "rush periods." Among those she assisted were the Chicago architects George Beaumont, Emery Stanford Hall, Arthur Woltersdorf, Harry B. Wheelock, L. Stanhope, and W. G. Kohfeldt. In 1921, Martini founded the Chicago Drafting Club, one of the first organizations for women architects. The club formed the core of a larger group, the Women's Architectural Club, which included Bertha Whitman and Juliet Peddle among its nine original members. The Women's Architectural Club was active from 1928 until the 1940s.

In 1934, Martini moved her practice to Michigan. She was a registered architect in Michigan when she became a member of the AIA.

LOCATION OF PAPERS. AIA membership files, Record Group 803, American Institute of Architects Archives, Washington, D.C. (note: Martini does not have a permanent box and folder number).

IIIIIIIIIIIIIIIIIIIIIIIIIIII
McCain, Ida (b. 1884)
IIIIIIIIIIIIIIIIIIIIIIIIIIII

Among the most prolific women architects of her day, Ida McCain tapped into the market in California for Bay Area bungalows and teamed up with developers to design hundreds of affordable houses. McCain was born in Fort Collins, Colorado, and attended local public schools before enrolling at Colorado State Agricultural College. In her second year, an architecture course was introduced that inspired her to launch a career in the field. After graduating, she moved to Los Angeles with her family and worked for a successful church architect, L. B. Valk, and for the firm of Lambert and Bartin. A partner in the firm just a year later, McCain designed and built several homes in the area. She and her family moved to Portland, Oregon, in 1909, where she also designed residences, before settling in San Francisco about 1915.

It was a time of rapid development in the Bay Area, and McCain was able to run the architectural department of the Stephen A. Born Building Company. During her years with the company, McCain was responsible for the design of many homes in what would become some of the region's most sought-after neighborhoods, such as Lincoln Manor and Westwood Park. Her work at Lincoln Manor included a tile-roofed "Spanish renaissance type" for her employer, Stephen Born. For the developer Baldwin and Howell, McCain supervised the architectural work on Westwood Park, which was considered a pioneering type of residential development with homes arranged on an oval plan. A 1920 advertisement for Baldwin and Howell's Westwood Park shows a caricature of McCain, a woman with an oversized head and a t-square as large as her body, standing near a house plan and the words "I'll design a bungalow especially for YOU" (fig. 32). The company clearly promoted its

Why I chose Westwood Park
for my Bungalows

A word about "Westwood"
by Miss Ida McCain, Expert
Bungalow Designer

"**B**ECAUSE I know it's the best place; best for me and most decidedly best for the home buyer.

"I can buy a fine big lot at from $750 to $1500 less than in any other equally desirable tract. 'Westwood' is more active; people like it and my bungalows sell much faster—I turn my money over quicker.

"And I am in good company. Fourteen of the best bungalow 'specialists' I know of are trying to outdo each other in artistic design, ideal arrangement and substantial construction. That keeps me keyed up to do my best and accounts for nearly 250 attractive homes already completed."

Take any bungalow in "Westwood" on same size lot and you cannot duplicate it at anything like the price for which you can buy at "Westwood Park." COMPARE — and you will buy at "Westwood."

I'll design a bungalow specially for YOU

We're glad to say that "Westwood Park" owes much to Miss McCain's skill and tireless energy, for, as our pictures show, she has designed and constructed some of the most notable bungalows in San Francisco.

Municipal "K" Car.
(Ingleside)

Direct to
WESTWOOD

BALDWIN & HOWELL
318-324 KEARNY ST
Phones Kearny 3810. Tract Office, Randolph 1454

FIGURE 32. Advertisement for Ida McCain bungalows, from the *San Francisco Chronicle*, June 5, 1920.

chief architect, declaring that Westwood Park owed much to McCain's "skill and tireless energy."[26]

After about six years with Born, McCain established herself as an independent architect, builder, and real estate agent. She focused her attention on the San Francisco Peninsula, where she helped to create the neighborhoods of San Mateo Park, St. Francis Woods, and Monterey Heights. McCain designed a corner house for herself in San Mateo Park, an unpretentious two-bedroom stucco bungalow. By 1930, she was living with her older sister and mother in a San Francisco apartment house, which she owned and supervised. Nothing is known about Ida McCain after 1937.

Partial List of Buildings

1916	Ernest Dettner House, 45 Upper Terrace, San Francisco
1918–23	Westwood Park Houses, 180 Westwood, 600 Miramar Ave., 701 Miramar Ave., San Francisco

Sources

Hunt, Rockwell D., ed. *California and Californians,* vol. 4. Chicago: Lewis Publishing, 1932.

Weinstein, Dave. "Ida McCain, Builder of Bungalows." *San Francisco Chronicle,* October 9, 2004.

"Why I Chose Westwood Park for My Bungalows" (advertisement). *San Francisco Chronicle,* June 5, 1920, 6.

|||||||||||||||||||||||||||
Mead, Marcia (1879–1967)
|||||||||||||||||||||||||||

Born in Pittsfield, Pennsylvania, Marcia Mead graduated from the State Normal College in Edinboro, Pennsylvania, in 1898. Despite these humble beginnings, Mead became the first woman to graduate from Columbia University's School of Architecture, in 1913, and set out to prove that women could succeed in the architectural profession. In March 1914, she and Anna Schenck organized their own firm in New York. The *New York Times* covered the story of the "first" firm of women architects, Schenck and Mead, noting that the venture was "expected to show that women need only opportunity." The confident pair announced that "other women architects, practicing independently have done fairly well; we are going to do very well."[27] A year after the interview, Schenck and Mead won a competition sponsored by the City Club of Chicago for a neighborhood center for children in the Bronx. The site they chose, between Washington Bridge and Macomb's Dam Park, was designed to provide services that residents would otherwise leave the area to obtain, such as social clubs, a gymnasium, library, and dance hall. Less than two years later, Anna Schenck died.

After her partner's death, Mead continued her own practice, although her firm retained the name Schenck and Mead for several years. At the time of her AIA application in 1918, Mead listed ten years of experience in an architect's office. During World War I she designed housing in Washington, D.C., for African American war workers. Her housing community at Bridgeport, Connecticut, was pictured in *Architectural Record* (October 1918), which noted that she was also the architect of the Wilson Memorial housing development in Washington, D.C. three years before. In 1925, Mead exhibited her work in the small house section of the "McCall Group" at the AIA/Architectural League and Allied Arts Exposition. Her major commissions include a series of projects for the Bridgeport Housing Company and YWCAs in Jersey City, New Jersey; Buffalo, New York; and Bridgeport, Connecticut. Mead was a member of the United States Housing Commission and a part-time professor at her alma mater, the School of Architecture at Columbia. In 1931, Mead interviewed Julia Morgan for the *Christian Science Monitor*.

Partial List of Buildings

1915	Ellen Wilson Memorial housing development, Washington, D.C. (designs accepted by the United States Housing Corporation; executed after World War I).
1918	Bridgeport Housing Company, planned community, Connecticut Ave., Bridgeport, Conn.
1927	YWCA, 270 Fairmount Ave., Jersey City, N.J.
n.d.	Marie McCaffery Cisneros House, Cranford, N.J.

Writings by Mead

"The Architecture of the Small House as Influenced by Our Modern Industrial Communities." *Architecture* 37 (June 1918): 145–54.

"The Bridgeport Housing Development." *American Architect* 113 (February 6, 1918): 129–48.

Homes of Character. New York: Dodd, Mead, 1926.

"Look Before You Leap." *McCall's,* April 1932, 40.

"Women's Versatility in Arts Enriches Field of Architecture." *Christian Science Monitor,* November 27, 1931, 5.

Sources

AIA and Architectural League, New York. *Architectural and Allied Arts Exposition*. New York: AIA and Architectural League, 1925. See esp. 46.

"Connecticut Development—Bridgeport Housing Co." *Architectural Record* 44 (October 1918): 303–4.

"Girl Architects Organize a Firm." *New York Times,* March 8, 1914, 15.

Paine, Judith. "Pioneer Women Architects." In *Women in American Architecture,* edited by Susan Torre, 68, photo. New York: Whitney Library of Design, 1977.

"The War-Boom City, Housing in Bridgeport." *Woman Citizen,* July 20, 1918, 150–51.

"Women Architects Win Chicago Prize," *New York Times,* March 6, 1915, 5.

"Women at Columbia: A Century of Change." *Progressive Architecture* 63 (June 1982): 22–23.

LOCATION OF PAPERS. Architectural drawings by Schenck and Mead for the Ellen Wilson Memorial Homes in Washington, D.C., are part of the Prints and Photographs Collection of the Library of Congress.

IIIIIIIIIIIIIIIIIIIIIIII
Mercur, Elise (1869–1947)
IIIIIIIIIIIIIIIIIIIIIIII

Elise Mercur, an architect from Pittsburgh, is remembered for winning a national competition to design the Woman's Building at the 1895 Cotton States and International Exposition in Atlanta, Georgia. In fact, this achievement was only the beginning of her short but significant architectural career in the Pittsburgh region. Before her successful competition entry, Mercur studied music abroad and art at the Pennsylvania Academy of the Fine Arts. She also had a year of experience as a drafter in the office of Thomas Boyd, an accomplished Pittsburgh architect. Over the next few years in Boyd's office, Mercur designed a variety of public buildings: the Children's Building (1896) for the firm's work at the Pittsburgh Home and Hospital, a building for Beaver College and Musical Institute (1896), St. Paul's Episcopal Church (1896), St. Martin's Episcopal Church (1897), and a building for Washington Female Seminary (1897), which now exists in a remodeled form as McIlvaine Hall at Washington and Jefferson College in Washington, Pennsylvania.[28]

By 1898, Mercur had clearly established herself as a successful architect of public buildings. She opened her own practice in the Times Building, a prominent building on Fourth Avenue designed by the well-known Pittsburgh architect Frederick J. Osterling, who occupied a nearby office. Shortly after Mercur's move, in April 1898, Mary Temple Jamison interviewed Mercur for the *Home Monthly,* a local magazine. In an article entitled "Pittsburgh's Woman Architect," Jamison reported on Mercur's presence at the construction site, noting that "she goes out herself to oversee the construction of the buildings she designs, inspecting the laying of foundations and personally directing the different workmen from the first stone laid to the last nail driven, thereby acquiring a practical knowledge not possessed by every male architect."[29] Although Mercur married Karl Rudolph Wagner during her first year of private practice, she kept her office open until the end of 1899, when she moved her practice to Economy, in Beaver County. She designed two public schools (demolished) and many houses before her retirement in 1910. Although she is virtually unknown today, at the height of her career in 1899 Mercur was listed on the *Interstate Architect & Builder's* list of "Leading Architects in Seven States."[30]

Partial List of Buildings

1895	Woman's Building, Cotton States and International Exposition, Piedmont Park, Atlanta, Ga.
	Beaver College and Musical Institute, building, College Ave. and Turnpike St., Beaver, Pa.
1896	Pittsburgh Home and Hospital, Children's Building, Bridgeville, Pa. (now Mayview Hospital; building demolished)
	St. Paul's Episcopal Church (now Christian Tabernacle Kodesh Church of Immanuel), 2601 Centre Ave., Pittsburgh
1897	St. Martin's Episcopal Church, Johnsonburg, Elk County, Pa. (demolished 1965)
	Washington Female Seminary building, now remodeled as McIlvaine Hall, Washington and Jefferson College, Washington, Pa. (to be demolished and replaced by a new science center by 2010)

Writings by Mercur (as Elise Mercur Wagner)

Economy of Old and Ambridge of Today. Ambridge, Pa., 1924.

Sources

Coons, F. H. Boyd. "The Cotton States and International Exposition in the New South, Architecture and Implications." M.A. thesis, University of Virginia, 1987.

Cooper, Walter G. *The Cotton States and International Exposition and South, Illustrated.* Atlanta: The Illustrator Co., 1896.

Roth, Darlene R., and Louise E. Shaw. *Atlanta Women: From Myth to Modern Times.* Atlanta: Atlanta Historical Society, 1980.

Tannler, Albert M. "Wagner Built a Career as Designer at Turn of the Century." *Tribune Review,* Sunday, May 9, 2004; posted on the Pittsburgh History and Landmarks Foundation News "Blog Archive" at http://wordpress.phlf.org/wordpress/?p=394 (accessed September 11, 2007).

"Valentine Issue." *Atlanta Journal,* February 16, 1895 (sketch of building interior).

||||||||||||||||||||||||
Moody, Harriet J. (1891–1966)
||||||||||||||||||||||||

Although Harriet Moody attended college in Santa Barbara, California, her birthplace, it is likely that her architectural education came from her father, a local building contractor. Moody began her career designing houses for her father in 1912, and when he retired in 1922 Moody found employment as assistant city engineer, a position she held until the earthquake of 1925. The Santa Barbara area lost many of its most prominent buildings in the quake, as well as a portion of its housing stock, and Moody took the opportunity to form an engineering partnership with her supervisor in the city engineer's office, George Morrison. Moody and Morrison created subdivisions in Goleta and Isla Vista, just north of Santa Barbara, for both public and private developers.

In 1932, Moody received recognition for an antiques shop she designed for her sister in Montecito with the help of her other two sisters and her contractor, Dixon MacQuiddy Sr. In 1937 she bought "The Peppers," a former Santa Barbara farmhouse with a 1915 ballroom addition by Julia Morgan. She lived in the house with her three sisters—Mildred, Brenda, and Wilma—until her death in 1966. During the 1930s and 1940s, Moody developed the style she would become known for—a kind of English "fairytale vernacular" that proved a charming addition to the fanciful architecture of this resort community. She coped with the hard times of the Depression era by recycling materials from demolished buildings and incorporating the leftover doors, windows, floors, and mantelpieces into new homes. This unusual juxtaposition of old and new gave a special quality to her cottages, which were all intended to seem old-world English, and preserved a sense of craftsmanship at a time when traditional building techniques were being lost. Moody's use of "found objects" influenced her residential design in many ways; she often planned a room around a single oddly shaped door or unusual set of windows, and because she made use of what was available, floor and wall coverings varied from room to room. During wartime Moody not only conserved materials, but actually recycled large estates by dividing them up into cottages. Once the housing shortage was over and building supplies were plentiful, Moody designed several houses for private clients that featured open ceilings, low plate rails, and wood paneling.

Harriet Moody retired in 1950 and died sixteen years later. She left behind about thirty-five cottages in the Santa Barbara area, each with a distinctive personality. Although Moody herself remains relatively unknown, her work has long been appreciated by local residents for its craftsmanship and sense of whimsy.

Partial List of Buildings

1932	Artist's studio, 1086 Coast Village Rd., Montecito, Calif.
1936	Swanson House, Santa Barbara, Calif.
1930s-40s	Six cottages, Barker Pass, George Knapp property, Santa Barbara
1940	Holly Hill House, 2207 Alameda Padre Serra, Santa Barbara Rosemary Lane and Periwinkle Lane, Montecito

Sources

Andree, Herb, et al. *Santa Barbara Architecture.* 3rd ed. Santa Barbara, Calif.: Capra Press, 1995.

McMahon, Marilyn. "Mildred Moody Dies at Age 99." *Santa Barbara News Press,* April 2, 1996, B1, B4.

"Real Challenge Decorating Unique Holly Hill House." *Santa Barbara News Press,* July 1, 1984, D8.

LOCATION OF PAPERS. The Santa Barbara Historical Society has a tape recording of an oral history interview with Mildred Moody.

Morgan, Julia (1872–1957)

Julia Morgan is undisputedly the most famous early woman architect and for good reason. The first female graduate of the Ecole des Beaux-Arts in

Paris, the elite architectural school of its day, Morgan ran one of the most successful firms in California during the first half of the twentieth century. In a career that spanned two generations, Morgan received more than seven hundred commissions that represent nearly every building type.

Morgan's effort to break down barriers in her chosen profession began in 1890, when she became the first woman enrolled in the Berkeley engineering department. She graduated four years later after submitting an undergraduate paper entitled "A Structural Analysis of the Steel Frame of the Mills Building." During her student years, Morgan was particularly influenced by one of her instructors, the architect Bernard Maybeck, who would become famous for both his Craftsman-style designs and his flamboyant personality. While still an undergraduate, she gained practical experience working on Maybeck's home and studio. After graduation she continued working for Maybeck while taking drawing classes at the Hopkins School of Art Instruction (now the San Francisco Art Institute), the school Mary Colter graduated from in 1890 (then the California School of Design). Because the architecture program at Berkeley did not accept women, Morgan began a quest to graduate from the Ecole des Beaux-Arts. She was accepted in 1898 (fig. 33).

Morgan spent the next four years working in Parisian studios (ateliers) and exhibiting her work in the required competitions that led to an Ecole certificate. The month of her thirtieth birthday, Morgan received a first mention for a drawing of a theater, an award that secured her graduation certificate in February 1902. After finishing up some projects and travel, Morgan returned to California and worked briefly for her former professor, John Galen Howard, the architect responsible for the Berkeley campus. During this time, she gained experience in revival styles, working on the Greek Theater at Berkeley for a very important client, Phoebe Apperson Hearst. Morgan also engaged in private work from her family's home in Oakland. Although she was offered employment from architects on both coasts, Morgan preferred to work on her own. After passing the California state architectural exam in 1904, she opened a private practice as a licensed architect. Her first office was demolished by the 1906 earthquake, but undaunted, Morgan set up shop in the Merchants Exchange Building on California Street in San Francisco. Ira Wilson Hoover worked as a junior partner in Morgan's office until 1910. For the remainder of her fifty-year practice, Morgan would lead the firm bearing her name.

Before she began seeking clients, Morgan was known as an accomplished architect, and within a decade she had gained a reputation as a hardworking, gifted supervisor. The city of San Francisco needed architects after the earthquake, and Morgan soon found herself with many commissions to remodel

FIGURE 33. Julia Morgan, "Carte d'Eleve, Ecole des Beaux-Arts" (student identification card), June 1899. Courtesy Julia Morgan Collection, Special Collections, California Polytechnic State University.

or repair damaged buildings. In addition, Morgan benefited from a network of powerful women, members of civic and philanthropic organizations, who became architectural patrons. Such groups had offered sorority to female architects in the past, but in California, many of the most accomplished leaders were wealthy and could help finance buildings that supported their causes. Beginning with a bell tower in 1903, Morgan worked for Susan Mills on several structures for Mills College in Oakland. Her work included the Margaret Carnegie Library, a gymnasium, the infirmary, a pool and recreation center, and a residence, the latter of which was completed in 1926. Among other commissions for women's organizations were the Oakland and San Jose YWCAs; a major YWCA conference center, Asilomar, in Pacific Grove, California, the design for which she worked on from 1913 to 1937; and the Saratoga Foothill Women's Club (1915) (figs. 34, 35), a commission that came to Morgan through a former college roommate.

With her work progressing at the YWCA's conference center, Morgan was a natural choice to design YWCA Hostess Houses when World War I

FIGURE 34. Saratoga Foothill Women's Club, Park Place, Saratoga, California. Designed by Julia Morgan in 1915. Drawings by HABS, 1979. Courtesy Library of Congress, Prints and Photographs Division, HABS.

FIGURE 35. Saratoga Foothill Women's Club, Park Place, Saratoga, California. Designed by Julia Morgan in 1915. Photograph by Jane Lidz, 1980. Courtesy Library of Congress, Prints and Photographs Division, HABS.

brought most building projects to a standstill. Morgan's residential style was particularly suited to the "houses," which were meant to provide a homelike environment where families and soldiers could gather for visits. From 1913 to the 1930s, Morgan designed dozens of Hostess Houses throughout the West and Hawaii, of which only the San Pedro and Camp Fremont buildings remain. An early view of the YWCA house at Camp Fremont (fig. 36), before it was moved and remodeled into a restaurant, illustrates Morgan's economical yet artistic use of wood piers to create a welcoming facade. Morgan's Hostess House designs demonstrate her flexibility in shifting from work for elite clients to utilitarian, low-budget commissions.

In addition to designing for women's organizations, Morgan also aided her female colleagues by providing professional opportunities in her firm. At different times, she employed Eleanor Jory, Alice Joy, Marjorie Tyng, Avesia Atkins, Harriet Young, and a Miss Delius as drafters. Charlotte Knapp worked her way through architectural school by drafting for Morgan and later became a state architect in New York City. One of the senior members of Morgan's office was C. Julian Mesic, a drafter and sculptor who changed her name

FIGURE 36. YWCA Hostess House, 27 University Ave. (now a restaurant), Palo Alto, California. Designed by Julia Morgan, 1917–19, and originally located at Camp Fremont. Photograph by Jack E. Boucher, 1975. Courtesy Library of Congress, Prints and Photographs Division, HABS.

from Charlotte to disguise her sex. Mesic made most of the models for Morgan in her early years, won an AIA award in 1929, and wrote several articles about her work. Dorothy Wormser, a Berkeley graduate, spent about four years working for Morgan. She remembered a rigorous training regime that gave drafters with experience in Morgan's office a reputation for excellence.[31] Although Morgan clearly opened her office to women, the number available was limited, and the majority of her staff was always comprised of men.

Since her early years working on the Berkeley campus, Morgan had a patron in Phoebe Apperson Hearst. The two became intimate while working together on improving Hearst's Hacienda del Pozo de Verona, a guesthouse and clubhouse, in Pleasanton from 1902 to 1910. It was through Phoebe Hearst that Morgan received the commission of an architect's dreams: to design a multi-million-dollar fantasy castle in the hills of San Simeon. From 1919 to 1940, Morgan worked as William Randolph Hearst's architect, commuting between her San Francisco office and Hearst's rapidly growing estate. The design and construction of Hearst Castle was a massive undertaking, requiring a staff of craftsmen imported from Europe, a museum's worth of art and architectural treasures, and the skill to please an exacting client with big dreams if not always the means to pay for them. The lavish main house contained one hundred fifteen rooms and was enhanced by several guesthouses and swimming pools, as well as eight acres of landscaped gardens within the 250,000-acre San Simeon ranch. In its grandeur and physical beauty, Hearst Castle is without precedent. The property was opened to the public in 1958 and became a National Historic Landmark in 1976.

In 1946, the AIA asked architects to fill out a questionnaire listing their most financially rewarding commissions. Morgan could boast of having three projects that each exceeded a cost of three hundred thousand dollars: the University of California Woman's Gymnasium, the Honolulu YMCA, and the Berkeley Woman's City Club; two projects, San Simeon and the Wyntoon Development in Shasta County, California, each reached a price tag of over a million dollars. More than seventeen million tourists visited Hearst Castle in its first thirty years as a public attraction and the estate continues to amaze visitors with the opulence of its design. If William Randolph Hearst has tended to overshadow Morgan as the designer of Hearst Castle, such is the nature of the architect/client relationship.

By any estimate, Morgan was a very successful architect. But her legacy is measured in more substantial terms than bricks and mortar. From her college years, Morgan broke gender barriers seemingly without acknowledging their existence. She proved to the world that a woman could design and supervise the construction of any kind of building and run a large, productive firm. Julia Morgan stands alone as the most accomplished and appreciated American woman architect of her day.

Partial List of Buildings

Morgan and her firm completed more than three hundred residential commissions. Due to the extent of Morgan's practice, this list does not include her houses, cottages, lodging houses, or apartment buildings. Unless noted otherwise, all locations are in California. For a more complete catalog of her work see Sara Holmes Boutelle's "revised and updated" biography, *Julia Morgan: Architect,* which includes an extensive list of buildings and projects documenting Morgan's work from 1896 to 1946.

1903–4	El Campanil (bell tower), Mills College, Oakland
1905–6	Margaret Carnegie Library, Mills College, Oakland
1905–17	Lakeview School, Perry and Grand Sts., Oakland [demolished]
1906	Fred Kuhle, stores and apartments, 3807 Grove St., Oakland [demolished]
1906–7	Law Brothers, Fairmont Hotel, reconstruction, California and Mason Sts., San Francisco
	First Baptist Church, Telegraph Ave. and 22nd St., Oakland
	Merchants Exchange Building, Trading Room interior, 465 California St., San Francisco
	Viavi Building, 636–52 Pine St., San Francisco [demolished]
1907	Parmelee Morgan and partners, Cook-Morgan-Warner warehouse, Linden and 22nd Sts., Oakland [demolished]
	Rose Morbio factory, Bluxome St., San Francisco [demolished]
	Mountain View Cemetery, Retiring Building, 4499 Piedmont Ave., Oakland [demolished]
	Vallejo Commercial Bank, alts., Main St., Vallejo [demolished]
1907	Methodist Chinese Mission School (Gum Moon), 920 Washington St. at Trenton Alley, San Francisco (1907–10)
1908	Fred Fisch storefront, 311 Georgia St., Vallejo [demolished]
	Friday Morning Club, Adams and Hoover Sts., Los Angeles
	Hamilton Methodist-Episcopal Church, 1525 Waller St., San Francisco

	Holy Trinity Episcopal Church, chapel, 235 Washington Ave., Point Richmond
	Kappa Alpha Theta Sorority House, 2723 Durant Ave., Berkeley
1908–10	St. John's Presbyterian Church and Sunday School, 2640 College Ave., Berkeley
1908–12	King's Daughters Home, main hospital and landscaped garden, north and east wings, 3900 Broadway
1908–16	Ransome and Bridges School for Girls, 9 Hazel Lane, Piedmont [demolished]
1909	Miss Grace E. Barnard School, 2748 Ashby Ave., Berkeley [demolished]
	Gymnasium, Mills College, Oakland
	Kapiolani Rest Cottage (infirmary), Mills College, Oakland
1910	Port Costa Water Company, Main St., Port Costa
1910–11	Montezuma School for Boys, dormitory and classroom, Bear Creek Rd., Los Gatos
	U.S. Immigration Station, Angel Island, San Francisco Bay [demolished]
1911	Girton Hall (social center for women students), University of California at Berkeley
1911–12	Bank of Yolo, 500 Main St., Woodland [demolished]
1913	St. Peter's Episcopal Church Mission, Lawton St., Oakland [demolished]
1913–15	Oakland YWCA, 1515 Webster St., Oakland
	San Jose YWCA, 1st St. at San Fernando, San Jose [demolished]
	YWCA Conference Center, Asilomar, Pacific Grove, various buildings, 1913–1937
1914	New Twentieth Century Club, alterations and auditorium, 1355 Franklin St., San Francisco
	San Francisco "Call" Building, alterations
	Santa Barbara Recreation Building, 100 E. Carrillo St., Santa Barbara
1914–15	King's Daughters Exposition Resting Room, Panama-Pacific International Exposition, San Francisco [demolished]
	YWCA Building, interior, restaurant, auditorium, and resting room, Panama-Pacific International Exposition, San Francisco [demolished]

YWCA Building for "Zone" employees, Panama-Pacific
    International Exposition, San Francisco [demolished]
ca. 1915   Modesto First Baptist Church, 12th St. and 527 Lottie Ave.,
    Modesto [demolished]
1915   Examiner Building, 1111 S. Broadway, Los Angeles
    Miss Sarah Dix Hamlin School, 2234 Pacific Avenue, San
        Francisco [demolished]
    Saratoga Foothill Women's Club, Park Place, Saratoga
1916   Katherine Delmar Burke School (now San Francisco
        University High School), 3025–65 Jackson St., San
        Francisco
    Kern County Sanitarium, Bakersfield [demolished]
    Marysville Grammar School, Marysville [demolished]
    Fred C. Turner, shopping center and apartments, Piedmont
        Ave. and 40th St., Oakland
    Social Center, Mills College, Oakland
1916–18   Sausalito Women's Club, 120 Central Ave., Sausalito
    Tulare and King Counties Sanitarium, Springville
    YWCA Beach House, alterations, Waikiki, Hawaii (ca. 1917)
        [demolished]
1917   United Presbyterian Church, 5951 College Ave., Oakland
1917–19   YWCA Hostess House, Camp Fremont (moved to 27
        University Ave., Palo Alto, now a restaurant)
    YWCA Hostess House 437 Ninth St. West, San Pedro
1918   Hobart Hall, Berkeley Baptist Divinity School, 2600 Dwight
        Way, Berkeley
    Oakland Post-Enquirer Building, 1751 Franklin St., Oakland
        [demolished]
    Santa Barbara County Tuberculosis Sanitarium, 300 N. San
        Antonio Rd., Santa Barbara
1918–19   Calvary Presbyterian Church, 1940 Virginia St., Berkeley
        [destroyed by fire]
1919   Marysville Bank, Marysville [demolished]
    Marysville Golf Clubhouse, Plumas Lake, Marysville
        [demolished]
    Vallejo YWCA, 245 York St., Vallejo [demolished]
1919–20   Salt Lake City YWCA, 322 E. Third St., South, Salt Lake City,
        Utah (interior by Elsie de Wolfe)

1919–42	William Randolph Hearst estate, San Simeon (multiple buildings)
1920	Ahwahnee Sanitarium, Merced, Madera, and Stanislaus Counties [demolished]
	Girls' Club, 545–47 Howard St. (now S. Van Ness St.), San Francisco [demolished]
	Kentfield Sanitarium, Kentfield, Marin County [demolished]
1921	Miss Julia Fraser antiques shop, 2014 Fifth Ave., Oakland [demolished]
	High Street Presbyterian Church, chapel, 1941 High St., Oakland
	Ocean Avenue Presbyterian Church, 32 Ocean Ave., San Francisco
	Pasadena YWCA, 78 N. Marengo Ave., Pasadena
	Potrero Hill Neighborhood House Community Center, 953 DeHaro St., San Francisco
	The Residence, remodel of Atherton House to YWCA dormitory, Honolulu, Hawaii [demolished]
	San Francisco Presbyterian Theological Seminary Faculty House, 118 Bolinas Ave., San Anselmo
1922	American Legion Veterans Building, Marysville [demolished]
	Berkeley YWCA, Union and Allerton Sts., Berkeley [demolished]
	Fresno YWCA residence, 1660 M St., Fresno (interior by Elsie de Wolfe)
	Pool and Recreation Center, Mills College, Oakland
1923	Delta Zeta Sorority House, 2311 Le Conte Avenue, Berkeley
	Hamilton Methodist Episcopal Church, gymnasium and offices, 1525 Waller St., San Francisco
	Long Beach YWCA and pool, 1865 E. Anaheim St., Long Beach [demolished]
	Sacramento Public Market, 1230 J Street, Sacramento
	St. James Presbyterian Church, 240 Leland Ave., San Francisco
	Saratoga Federated Community Church, Park Place, Saratoga
1924	Fresno YWCA offices, Tuolomne and L Sts., Fresno

	Thousand Oaks Baptist Church, 1821 Catalina St., Berkeley
1924–25	Ladies Protection and Relief Society residence, 3400 Laguna St., San Francisco
	Ming Quong Chinese School for Girls, 367 McClellan St., Oakland
1924–43	Wyntoon, William Randolph Hearst estate, Near McCloud and Mt. Shasta
1925	Cosmopolitan Headquarters, projection room and additions, Hollywood [demolished]
	San Francisco Examiner Building, major alterations, Fifth and Market Sts., San Francisco
	San Francisco Presbyterian Orphanage, Tooker Memorial (Sunnyhill), San Anselmo [destroyed by fire]
1925–26	Margaret Baylor Hotel for Women (now the Lobero Building), 924 Anacapa St., Santa Barbara
	Phoebe Apperson Hearst Memorial Gymnasium for Women (with Bernard Maybeck), University of California at Berkeley
1926	First Swedish Baptist Church, Third Ave. and Fifteenth St., Oakland
	YWCA at University of Hawaii, Honolulu
1926–27	YWCA Metropolitan Headquarters, 1040 Richards St., Honolulu
1926–30	Columbarium, Chapel of the Chimes, 4400 Piedmont Ave., Oakland
1927	Berkeley Day Nursery, auditorium and apartment/office, Sixth St., Berkeley
	Minerva Club (Santa Maria Women's Club), Lincoln at Boone St., Santa Maria
1928	The Hearthstone, California Federation of Women's Clubs, Redwood Forest, Humboldt County
	Native Daughters of the Golden West, San Francisco Central Headquarters, 500 Baker St., San Francisco
1929	Riverside YWCA (now Riverside Art Center and Museum), 3245 Seventh St., Riverside
1929–30	Berkeley Women's City Club, 2315 Durant Ave., Berkeley
	The Residence, YWCA, 940 Powell St., San Francisco
1930s	Hearst Globe Wireless Company Station, Cahill Ridge, San Mateo

	Principia College women's dormitories, Elsah, Illinois (with Bernard Maybeck)

Principia College women's dormitories, Elsah, Illinois (with
    Bernard Maybeck)
San Francisco Hearst Building, interior alterations, Third
    and Market Sts., San Francisco
1930   Chinese YWCA, 965 Clay St., San Francisco
Marion Davies Foundation, Pediatric Clinic, 11672 Louisiana
    Ave., Los Angeles
Japanese YWCA, 1830 Sutter St., San Francisco
1930–37   Homelani Columbarium, 388 Ponahawaii St., Hilo, Hawaii
1933–34   Monday Club (now Women's Club), 1800 Monterey St., San
    Luis Obispo
San Francisco Examiner Building, alterations, Stevenson and
    Jessie Sts., San Francisco
1936   Fred C. Turner laboratory and medical building, Bancroft
    Way, Berkeley [demolished]
VKUP Transmitting and Receiving Station, Redwood City
1938–41   Fred C. Turner stores, offices, and Black Sheep Restaurant,
    2546 Bancroft Way, Berkeley
1940   Russian Day School and Nursery, Sutter St., San Francisco

Sources

This is a selected list of references referring directly to Morgan. For more information about architecture in the Bay Area, the Hearst family, and Morgan's place in the Arts and Crafts movement, see Sara Holmes Boutelle's *Julia Morgan: Architect*.

Boutelle, Sara Holmes. "Julia Morgan: An Architect from Oakland." In *Architectural Drawings by Julia Morgan,* exhibition catalog. Foreword by Therese Heyman. Chronology by Sara Holmes Boutelle. Oakland, Calif.: Oakland Museum, 1976.

———. *Julia Morgan: Architect.* New York: Abbeville Press, 1995.

Brewer, Henrietta. "Julia Morgan, Our Architect." *Kappa Alpha Theta Journal,* 1909, 473–74.

"Morgan, Julia." In *Notable American Women: The Modern Period,* edited by Barbara Sicherman and Carol Hurd Green, 499–501. Cambridge, Mass.: Belknap Press of Harvard University Press, 1980.

National Cyclopedia of American Biography. Vol. G, 151. New York: James T. White and Co., 1946.

Riess, Suzanne B., ed. "The Julia Morgan Architectural History Project." Manuscript, 2 vols. Regional Oral History Office, Bancroft Library, University of California, Berkeley, 1976.

LOCATION OF PAPERS. Archival sources about Julia Morgan are located at the following repositories: Bancroft Library, University of California, Berkeley; Documents Collection, College of Environmental Design, University of California, Berkeley; Julia Morgan Collection, Robert E. Kennedy Library, California Polytechnic State University, San Luis Obispo; M. H. de Young Memorial Museum, San Francisco.

||||||||||||||||||||||||
Morrow, Gertrude E. Comfort (ca. 1892–1987)
||||||||||||||||||||||||

Gertrude E. Comfort graduated in 1913 from the University of California, Berkeley, with a bachelor's degree in architecture and completed her master's degree the next year. While a student she belonged to the Architectural Association and published renderings of a city residence and a bridge terminal in the club's yearbook. A native Californian, Comfort was surrounded by role models during her student years; Berkeley alumnae and classmates included Julia Morgan, Lilian Rice, and Helen G. Waterman, to name a few. After graduation, Comfort worked independently, designing the Women's Athletic Club in Oakland and the music building at the College for Women in Bethlehem, Pennsylvania, among other public buildings. During World War I she was supervising architect for St. Francis Woods, a San Francisco neighborhood based on City Beautiful principles.

After Comfort married the architect Irving F. Morrow in 1920, the two worked together as Morrow and Morrow. The firm served as consulting architects for the Golden Gate Bridge from 1932 to 1937 and designed the Alameda–Contra Costa County Building for the 1939 Golden Gate International Exposition. In 2007, Gertrude and Irving Morrow received considerable publicity for their Art Deco design of the Golden Gate Bridge after it was ranked fifth in an AIA public poll of America's favorite architectural structures.

Partial List of Buildings

1918	R. C. Mason House, St. Francis Wood, San Francisco, Calif.
ca. 1918	James F. Rice House, St. Francis Wood, San Francisco
1919	S. E. Heckscher House, addition, St. Francis Wood, San Francisco
	C. J. Sauter House, St. Francis Wood, San Francisco
1921	Terrace Drive Houses, St. Francis Wood, San Francisco

1932–37	Golden Gate Bridge, San Francisco (Morrow and Morrow, consulting architects)
1939	Alameda–Contra Costa County Building, Golden Gate International Exposition
n.d.	Music Building, Moravian Seminary and College for Women, Bethlehem, Pa.
	Women's Athletic Club, Oakland, Calif.

LOCATION OF PAPERS. The Morrow (Irving F. and Gertrude Comfort) Collection, 1914–58, is in the Environmental Design Archives, University of California, Berkeley. The collection includes professional papers and project reports dating from 1914, as well as files and drawings. The Harriet Rochlin Collection of Material about Women Architects in the United States, 1887–1979, Department of Special Collections, UCLA Library, contains notes, correspondence, articles, and personal papers collected by Rochlin for her research on Gertrude Morrow.

IIIIIIIIIIIIIIIIIIIIIIIII
Mother Joseph of the Sacred Heart, Sister of Providence (Esther Pariseau) (1823–1902)
IIIIIIIIIIIIIIIIIIIIIIIII

A native of Quebec, Canada, Esther Pariseau spent most of her life in the Pacific Northwest. She made her religious vows in 1845 as a member of the Sisters of Providence, a Catholic religious community of women in Montreal. She came to be known as Mother Joseph of the Sacred Heart and was one of the founders of the order's branch in the American West that pioneered providing health care, education, and social services. Mother Joseph was responsible for designing and directing the construction of many of the more than thirty institutions created during her forty-five years in the West. One of these, Providence Academy in Vancouver, Washington (1873), was once the largest brick building in the territory and is on the National Register of Historic Places. Mother Joseph completed her last work, Providence St. Genevieve Orphanage (New Westminster, British Columbia) in 1900. The extent of her participation in the design and construction of individual buildings is unknown. However, multiple sources have noted that, if not the sole architect of every building, Mother Joseph played an important role in many aspects of each design. It is clear that, as most of the buildings were related to the sisters' charitable mission, she was the most capable person to supervise and advise on matters of program.

In 1980, a statue of Mother Joseph became the fifth sculpture of a woman to be installed in the National Statuary Hall, the U.S. Capitol's collection of statues from each state in the union. The statue depicts Mother Joseph kneeling in prayer, with drafting tools at her feet, upon a rectangular base inscribed with images of her most significant buildings (fig. 37). The statue renewed a long-standing controversy among members of the American Institute of Architects. An article published in 1953 claimed that the AIA had declared her "the first architect in the Pacific Northwest." Although this was the opinion of individual architects attending the AIA conference that year, and not of the entire organization, it has been widely quoted. Regardless of such debate, Mother Joseph's contribution to the architecture of the Northwest is beyond dispute. In 2005 her lasting influence as a true pioneer architect was recognized by the Washington State House of Representatives in a resolution in honor of her 182nd birthday.[32]

Partial List of Buildings

1856	Providence Academy, Vancouver, Wash.
1858	St. Joseph Hospital, Vancouver
1863	Providence St. Joseph (school), Steilacoom, Wash.
1864	St. Vincent Academy, Walla Walla, Wash.
	Holy Family Hospital, St. Ignatius, Mont.
1868	Providence of Our Lady Seven Dolors (school), Tulalip, Washington Indian Reservation
1873	Providence of the Sacred Heart (school), Colville, Wash.
	St. Patrick Hospital, Missoula, Mont.
1874	St. James Residence, Vancouver
1875	St. Joseph Academy, Yakima, Wash.
	St. Vincent Hospital, Portland, Ore.
1876	Providence of Our Lady of the Sacred Heart (School), Cowlitz, Wash.
1877	Providence Hospital, Seattle, Wash.
1880	St. Mary Hospital, Walla Walla
	St. Mary Hospital, Astoria, Ore.
1881	St. Michael School, Olympia, Wash.
	Providence St. Martin, Frenchtown, Mont.
1885	Sacred Heart Academy, Missoula
1886	Sacred Heart Hospital, Spokane, Wash.
	St. Clare Hospital, Fort Benton, Mont.

FIGURE 37. Statue of Mother Joseph by Felix DeWeldon. The photograph was taken in 1980, when the statue was placed in the United States Capitol. Courtesy Providence Archives, Seattle.

St. Joseph Academy, Sprague, Wash.
1887   St. Peter Hospital, Olympia
1890   St. John Hospital, Port Townsend, Wash.
Mission St. Eugene, Kootenay, Canada
1891   Providence Hospital, Wallace, ID
St. Elizabeth Hospital, Yakima
1892   Columbus Hospital, Great Falls, Mont.
1893   St. Ignatius Hospital, Colfax, Wash.
1900   Providence St. Genevieve, New Westminster, Canada

Sources

McDonald, Lucile. "Mother Joseph, State's Pioneer Architect-Nun." *Seattle Times,* May 12, 1957.
McQuaid, Matilda. "Educating for the Future: A Growing Archive on Women and Architecture." In *Architecture: A Place for Women,* edited by Ellen Perry Berkeley and Matilda McQuaid, 250–54. Washington, D.C.: Smithsonian Institution Press, 1989.
Sjoblom, Cheryl. "Mother Joseph of the Sacred Heart (Esther Pariseau)." In *Shaping Seattle Architecture,* edited by Jeffery Ochsner, 6–9. Seattle, Wash.: University of Washington Press, 1994.
Stevens, James. "Region's First Architect." *Seattle Times,* June 14, 1953.

LOCATION OF PAPERS. Primary and secondary sources relating to Mother Joseph are located in the Archives of the Sisters of Providence, Mother Joseph Province, Seattle, Washington.

|||||||||||||||||||||||||
Muir, Edla (1906–71)
|||||||||||||||||||||||||

Of the architects described in this book, none began her architectural career at an earlier age than Edla Muir. When just thirteen, Muir worked after school, on weekends, and during the summer in the office of a Los Angeles architect, John Byers. After graduating from Inglewood High School in 1923, Muir worked for Byers full time, serving as office manager but also drafting and assisting on site. During her long apprenticeship with Byers, Muir designed homes in a wide variety of styles that appealed to wealthy clients in Santa Monica, Brentwood, Pacific Palisades, and Beverly Hills. The firm became known for its ability to appeal to a client's desire for a residence with traditional components while also using modern elements that provided convenience and a sense of modernity. In 1934, Muir received her license to practice architecture in California. She worked as Byers's associate until 1942.

Although she never received a college degree or any formal architectural education, Muir was able to establish her own office after World War II. She worked independently from 1946 to 1968 on more than one hundred commissions. Her work was primarily residential but included a building for Paddock Pool Company and a remodel of an office building for Grant Oil Tool Company. According to one biographer, Harriet Rochlin, Muir found her greatest success designing in the modern style, which her mentor Byers "reviled." Two of her most prominent modern residences, the John Rex House in Mandeville Canyon and the Russell Law House in Malibu, were "horizontal and ground-hugging" buildings "constructed of rough-sawn redwood and glass."[33]

Muir was married to Clyde Lambie and had a son, but she kept her professional name throughout her career.

Partial List of Buildings

Listed buildings are located in California. Pre-1945 buildings were designed in partnership with John Byers.

ca. 1925	Boland House, 12322–23 Helena Dr., Brentwood, Los Angeles
1930	Kerr House, 428 N. Carmelina Ave., Brentwood
1931–33	Hamilton House, 193 N. Carmelina Ave., Brentwood
ca. 1935	Murray House, 436 N. Carmelina Ave., Brentwood
1935–36	Stedman House, 363 N. Carmelina Ave., Brentwood
	Temple House, 231 N. Rockingham Ave., Los Angeles
1936	G. Young House, West Los Angeles
1936–37	R. A. Sperry House, Encino
1940	Grove Bungalow Court, 10500 Santa Monica Blvd., Westwood, Los Angeles
ca. 1946–48	Grant Oil Tool Company, office building remodel, n.p.
	V. D. King House, Mandeville Canyon, Los Angeles
	Dr. and Mrs. James L. McPherson House, n.p.
	Paddock Pool Company Building, n.p.
	Robert Taylor and Barbara Stanwyck House, n.p.
	Henry Thiem House, n.p.
1949	John Rex House, 1888 Mandeville Canyon Rd., Los Angeles
1956	Russell Law House, Malibu

Sources

Gebhard, David, and Robert Winter. *Los Angeles: An Architectural Guide*. Layton, Utah: Gibbs-Smith, 1994.

"House in Santa Monica Canyon, California, Edla Muir, Architect." *Architectural Forum* 9 (August 1943): 90–91.

Rochlin, Harriet. "A Distinguished Generation of Women Architects in California." *AIA Journal* 66 (August 1977): 38–42; see esp. 41.

"A Thousand Women in Architecture." *Architectural Record* 103, part 2 (June 1948): 108–15.

LOCATION OF PAPERS. The Art Museum at the University of California at Santa Barbara has drawings for more than a hundred projects by Muir from the 1940s through 1968. The Harriet Rochlin Collection of Material about Women Architects in the United States, 1887–1979, in the Department of Special Collections, UCLA Library, contains primary and secondary source material on Muir that Rochlin collected for her work on early twentieth-century women architects in California.

||||||||||||||||||||||

Nedved, Elizabeth Kimball (1897–1969)

||||||||||||||||||||||

Elizabeth Nedved was born in Chicago in 1897 and graduated from the Church School of Art in 1918. During a year spent at Northwestern University, Nedved worked as a drafter for the firm Tallmadge and Watson, a partnership established by Thomas Eddy Tallmadge and Vernon Spencer Watson, former employees of D. H. Burnham and Company. The firm had a reputation for designing modestly priced Prairie-style residences and would employ Alberta Pfeiffer (see entry) a few years later. Nedved went on to study for two years at the University of Illinois and for two and a half years at the Armour Institute of Technology in Chicago, graduating with a B.S. in architecture in 1925. This was an exciting era in the history of skyscraper design, with the 1922 competition for the Chicago Tribune building challenging architects to design "the world's most beautiful office building."

During 1926–28, Nedved worked in partnership with a fellow Armour Institute graduate, Rudolph J. Nedved, who would later become her husband. In this period she was elected to the AIA (1927) and earned a license to practice architecture in Illinois (1928). From 1928 to 1935, Elizabeth Nedved was a silent partner in the firm of Hamilton, Fellows, and Nedved Architects. By the early 1930s, the firm had gained a reputation for school-building design and had begun work on Wyandotte High School in Kansas City, now a National

Register property. Nonetheless, Nedved resigned from the AIA in 1931, most likely as a result of the Depression.

Nedved was employed by the U.S. Navy, Bureau of Ships, during World War II as a marine engineer specializing in naval architecture. In the 1940s, the Nedveds entered a house design in the Chicagoland Prize Homes Competition sponsored by the *Chicago Tribune*. Elizabeth Nedved was readmitted to the AIA in 1962 and in 1969 became a member emeritus after having the fifteen-year requirement for membership waived.

Partial List of Buildings

ca. 1925   Sunset Point House, 1024 Everett Rd., Eagle River, Wis. (National Register), attributed to Elizabeth Kimball and Rudolph Nedved)

LOCATION OF PAPERS. The American Institute of Architects Archives, Washington, D.C., has records documenting Nedved's membership in the AIA membership files, Record Group 803, box 133, folder 12.

|||||||||||||||||||||||||||
Nichols, Minerva Parker (1863–1949)
|||||||||||||||||||||||||||

Minerva Parker grew up in Chicago, where she was influenced in her choice of career by her grandfather, the architect Seth A. Doane. After graduating from the Philadelphia Normal Art School in 1882, Parker spent four terms at the Franklin Institute Drawing School, completing the course with honors and a certificate in 1885. While still finishing classes, she entered the office of Frederick Thorn Jr., a prominent Philadelphia architect. Parker worked for Thorn until his retirement in 1888, whereupon she took charge of his business at 14 South Broad Street.

In her early years, Parker concentrated on residential architecture in the wealthy suburbs of Philadelphia—Radnor, Cynwyd, Berwyn, Germantown, and Overbrook. By 1890 she had established herself in the profession and was chosen by the Queen Isabella Society in Chicago to design a pavilion for the 1893 World's Columbian Exposition. Although her design was never executed, her role in the controversy over a women's building at the fair made her a public figure. The next year Nichols married a Unitarian minister, William Nichols, and completed her most famous commission, the New Century Club building (figs. 38, 39). The New Century Club, founded in 1877, was one of Philadelphia's first organizations committed to promoting women's interests. The Renaissance-style building with a mansard roof, located in a prominent section of downtown Philadelphia, would become Nichols's signature work. It garnered her a commission for the New Century Club in Wilmington, Delaware, a year later. In a relatively short career, Nichols would design more than fifty buildings, including residential blocks for J. H. Carter, two factories for the Philadelphia spaghetti manufacturer Geano and Raggio, and a residence and office in Santa Barbara, California.

FIGURE 38. New Century Club, 124 South Twelfth St., Philadelphia (demolished). Designed by Minerva Parker Nichols, 1891. George A. Eisenman, photographer, 1973. Courtesy Library of Congress, Prints and Photographs Division, HABS.

FIGURE 39. New Century Club, entrance hall, first floor looking west. Designed by Minerva Parker Nichols, 1891. George A. Eisenman, photographer, 1973. Courtesy Library of Congress, Prints and Photographs Division, HABS.

Along with her architectural practice, Nichols taught courses on historic ornament and classical architecture at the Philadelphia School of Design for Women. She and her husband moved out of Philadelphia in 1896, when she appears to have been retired. Over twenty years later, Nichols would design a home for her daughter, Adelaide.

Partial List of Buildings

1888 George M. Christy House, Elm Station, Pa. (now Narberth, Pa.)

    Max M. Suppas House, Johnstown, Pa.

1889 James F. Beale House, n.p.

S. E. Bewley House, Elm Station
Louis T. Brooke House, Radnor, Pa.
E. J. Davis House and stable, Elm Station
E. C. Harfell House and store, Lansdowne, Pa.
Miller Justice House, Elm Station
Maxwell House, Oak Lane, Philadelphia
Parksley Land and Improvement Company, inn, Parksley, Va.
J. A. Patterson House, Overbrook, Philadelphia
W. R. Wright houses (2), Elm Station

1890   Rachel Foster Avery House and stable, Somerton, Pa.
Baugh House, n.p.
Henry R. Bennett House, Parksley, Va.
Mary Botts House, Germantown, Philadelphia
J. H. Carter houses (14), 49th and Market Sts., Philadelphia
J. H. Carter houses (16), 49th and Ludlow Sts., Philadelphia
F. B. Crooke House, n.p.
L. E. Gallagher House, Moore's Station, Pa.
Hartell House, Lansdowne, Pa.
Jardan House, Bala, Pa.
C. F. Johnson, Beaumont, Tex.
Wallace Munn House, 1012 E. Oak Lane, Philadelphia
Elizabeth Newport, cottage, Longport, N.J.
Overbrook Land Company, house, Philadelphia
Overbrook Land Company, houses, 61st St. and Columbia
    Ave., Philadelphia
W. P. Painter House, n.p.
Parksley Land Improvement Company, residential
    operation, Parksley, Va.
J. A. Patterson, stable, Overbrook, Philadelphia
Queen Isabella Pavilion (unexecuted design), Chicago, Ill.
Stewart Cottage, Avon-by-the-sea, N.J.
E. Y. Taylor House, n.p.

1891   Mary Campbell, houses (2), School House Lane,
    Philadelphia
David S. Cresswell, foundry, Nicetown, Pa.
E. R. Gaskill House, Canton, Ohio
E. L. McGammom House, Gettysburg, Pa.
New Century Club, 124–26 S. 12th St., Philadelphia
    (demolished 1973)

W. J. Nichols, summer cottage, Bellefonte, Pa.

Abraham Pennock House, alterations and additions,
Lansdowne, Pa.

Ida V. Stambauch House and offices, Santa Barbara, Calif.

Unitarian Church, alterations and additions to school,
Wilmington, Del.

1892   M. Barbour House, Broad and Dauphin Sts., Philadelphia

Geano and Raggio, factory and stable, 924 S. 7th St.,
Philadelphia

F. L. Harrington House, Upsal St., Germantown,
Philadelphia

M. N. Johnson House, San Francisco, Calif.

Moore Brothers., residential operation, n.p.

New Century Club, Wilmington, Del.

1893   John O. Keim House, Cheltenham, Pa.

Irwin N. Megargee House, Roseglen, Pa.

John O. Sheetz House, alterations and additions, 3313
Hamilton St., Philadelphia

Ida V. Stambach House, alterations and additions, Santa
Barbara, Calif.

1929   Adelaide Nichols House (Mrs. John A. Baker), Westport,
Conn.

Writings by Nichols

"A Woman on the Woman's Building." *American Architect and Building News* 38 (December 10, 1892): 169.

Sources

"House at Cynwyd, Pennsylvania." *American Architect and Building News* 39 (February 11, 1893), 95+, plate.

Logan, Mary S. *The Part Taken by Women in American History.* Wilmington, Del.: Perry-Nalle, 1912. See esp. 786–87.

"Minerva Parker Nichols: Obituary." *New York Times,* November 20, 1949, 94.

"Nichols, Minerva Parker." In *Notable American Women, 1607–1950,* edited by Edward T. James, Janet Wilson James, and Paul S. Boyer, vol. 2, 629–30. Cambridge, Mass.: Belknap Press of Harvard University Press, 1971.

Philadelphia Real Estate Record and Builder's Guide, August 14, 1889; March 26, 1890; April 1, 1893.

"Representative Women: Minerva Parker Nichols." *Woman's Progress* 1 (May 1893): 57–58.

Tatman, Sandra L., and Roger W. Moss. *Biographical Dictionary of Philadelphia Architects: 1700–1930*. Boston: G. K. Hall, 1985. See esp. 573–75.

Willard, Frances E., and Mary A. Livermore, eds. *A Woman of the Century*. Buffalo: Charles Wells Moulton, 1893.

LOCATION OF PAPERS. The Schlesinger Library at Radcliffe College has the papers of Adelaide Nichols Baker, Nichols's daughter, which include architectural drawings said to be by her mother. One of Nichols's projects, "Architectural Drawings for a Pair of Houses for M. and J. Campbell, ca. 1891," is in the architectural collection of the University of Pennsylvania. The Historical Society of Delaware, in Wilmington, has some drawings by Nichols.

IIIIIIIIIIIIIIIIIIIIIIIIII
Northman, Edith Mortensen (b. 1893)
IIIIIIIIIIIIIIIIIIIIIIIIII

Born in Copenhagen, Denmark, Edith Mortensen Northman studied for two years at the Studio School of Arts in the atelier of Frede Aamodt before immigrating to the United States in 1914. She and her family settled in Brigham City, Utah, where Northman worked as a librarian for two years. In 1918 she decided to become an architect, moved to Salt Lake City, and joined the office of Eugene R. Wheelon as a junior drafter. After two years, a doctor suggested that Northman move to Southern California for her health. In 1920 she settled in Los Angeles, where she worked for Henry J. Knauer's firm. Later she would become chief drafter for Clarence J. Smale. Northman studied architecture at the University of Southern California from 1927 to 1930. She passed the state licensing examination in 1931.

During the Depression, Mortensen carried on a remarkably successful private practice aided by a single drafter. The hundreds of projects she completed included a commission from the Union Oil Company to design more than fifty service stations on the West Coast. Among other significant buildings, she designed a Beverly Hills mansion for the Danish actor Jean Hersholt, the Danish Lutheran Church in Los Angeles, and the Normandie Mar Apartment Hotel. A Fresno newspaper reporter, John Edward Powell, described the hotel as in "the West Los Angeles tradition of swank French-inspired apartment buildings." During World War II, Mortensen worked in fortifications and engineering for the U. S. Army Corps of Engineers. Her assignments ranged from designing crude camp toilets to planning state-of-the-art medical buildings. After the war, Northman's commissions were primarily apartment buildings and hotels in the Los Angeles area.

Partial List of Buildings

1928–29	Apartment Building, New Jersey St., Los Angeles, Calif.
1937	Leimert Park Apartment Building, Garthwaite Ave. and Stocker Court, Los Angeles
	Danish Lutheran Church, Los Angeles
1939	Normandie Mar Apartment Hotel, N. Wishon Ave. and E. Home Ave., Fresno, Calif.
n.d.	Spanish revival house, 4216 6th Ave., Los Angeles

Sources

John Edward Powell. "Edith Mortensen Northman: Tower District Architect." *Fresno Bee,* May 11, 1990, F4.

|||||||||||||||||||||||||
Parker, Marion Alice (1875?-1935)
|||||||||||||||||||||||||

Marion Alice Parker grew up in New Hampshire, where she attended a drafting school and learned about running a business at her uncle's wood mill. Parker had experience working for several firms before becoming the first drafter in the Minneapolis office of William Gray Purcell and George Feick Jr. Although the only woman in the firm, Parker was considered an ordinary member of the team. In 1909, the firm of Purcell and Feick added George Grant Elmslie, who had gained recognition as a superb drafter during his twenty years working with the famous Chicago architect Louis Sullivan. Feick left the firm four years later, and it became Purcell and Elmslie until the dissolution of the partnership in 1921. Purcell and Elmslie designed more than seventy buildings and projects throughout the Midwest, prompting historians to describe the firm as the most productive of the Prairie School. Marion Parker was an important member of the design team for most of the firm's existence.

As a drafter, Marion Parker was known to be "competent and dependable," and her work was spoken of with admiration by William Purcell, who left behind oral history accounts of the firm's achievements. Purcell recounted watching her "faithful study of the working drawings," but it is clear that she began to take on a larger role in the firm as early as 1912. In his reminiscences of the commission for the Charles I. Buxton Bungalow,

Purcell described collaborating with Parker: "Our Miss Parker took a great interest in this house, and together she and I spent time and study on every smallest arrangement and detail. The plan is a perfect piece of articulation and the whole project made functional from every view we could bring to bear upon it. Miss Parker and I take credit for the design. George Elmslie seems to have been busy elsewhere."[34]

Parker left the firm in 1919 and set up her own office in Minneapolis. Details of her private practice are unknown, but Purcell noted that one of his firm's projects, the Business Women's Dormitory for Gratia Countryman, a longtime director of the Minneapolis Public Library and a social activist, was "later revised and built by Marion Parker as her own commission."[35] When Parker retired, she moved to Laguna Beach, California, and opened an arts and crafts shop. She died in California in 1935.

Partial List of Buildings

The extent of Parker's collaboration on many projects is unclear, and the work she did as a private architect is undocumented. The following two attributions have been made from William Gray Purcell's account.

ca. 1912   Business Women's Dormitory (for Gratia Countryman), Minneapolis, Minn.

1912   Charles I. Buxton, bungalow, Owatonna, Minn. (with William Gray Purcell)

1920s   Frank P. Stover House, 1320 W. Oak St., Fort Collins, Colo.

Sources

Mark Hammons. "Purcell and Elmslie, Architects." In *Art and Life on the Upper Mississippi, 1890–1915,* edited by Michael Conforti. Newark: University of Delaware Press, 1994.

LOCATION OF PAPERS. The Marion Alice Parker Collection, consisting of blueprints and pencil sketches of two structures, is in the Northwest Architectural Archives, University of Minnesota Libraries, Minneapolis. A few details of Parker's life and information about her role in the firm of Purcell and Elmslie were recorded by William Gray Purcell. The William Gray Purcell Papers, also at the Northwest Architectural Archives, include a useful introduction by Mark Hammons, who also offers an internet site devoted to the firm: http://www.organica.org/purcell.htm (accessed September 12, 2007).

||||||||||||||||||||||||||
Pattee, Elizabeth Greenleaf (b. 1893)
||||||||||||||||||||||||||

In a career that would span nearly three generations, Elizabeth Greenleaf Pattee worked as a drafter, an architect, a landscape architect, and a professor. She was born in Quincy, Massachusetts, in 1893. Prior to her graduation from MIT in 1916, Pattee submitted a thesis entitled "Design for the Main Building of a Day School for Girls." She may have spent the next two years at Lowthrope School of Landscape Architecture in Groton, Massachusetts, an institution that would become an important part of her professional life. Pattee was employed by the architectural firm Stone and Webster from 1919 to 1921 and worked briefly as a drafter for Lois Howe and Eleanor Manning in Boston. She then established her own Boston architectural office with Constance E. Peters, a landscape architect. The firm of Pattee and Peters gradually focused on landscape architecture, though always with special attention to building and site design. One of Pattee's early commissions was the landscape of Killian Court, arguably the most important public space at MIT. Along with her practice, Pattee taught architectural subjects at Lowthrope, where she was listed as the acting principal in 1924 and would remain for over twenty years. She was also an instructor at the Rhode Island School of Design. Pattee and Peters worked together until the 1940s.

Pattee attended International Federation of Landscape Architecture (IFLA) conventions in Stockholm, Vienna, Zurich, and Stuttgart. She became a member of the AIA in 1933 and was also a member of the American Society of Landscape Architects. In 1950, Pattee married the landscape architect and city planner Arthur Coleman Comey (1886–1954) in Lincoln, Massachusetts.

Partial List of Buildings

1920s-30s   "All-the-year-round garden treatment," offices of Kidder Peabody Company, Devonshire St., Boston
Robert Winsor House, Weston, Mass.
John R. McLane House, Manchester, Mass.
Henry S. Woodbridge House, Pomfret, Conn.
Ernest R. Behren House, Second Beach, Newport, R.I.
Headquarters for Colonial Dames of America, garden, Wethersfield, Conn.

Writings by Pattee

"An Account of IFLA's Scenic Tour through Austria." *Landscape Architecture* 45:32–35.
"Impressions from IFLA's Scenic Tour through Switzerland." *Landscape Architecture* 47:327–34.
"Little Lessons in Landscape Design." Unattributed magazine clipping, 1939, possibly from *House Beautiful* or *House and Garden*.

Sources

"Elizabeth Greenleaf Pattee." In *American Women, 1935–1940*, edited by Durwood Howes, 690. Detroit: Gale, 1981.

LOCATION OF PAPERS. Records relating to Pattee's membership in the AIA are located in the AIA membership files, Record Group 803, American Institute of Architects Archives, Washington, D.C.

IIIIIIIIIIIIIIIIIIIIIIIII
Peddle, Juliet (1899–1979)
IIIIIIIIIIIIIIIIIIIIIIIII

Juliet Peddle's architectural career was unusual for a woman of the day, and her upbringing made her success even more remarkable. Born in Terre Haute, Indiana, Peddle was the daughter of a professor of machine design, and, according to family history, became "son" of the family after the death of her infant brother. Peddle's father taught her drafting and photography in preparation for a career in architecture, and she entered the University of Michigan, Ann Arbor, in 1918. During her college years, Peddle became friends with Bertha Yerex Whitman, who was the first female graduate of the university's school of architecture in 1920. The two are pictured together in a yearbook photograph of the T-Square Society, a social club for female architecture students of which Peddle was treasurer. After her graduation in 1922, Peddle followed Whitman to Chicago and was welcomed to the firm of Perkins, Fellows, and Hamilton, which specialized in the design of regional schools. During this time, Peddle took courses at the Art Institute of Chicago (where she taught briefly) and at the Berkshire Summer Art Institute. In 1926 Peddle received a license to practice architecture in the state of Illinois.

Before settling down in the Midwest for the remainder of her career, Peddle took a six-month sketching trip through England, France, and Italy. When she returned home, Peddle designed a small house for family friends in the Terre Haute suburb of Allendale and may have been employed briefly by the architect Herbert Foltz of Indianapolis. Between 1927 and 1931, Peddle worked for Edwin H. Clark, Inc., of Chicago, where she learned to draw plans, make inspections, and tackle practical aspects of the profession, such as figuring specifications for contractors, estimating costs, and understanding the physics of construction materials. In the late 1920s, Peddle lived at the Three Arts Club, a residence for female artists and designers. During this time, Peddle and her friend Bertha Whitman were among the founders of the Chicago Women's Architectural Club, one of the first professional organizations for female architects. Club members exhibited architectural work at the first Women's World's Fair in Chicago, in 1927, and at other locations throughout the 1930s. In 1932 the club had fourteen members and Peddle served as editor of its publication, the *Architrave.*

In 1931, Peddle lost her job as a result of the Depression but found some temporary employment in local firms and then with the government-sponsored Historic American Building Survey (HABS). During her brief employment with HABS, Peddle gained considerable knowledge in the field of historic preservation and restoration, in part by attending a seminar in Colonial Williamsburg. This training would play a significant role in her postwar career.

Peddle moved back to Terre Haute in 1935 and struggled to find temporary work for several years. Despite the hard times, Peddle received an Indiana architectural license in 1939 and immediately opened her own office. Her second year in business, Peddle received a commission to remodel the tower of the First Congregational Church and to design federally sponsored low-rent housing for the Vigo County Housing Authority. By 1941, Peddle recorded working on twenty jobs, and although many must have involved remodeling old buildings, she considered herself off to a good start. Unfortunately, World War II resulted in the closing of the office in March 1942. As residential building came to a standstill, Peddle was fortunate to find work as a drafter with the firm of Miller, Vrydagh, and Yeager, and to work on the design for a twin-engine training facility for the U.S. Air Force. Another temporary job with a commercial solvents manufacturer included designing plans for an animal research building.

In 1946, Peddle was able to reopen her office on the fifth floor of the Opera House Building in Terre Haute. This professional building housed doctors, lawyers, a civil engineer who frequently worked with Peddle, and the firm of Miller, Vrydagh, and Yeager. Over the next three years, she found few clients but was able to establish a good working relationship with several local contractors who would serve her well in the future. Business began to pick up in 1949, when Peddle designed her first postwar house and received a contract to remodel the main building of Rose Polytechnic Institute and to work on other aspects of campus planning. During the early 1950s, Peddle continued to build up her social connections, which included community members involved in the historical society, the local theater, and the medical profession. In the mid-1950s, Peddle designed her most challenging structure to date, a modern medical facility for six doctors, known as the Medicenter. The building was considered a notable contribution to the city upon its completion in 1957, and in 1959 the *Practical Builder* praised its efficient organization. By this time, Peddle herself had become a well-known regional architect and the subject of a series of newspaper articles. During the height of her career, from 1958 to 1968, Peddle designed several schools, took on two extensive remodeling projects at Rose Polytechnic, and, in 1972, designed a new Social Security office commissioned by the federal government. Throughout this time, she received a steady stream of residential commissions.

During the 1970s, Peddle continued to take on architectural work, but her home became her office, and the jobs were mostly small domestic remodeling projects. As she eased into retirement, Peddle enjoyed working as a historian, contributing a series of articles on old houses to the local newspaper, lecturing, and, most important, developing a collection of more than one thousand slides of historic buildings. Many of the images were taken moments before demolition. A few months after Peddle's death in 1979, an apartment building for senior citizens was named Peddle Park in her honor.

Partial List of Buildings

1939	Mary Phillips, cottage, Terre Haute, Ind.
1940	Paul N. Bogart House, Allendale, Ind.
	First Congregational Church, tower remodel, Ohio St., Terre Haute
1941	Dr. Alexander W. Cavins House, Allendale
	Vigo County Housing Authority, near Riley, Ind.
1946	J. C. Wakeman House (built 1952), n.p.
1947	Associated Physicians and Surgeons, clinic addition (AP & S Clinic), Poplar and Sixth, Terre Haute
1948–49	Dr. Frank Sayre House, Robinwood, east of Terre Haute
	Rose Polytechnic Institute, remodeling of main building, Terre Haute
1951	Modesitt House (built 1956), north of Terre Haute

1953–54	Indiana Room, Emeline Fairbanks Public Library, Terre Haute
1954	Community Theater, remodel of old movie house (additions, 1965), Terre Haute
1955–56	John Ennis House, Woodridge, Ind.
1955–57	Dr. Roy J. Ault, Medicenter, East Poplar, Terre Haute
1957	Benjamin and Fannie Blumberg House, Terre Haute
1958	George Mitchell House, Marshall, Ill.
	Lincoln Elementary School (Benjamin Franklin School) remodel, n.p.
1959	Paul Martin House, west of Marshall, Ill.
1959–61	Crawford School, Terre Haute
early 1960s	Dr. and Mrs. William Mankin House, n.p.
	Dr. and Mrs. Robert Reed House, n.p.
1962	First Congregational Church remodel, n.p.
	Rose Polytechnic Institute, remodel of student center and conversion to Templeton Administration Building; main building remodel, lecture hall and computer room (1964), Terre Haute
1972	Social Security Office, Meadows Shopping Center, Terre Haute

Writings by Peddle

"Early Terre Haute Architecture." (Weekly essays and sketches.) Terre Haute *Tribune-Star,* Feb. 2, 1941–April 19, 1942.
Leaves of Thyme, 1949–79. Vigo County Historical Society newsletter edited by Peddle.

Sources

Caplow, Harriet M., et al. *Juliet Peddle of Terre Haute: The Architect, the Historian, and Her City, 1899–1979.* Terre Haute, 1990.
"Medical Center." *Practical Builder* (July 1959): 80–84.

LOCATION OF PAPERS. The Vigo County Historical Society, Terre Haute, holds the Peddle Family Letters, 1912–37, as well as Peddle's personal papers relating to the historical society and various professional resumes, slide collections, and manuscripts. The Vigo County Public Library has minutes of the Terre Haute Pen and Brush Club and clippings files. Information on Peddle's work on school buildings can be found in the minutes of the Terre Haute School Trustees, Vigo County School Corporation, Terre Haute.

|||||||||||||||||||||||||
Peters, Nelle Elizabeth Nichols (1884–1974)
|||||||||||||||||||||||||

One of the most remarkable and prolific female architects of her generation, Nelle Elizabeth Nichols Peters was born in a sod house on the North Dakota prairie. After graduating from Buena Vista College at Storm Lake, Iowa, in 1903, she decided that her talents in art and mathematics were most appropriate for an architect. Nichols found work as a drafter at the firm of Eisentrout, Colby, and Pottenger in Sioux City and remained with the firm for about four years. She supplemented her practical education with correspondence courses in architecture. In 1907 Eisentrout, Colby, and Pottenger sent her to its Kansas City office, and two years later she left the firm to establish her own practice in the city.

Nelle Nichols married William H. Peters, a designer for the Kansas City Railroad, in 1911. Two years later, she received commissions from the Phillips Building Company, which included the stately apartment buildings surrounding courtyards that would become her trademark. One of her most successful apartment groupings was the "literary group," seven apartment buildings named after famous authors such as Robert Louis Stevenson and Mark Twain, located on the west side of Country Club Plaza. At the highpoint of her career, in the 1920s, Peters designed two Kansas City landmarks, the Ambassador Hotel and the Luzier Cosmetic Company, as well as churches and office buildings. A 1931 photograph of the Luzier building declared it "the largest laboratory of its kind in the world" (fig. 40). Peters completed twenty-nine commissions in 1924 alone. Although hardly acknowledged at her death fifty years later, Peters's exceptional career resulted in nearly one thousand buildings that helped shape the character of Kansas City.

Partial List of Buildings

1920	Del Monte Apartments, 200–202 West Armour Blvd., Kansas City (unless noted otherwise, all locations are in Kansas City)
1921	Belnord Court, 4024–4050 Warwick Blvd.
	King Cole Apartments
	Armour-Gillham Apartments
	Poet Apartments, "literary block," West Forty-eighth St. on Country Club Plaza
1924	Ambassador Hotel, 3560 Broadway

FIGURE 40. Luzier Cosmetic Company, Kansas City, Missouri. Designed by Nelle Peters, 1928. Courtesy Jackson County Historical Society, Independence, Missouri.

1926	Ellison Apartments, 306 West Armour Blvd.
1927	Belleclaire Apartments, 401–403 East Armour Blvd.
	Melbourne Apartments, 303 Brush Creek
	Valentine Hotel, 3724 Broadway
1928	Apartment building, Tulsa, Okla.
	House, 5825 Overhill Rd., Mission Hills, Kans.
	Luzier Cosmetic Company, 3216 Gillham
	Pendennis Apartments, Topeka, Kans. (demolished)
	Hillcrest Apartments, 509–11 Gladstone Blvd.
n.d.	Apartments, 420 West Forty-sixth Terrace
	Hanover Apartments, 3603–3605 Central St.
	James Russell Lowe Apartments, 722 Ward Parkway
	House, 1008 E. Forty-fourth St.
	House, 1255 Stratford Rd.
	Country Club Plaza

Sources

Ehrlich, George, and Sherry Piland. "The Architectural Career of Nelle Peters." *Missouri Historical Review* 83, no. 2 (January 1989): 161–76.

Flynn, Jane. "The Amazing Nelle E. Peters." *Preservation Issues* 3, no. 2.

Wright, Henry. "The Place of the Apartment in the Modern Community." *Architectural Record* 67, no. 3 (March 1930): 245–46, 296.

LOCATION OF PAPERS. The University of Missouri, Kansas City, has fourteen rolls of Nelle Peters's drawings in its Western Historical Manuscript Collection.

‖‖‖‖‖‖‖‖‖‖‖‖‖‖‖‖‖‖‖‖‖
Pfeiffer, Alberta Raffl (1899–1994)
‖‖‖‖‖‖‖‖‖‖‖‖‖‖‖‖‖‖‖‖‖

Alberta Pfeiffer graduated at the top of her class from the University of Illinois School of Architecture in 1923 and was the first woman ever to win the AIA school medal, awarded for excellence throughout four years achieved by a graduating student at each school recognized by the institute. Pfeiffer received a master's degree from the university two years later. Her fifty-five years in the profession began at the Chicago firm Tallmadge and Watson in 1923. From 1925 to 1931, Pfeiffer was employed by the New York architect Harrie T. Lindeberg, one of the most sought-after residential designers in the region. During her years with Lindeberg, Pfeiffer worked on country estates for wealthy clients, sometimes serving on a team of as many as six architects. Some of her drawings for such houses appear in *Domestic Architecture of H. T. Lindeberg* (1940).

In 1930 Alberta married Homer Pfeiffer, a 1925 graduate of the University of Illinois who had earned an architecture degree from Yale in 1926. While Alberta was still employed by Lindeberg, Homer won the prestigious Prix de Rome, and during his years as a fellow at the American Academy in Rome (1927–30) she was able to visit him at least twice. The couple opened their own firm in 1933. The Pfeiffers were primarily residential architects, with more than two hundred fifty commissions to their credit, mostly in Hadlyme, Connecticut.

In 1940, Homer joined the navy and supervised the construction of naval housing, hospitals, and other facilities. Alberta carried on their firm during the war and established her own practice afterward. According to the IAWA newsletter, Pfeiffer recalled that "during the 1950s and 1960s she was never without a project, and often had as many as ten designs on her desk at the same time."[36] During her career, Pfeiffer completed more than one hundred seventy residential designs, renovations, and alterations, as well as a bank and a church in Connecticut. In addition to her local work, she designed two Arizona ranches, a house in Illinois, and a house in Wisconsin.

Pfeiffer was involved in local organizations, such as the Hadlyme board of education and its zoning board. In 1935 she joined the board of directors of the Society of Connecticut Craftsmen. She retired and closed her office in 1977.

Sources

"Alberta Pfeiffer." *International Archive of Women in Architecture Newsletter* 2, no. 1 (Fall 1990): 1–2.
"Architects in Lifetime Partnership." *Illinois Alumni News* 56, no. 6 (September 1977): 5.
Obituary. *Hartford Courant,* August 10, 1994.
Obituary. *Sun,* Westerly, R.I., August 10, 1994.

LOCATION OF PAPERS. The International Archive of Women in Architecture, Blacksburg, Virginia, is the repository for Alberta Pfeiffer's project files.

IIIIIIIIIIIIIIIIIIIIIIIIII
Pierce, Marjorie (1900–1999)
IIIIIIIIIIIIIIIIIIIIIIIIII

Marjorie Pierce is still remembered at MIT, both for her accomplishments as an architect and for her contributions to the institute (fig. 41). A native of Malden, Massachusetts, Pierce received her architectural degree from MIT in 1922 and earned her master's degree the next year. Oral history records and articles on Pierce in MIT publications describe how she helped pay for her education by working as a theater usher and selling homemade fudge. After graduation, Pierce won a fellowship from the Boston Society of Architecture for studying art and architecture abroad. From 1940 to 1944, she was president of the MIT Women's Association, and during her tenure she endowed the Ellen Swallow Richards Professorship. Later, Pierce created the first fully endowed graduate fellowship in the MIT Department of Architecture, the William Emerson Fellowship, in memory of her teacher and the first dean of the architecture school. In 1999, Pierce was remembered as the oldest alumna. A new women's independent living group, an off-campus residence for female students at MIT, was named in her honor.

Pierce spent most of her career working in Weston, Massachusetts, where

FIGURE 41. Marjorie Pierce. Courtesy MIT Museum.

she designed residences and commercial buildings for most of her fifty years as a practicing architect. Her generous financial contributions to MIT and the more than eighty rolls of architectural drawings she donated to the MIT Museum suggest that she had a successful business.

Partial List of Buildings

1953	Lexington Arts and Crafts Society Headquarters, 130 Waltham St., Lexington, Mass.
1972	Old Hardy County Courthouse, remodel, Winchester Ave. and Elm St., Moorefield, W. Va.

Sources

"Architect Marjorie Pierce, Oldest Alumna, Dies at Age 99." *Tech Talk*, Massachusetts Institute of Technology, December 15, 1999.

Oral History. Pierce, Marjorie. MC 356, Alumnae Oral History Collection, Institute Archives and Special Collections, MIT.

LOCATION OF PAPERS. The MIT Museum and the Institute Archives and Special Collections at MIT hold more than eighty rolls of Pierce's drawings.

|||||||||||||||||||||||||||
Pope, Theodate (1867–1946)
|||||||||||||||||||||||||||

It was unusual for a woman to pursue an architectural career in the 1890s, but for the daughter of a wealthy industrialist in Cleveland, Ohio, becoming a professional architect could hardly have seemed possible. Born into an upwardly mobile family in 1867, Theodate Pope attended private girls' schools, traveled frequently, and moved to an elite Cleveland neighborhood in the early 1880s. At age nineteen, she was sent to Farmington, Connecticut, to complete her education at Miss Porter's School. After graduation, Pope spent a year touring Europe with her family but returned to Cleveland briefly before becoming a permanent resident of Farmington in 1890. Evidently, she had developed a passionate interest in colonial revival architecture during her school years, and she immediately began work on restoring a local eighteenth-century farmhouse to its former glory. In keeping with the romantic sensibility of the day, Pope called the farmhouse the "O'Rourkery" after the man she bought it from, James O'Rourke. As she indulged her interest in the colonial era, living in the house as if she were of that time, Pope envisioned designing a lavish country estate for her family in Farmington.

Pope had loftier ambitions than simply devoting herself to amateur restorations. She set off for Princeton University during the 1890s and was privately tutored in architecture by faculty members. In 1898, Pope wrote to the firm of McKim, Mead, and White, the country's most famous colonial revival architects, to solicit help in creating "Hill-Stead," the future family estate (fig. 42). She directed the firm to make scaled plans and elevations from her country house designs and announced that she expected "to decide on the more important questions that may arise." It was to be "a Pope house, instead of a McKim, Mead and White house."[37] Her father, Alfred Pope, then hired McKim, Mead, and White to follow his daughter's ideas. When the house was finished in 1901, Theodate had contributed enough to the design to cause the firm to lower its fee, in honor of her collaboration. By 1906, Pope had established a private office in New York City, but her first major commission came from a close friend and former teacher. Mary Hillard hired Pope to design a girls' school in Middlebury, Connecticut (fig. 43). The Westover School, designed and constructed from 1906 to 1909, received high praise from the skyscraper architect Cass Gilbert as "the best girls' school . . . in the country."[38] Pope became a registered architect in New York and Connecticut in 1910.

The Nugent Publishing Company apparently considered Pope a prominent New York architect in 1915, on the basis of her reputation, for it requested her photograph for publication in a book of the state's notable practitioners. Pope recounted the company's request in a letter to her mother:

> You will be most amused to know that I was called up by telephone from their office and a masculine voice at the other end asked incredulously if I were really Theodate Pope the architect, and when I said I truly was this voice apologetically explained that it would be impossible for them to use my photograph as they had just heard I was a woman. They had not

FIGURE 42. Hill-Stead Museum, Farmington, Connecticut. Ethan Carr photographer, 2004.

FIGURE 43. Theodate Pope Riddle on the Westover School building site, c. 1907. Courtesy Westover School, Middlebury, Connecticut.

believed the rumor, hence the incredulous voice over the telephone. So you see, although art has no sex, I am discriminated against, though on the merits of my work they had selected me as one of the architects whom they wished to mention.[39]

If Pope's marriage to a diplomat, John Wallace Riddle, in 1916 affected her career, it was only to make her work more profitable. Theodate Pope had already gained a reputation for her creative designs in revival styles. The year of her marriage, Pope completed the Hop Brook School, a public elementary school in Naugatuck, Connecticut. She became a member of the American Institute of Architects in 1918. Upon learning of her membership, Pope wrote to the AIA insisting that she be listed as Theodate Pope, not

Theodate Pope Riddle, and noting that it was by her maiden name that she was known professionally. The correspondence was on stationery with the heading, "Theodate Pope, Architect, Farmington, Connecticut."[40]

In the early 1920s, Pope received an important restoration commission from the Women's Roosevelt Memorial Association to reconstruct Theodore Roosevelt's birthplace at 28 East Twentieth Street in New York City (fig. 44). The Roosevelt Birthplace was finished before the completion of Avon Old Farms School, a school for boys that Pope created as a memorial to her father in Avon, Connecticut. The school, designed in the style of sixteenth-century English architecture, was intended to resemble the cottages of the Cotswolds. It is characteristic of Pope that she visited the Cotswolds in 1920 to better understand native building traditions, and she hired British craftsmen to work

FIGURE 44. Theodate Pope Riddle with trustees of the reconstructed birthplace of Theodore Roosevelt, ca. 1923. Courtesy Hill-Stead Museum, Farmington, Connecticut.

on the school. In 1925, some of her drawings of the Avon Old Farms School were exhibited at the Architectural and Allied Arts Exposition cosponsored by the AIA and the Architectural League in New York.

Theodate Pope did not design a great number of buildings during her career, but her homes and schools were universally admired by her peers at a time when historicism in architecture was highly valued. Not only did she demonstrate remarkable ability and creativity as an architect, but her work and life cut across class lines, showing how an upper-class woman could be more than a dilettante and rise to become a professional capable of supervising at a construction site. This society woman's greatest achievement may have been that her work spoke to those of her class, such as Henry James, and gave their elite social circle ample evidence of the capabilities of women. Hill-Stead, a National Historic Landmark, became a museum upon Pope's death in 1946.

Partial List of Buildings

1898–1907	Alfred Pope House, Hill-Stead (with the firm of McKim, Mead, and White), Farmington, Conn.
1906–9	Westover School, Middlebury, Conn.
1911–14	Highfield (Joseph P. Chamberlain Estate), Middlebury
1913–14	Dormer House (Mrs. Charles O. Gates Estate), Locust Valley, Long Island, N.Y.
1914–15	Hop Brook School (later altered), Naugatuck, Conn.
1915	Worker's Housing (three duplexes), Farmington
1918–27	Avon Old Farms School, Avon, Conn.
1919–22	Theodore Roosevelt Birthplace (reconstruction, interior restoration, and design of adjacent building), New York City

Writings by Riddle

A Letter. Paris, 1924. Private signed edition of twenty-five numbered copies.
"Sinking of the *Lusitania.*" *American Heritage* 26 (April 1975): 98–101.

Sources

"Avon." *House Beautiful,* January 1926, 44–45.
"Avon Old Farms: A School for Boys." *American Architecture* 128 (November 5, 1925): 391–94.
Boyd, John Taylor, Jr. "Some Principles of Small House Design." *Architectural Record* 46 (1919): 408.

Callahan, Tara. *Theodate Pope Riddle: A Pioneer Woman Architect.* Eastern National, 1998.

"Dormer House." *Country Life in America* 35 (1919): 56–57.

Ferree, Barr. "Notable American Homes: Hill-Stead." *American Homes and Gardens* 7 (February 1910): 45–51.

"The Home of Mrs. Charles O. Gates." *Architecture* 37 (April 1918).

Katz, Sandra L. *Dearest of Geniuses: A Life of Theodate Pope Riddle.* Windsor, Conn.: Tide-mark Press, 2003.

"Mr. Alfred A. Pope's House." *Architectural Record* 20 (August 1906): 122–29.

Paine, Judith. "Avon Old Farms School: The Architecture of Theodate Pope Riddle." *Perspecta* 18 (1982): 42–49.

———. "Pioneer Women Architects." In *Women in American Architecture,* edited by Susan Torre, 65–66. New York: Whitney Library of Design, 1977.

"Residence of J. P. Chamberlain, Esq." *Architectural Record* 46 (November 1919): 408–9.

"Theodate Pope Riddle." *Biographical Cyclopedia of American Women,* vol. 1, 310–12. New York: Halvord, 1924.

"Theodate Pope Riddle." *Macmillan Encyclopedia of Architects,* vol. 3, 577–78. New York: Free Press, 1982.

Withey, Henry F., and Elsie R. Withey. *Biographical Dictionary of American Architects.* Los Angeles: Hennessey and Ingalls, 1970, 512.

LOCATION OF PAPERS. The Theodate Pope Riddle Papers are in the archival collection of the Hill-Stead Museum in Farmington, Connecticut. In nearby Avon, the Avon Old Farms School has Theodate Pope Riddle's manuscript "Memoirs" and some correspondence, drawings, and photographs. The Westover School Archives also have photographs and documents related to Riddle's work at the school.

|||||||||||||||||||||||||
Power, Ethel Brown (1881–1969)
|||||||||||||||||||||||||

A member of the first graduating class of the Cambridge School of Architecture and Landscape Architecture, Ethel Brown Power was one of five architects who received the school's certificate in 1920. *American Women, 1935–1940,* a biographical dictionary, describes Power as an architect who specialized in designing "service parts of the house." An undated circular in the Smith College Archives advertises Power's practice in Boston and her expertise in kitchen design. Power lectured at Smith in 1936, after the Cambridge School had merged with it and added a graduate program.

From the early 1920s to 1934 Power was the architectural editor of *House Beautiful,* which featured many articles by Cambridge School graduates and unusually good coverage of their work. Her career at the magazine ended when *House Beautiful* moved its editorial offices to New York City. Doris Cole devotes a chapter of *Eleanor Raymond, Architect* to Power and the importance of her work as an editor. Power not only set high editorial standards, but she also brought a professional level of expertise to the magazine, published architectural plans, and discussed a range of issues from building technology to the social ramifications of design. According to Cole, the magazine "surpassed many of the contemporary professional journals with its thorough, clear, and useful architectural commentary."[41] Power did more than any writer or editor of her day to promote the work of women architects, both in her magazine and through her relationships with classmates and friends. In her later years, Power saved the papers and drawings of her companion, Eleanor Raymond, preserving the work of an important architect for future generations.

Writings by Power

"A Beacon Hill Renovation." *House Beautiful,* November 1924, 462–63.
"Echoes from the Chicago Fair," *House Beautiful,* September 1933.
"High Spruces." *House Beautiful,* March 1932.
"Modern in New England." *House Beautiful,* August 1934.
The Smaller American House. Boston: Little Brown, 1927.

Sources

Alumni News Journal, Cambridge School of Architecture and Landscape Architecture, 1930–33. College Archives, Smith College, Northampton, Mass.
Cole, Doris. *Eleanor Raymond, Architect.* Philadelphia: Art Alliance Press, 1981.
"Ethel Brown Power." In *American Women, 1935–1940,* edited by Durwood Howes, 722. Detroit: Gale, 1981.

LOCATION OF PAPERS. Diaries by Power are part of the Eleanor Raymond Collection at the Frances Loeb Library, Graduate School of Design, Harvard University.

|||||||||||||||||||||||||||
Raymond, Eleanor (1888–1989)
|||||||||||||||||||||||||||

As a senior at Wellesley College, Eleanor Raymond attended an hour-long lecture on landscape architecture that changed her life. After graduating in 1909, Raymond spent a year traveling in Europe and began taking informal landscape courses offered by the Boston landscape architect Fletcher Steele. Raymond worked in Steele's office without pay for some time, and when she enrolled in the Cambridge School of Architecture and Landscape Architecture in 1917, she entered with considerable experience. In fact, she formed a partnership with one of her instructors, Henry Atherton Frost, just two years later and received her first commission, the Cleaves House in Winchester, Massachusetts. Raymond graduated from the Cambridge School in June 1920.

The 1923 renovation of 112 Charles Street on Beacon Hill in Boston was particularly important to Raymond, who transformed the derelict property into a townhouse she would share with friends and relatives for the next thirty years. Raymond, her sister Rachel, and Ethel Power lived on the third and fourth floors; the second floor became a private apartment for the Raymond sisters' mother; the ground floor belonged to Mary Cunningham, a landscape architect and Cambridge School graduate, and her twin sister, Florence, an educator. The residents shared common areas on the ground floor, the laundry, and a small garden. Over the years, the Charles Street house would increasingly come to represent the importance of a female network of professionals, for the purposes of both collaboration and personal strength.

Raymond opened her own office in 1928 and traveled to Germany with Power for a visit to the Bauhaus the next year. Raymond's private practice began with one of the first International style buildings in New England, the Raymond House, designed for her sister in 1931. The Raymond House was made of wood rather than concrete or stucco and featured factory-made windows and other prefabricated items. Like nothing ever seen in the region, the Raymond House was both cutting-edge modern and a building that borrowed from hundreds of years of vernacular architecture. The year of its design, Raymond published her only book, *Early Domestic Architecture of Pennsylvania*, a study that has since been distinguished as among the earliest systematic inventories of American vernacular architecture. Photographs of the Raymond House were featured in an exhibition sponsored by the Women's Architectural Club of Chicago for the Century of Progress, the world's fair held in the city during 1933–34. In 1936, Raymond received an architectural degree from Smith College for studies at the Cambridge School, and in 1939 she was appointed a Smith College trustee.

Raymond profited not only from the advice and expertise of her Cambridge School colleagues, but also from the collaboration of the school's talented graduates who were eager for office experience. Raymond employed Laura Cox, a Cambridge School graduate and architect in her own right, as a drafter for thirty years, but she also encouraged Cox to take on her own independent commissions. Cox designed several houses in Maine and was responsible for the renovation of the Women's College Club in Boston, among other projects.

Throughout her career, Raymond experimented with new technologies to learn how they could help her design simple buildings that suited the landscape, referred to the past, and were pleasant to occupy. She designed thirteen projects for the sculptor and art patron Amelia Peabody, including an experimental plywood house in 1940 (Peabody Plywood House) and an all-Masonite house (Peabody Masonite House) in 1944. Raymond worked with Dr. Maria Telkes of the MIT solar laboratory to design the Peabody or Dover Sun House (1948), in Dover, Massachusetts, one of the first successful solar buildings and probably the country's first occupied solar-powered house (fig. 45). In 1940 she took charge of the drafting room at the Radar School of MIT.

Raymond believed that a residential architect should be responsible for the comprehensive design of a home: its interior, exterior, and landscape.

FIGURE 45. Eleanor Raymond (right) and Maria Telkes of MIT at the Dover Solar House, Powisset St., Dover, Massachusetts. The house was constructed in 1948 and featured in the March 1949 *Architectural Record.* Courtesy Harvard University, Loeb Library.

Her interest in architectural history stemmed from a desire to learn from the past, in order to apply the best in traditional construction to modern design. Her innovative designs always involved the application of historical details to modern architecture, and in this she stands out as one of the creative thinkers of her day. In 1961, Raymond was elected a Fellow of the AIA. Her book was reprinted in 1973, and a retrospective exhibition of her work was presented in 1981 at the Institute of Contemporary Art, Boston.

List of Buildings

1919	Cleaves House, 10 Lawrence St., Winchester, Mass.
1922	TZE Society House, Wellesley College, Wellesley
1923	Building renovation, 112 Charles St., Boston
	Jackson House, Chestnut Hill Rd., Chestnut Hill, Mass.
1924	McNair House, 11 Gray Gardens East, Cambridge, Mass.
1926	Smith House and Barn, 57 Central St., Andover, Mass.
	Cross House, 255 Dudley St., Brookline, Mass.
1928	Safford House, Brook Hill Rd., Milton, Mass.
1929	Mitchell studio, 111 South St., Weston, Mass.
1931	Raymond House, Park Ave., Belmont, Mass.
1933	Peabody studio, Mill Farm, Dover, Mass.
	Peabody farm group, Mill Farm, Dover
	Peabody piggery, Powisset St., Dover
1935	Farnsworth House addition, Boston Post Rd., Weston, Mass.
	Elliott House, Westford, Mass.
	Sugarman House, 72 Arlington St., Brookline
	Frost House, 16 Longfellow Park, Cambridge
	Peabody greenhouse, Mill Farm, Dover
1936	Miller House, Juniper Rd., Belmont
	Smith House, addition, 59 Central St., Andover
1937	Ballantine House, addition, Vineyard Haven, Mass.
	Olmsted House, 35 Glencoe Rd., Chestnut Hill
	Bartel House, Gleason Rd., Wayland, Mass.
1939	Besse House, Vineyard Haven
	Peabody garage, Mill Farm, Dover
1940	Peabody Plywood House, Powisset St., Dover
1941	Hammond compound, Dolliver's Neck, Gloucester, Mass.
	Parker Plywood House, 7 Ledgewood Road, Winchester
1942	Smith House, addition, Biddeford, Me.
1943	Blewer House, addition, Sugar Hill, N.H.

1944	Wile House, 141 Meadowbrook Rd., Weston
	Barnes House, renovation, Haverhill, Mass.
	Peabody Masonite House, Powisset St., Dover
1945	Williams House, Concord
	Stackpole House, addition, Biddeford
1946	Olmsted House, addition, New Boston, N.H.
1947	Dickerson House, Hancock Point, Me.
	Burrill House, Marmion Way, Rockport, Mass.
1948	Stackpole House, 56 Morton Rd., Milton, Mass.
	Mason House, Simon Willard Rd., Concord
	Peabody Sun House, Powisset St., Dover
	Peabody Borden House, Powisset St., Dover
1949	Pope House, Manchester, Mass.
1950	Whiting House, Tyler Rd., Belmont
	Donovan House, Eastern Point Rd., Gloucester
1951	Warner House, Argilla Rd., Ipswich, Mass.
1952	Peabody, aluminum barn, Powisset St., Dover
1953	Podren House, Swampscott, Mass.
	Boditch House, addition, Fayerweather St., Cambridge
1954	Hunt House, addition, 725 Boston Post Rd., Weston
1955	Cove Chapel, Western Ave., Gloucester
1956	McCreary House, Kenmore Rd., Belmont
	Meyer House, 240 Somerset St., Belmont
1959	Nichols, factory addition, Waltham
	Barr House, Concord Heights, Haverhill
1961	Damon House, Squam Lake, Holderness, N.H.
	Peabody Dave's House, Powisset St., Dover
1966	Wile House, Pittsford, Vt.
	Hart House, addition, Argilla Rd., Ipswich
1968	Peabody Deck House, Powisset St., Dover
1969	Von Mertens House, 200 Lexington Ave., Weston
1970	Baxter-Ward antiques shop, East Brewster, Mass.
1972	Peabody Westville prebuilt house and garage, Dover
1973	Smith House, Biddeford, Me.

Writings by Raymond

Architectural Record (August 1933) (tenant house on the estate of Mrs. Carolene H. Dupont, Kent City, Md.).

"Barn into Studio." *House Beautiful,* September 1933.

Early Domestic Architecture of Pennsylvania, with Photographs and Measured Drawings by Eleanor Raymond, A.I.A. New York: W. Helburn, 1931.
"Giving Character to a Nondescript House." *House Beautiful,* August 1933.
"A Model Kitchen—Designed for the Woman Who Does Her Own Work." *House Beautiful,* June 1932.

Sources

Campbell, Robert. "Eleanor Raymond: Early and Indomitable." *AIA Journal* 71 (January 1982): 52–53.

Cole, Doris. *Eleanor Raymond, Architect.* Philadelphia: Art Alliance Press, 1981.

"Economy Still Favored the Two-Story Type." *Architectural Record* (June 1948).

Greely, Rose. "An Architect's Garden in the City." *House Beautiful,* November 1926.

———. "A Small House of Distinction." *House Beautiful,* November 1922, 423.

Gruskin, Nancy Beth. "Building Context: The Personal and Professional Life of Eleanor Raymond, Architect, 1887–1989." Ph.D. diss., Boston University, 1998.

"House for James H. Cleaves, Winchester, Massachusetts." *Architectural Record* 66 (November 1929): 442–43.

"House of James H. Cleaves, Esq., Winchester, Massachusetts." *Architectural Forum* (January 1927): 95–96.

Institute of Cotemporary Art, Boston. *Eleanor Raymond: Architectural Projects, 1919–1973.* Catalog for exhibition, September 15–November 1, 1981. Boston: Institute of Contemporary Art, 1981.

Kingsbury, Edith. "Spring Pasture—Our Experiment in the Country." *House Beautiful,* October 1932.

Mitchell, Marguerite MacKellar. "Barn into Studio." *House Beautiful,* September 1933.

Smith, Mary Byers. "Two Houses from One." *House Beautiful,* September 1928.

"Test House Heated Only by Solar Heat," *Architectural Record* 105 (March 1949): 136–37.

LOCATION OF PAPERS. The Eleanor Raymond Collection is part of Frances Loeb Library at the Graduate School of Design, Harvard University. The collection includes records related to three hundred architectural projects, photographs, personal papers, and memorabilia, as well as diaries kept by Ethel Power.

|||||||||||||||||||||||||
Rice, Lilian Jeanette (1888–1938)
|||||||||||||||||||||||||

Although Lilian Rice was one of the first women to graduate from the new architectural school at the University of California, Berkeley, she was exposed to an unusual number of female role models in the profession. For example, Julia Morgan had received a degree from the Berkeley School of Engineering many years before; Morgan had been accepted into Bernard Maybeck's circle of aspiring pupils and had recently opened her own office in the Bay Area. Rice's first architectural employment was with Hazel Wood Waterman, an architect in San Diego who attended Berkeley as an art student in the 1880s.

Rice was born in National City, California, a border town between San Diego and Tijuana, in 1888. Her education was encouraged by her father, Julius, an innovative teacher in local public schools, and her mother, Laura, known for her miniature paintings and flair for design. After earning a Berkeley degree in 1910, Rice returned to National City to nurse her invalid mother. For the next ten years she worked on her own, as a drafter for Waterman, and for the local firm of Richard S. Requa and Herbert L. Jackson. To supplement her income, Rice taught mechanical drawing and descriptive geometry at San Diego High School and San Diego State Teachers College during the early 1920s.

The 1915 Panama-California Exposition, a celebration of the opening of the Panama Canal, made this an exciting time to be in San Diego. Rice's move back to her hometown may have been for personal reasons, but she found herself surrounded by the work of some of the most creative California architects of the day, including Waterman's mentor, Irving Gill; Julia Morgan's teacher, Bernard Maybeck; and the Spanish baroque exposition buildings of the New York architect Bertram Goodhue. The exposition popularized a California style that drew from the region's Spanish history and combined innovative concrete construction, the exotic "resort" architecture of the Mediterranean, and the Arts and Crafts movement's emphasis on traditional wood craftsmanship. The romance of the California mission style was perhaps epitomized by Helen Hunt Jackson's popular novel *Ramona* (1884), a story associated with the Estudillo House (Ramona's Marriage Place) restored by Hazel Waterman in 1909.

Rice must have developed a taste for the popular California architectural idiom. In 1922, her employers, Requa and Jackson, suggested that she design and supervise Rancho Santa Fe, a small city planned by the Santa Fe Land Improvement Company, a division of the Santa Fe Railroad. Sixteen years earlier, the company had purchased land on which it planned to grow eucalyptus trees for railroad ties, but when that experiment failed, officials decided to invest instead in urban development. From 1922 through 1927, Rice worked on the fourteen-mile tract about twenty miles northeast of San Diego, designing a community complete with residences, shops, an inn, school, administration building, library, and other service buildings (figs. 46, 47). Here, Rice was given free rein to create a miniature world in the desert, often acting as landscape architect and city planner as well as supervisor of construction. She maintained an office on the property under her own name.

FIGURE 46. Santa Fe Land Improvement Company Administration Building, Rancho Santa Fe, San Diego County, California. Designed by Lilian Rice, ca. 1922. Jack E. Boucher, photographer, 1991. Courtesy Library of Congress, Prints and Photos Division, HABS.

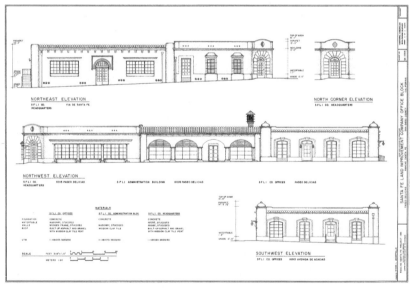

FIGURE 47. Santa Fe Land Improvement Company, Office Block, Paseo Delicias, Rancho Santa Fe. San Diego County, California. Designed by Lilian Rice, ca. 1922. Drawing by HABS. Courtesy Library of Congress, Prints and Photographs Division, HABS.

The appealing and somewhat exclusive character of Rancho Santa Fe was not lost on writers compiling *The WPA Guide to California* during the 1930s, who noted that "Rancho Santa Fe is the home of wealthy ranchers, among them Douglas Fairbanks Sr., whose 3,000-acre tract contains 300 acres of Valencia oranges irrigated by an expensive overhead sprinkling system."[42] Another well-known resident, Bing Crosby, lived in the remodeled Osuna Adobe, which had been the home of the first mayor of San Diego under Mexican rule a hundred years earlier.

In 1929, Rice left Requa and Jackson and opened her own office. She immediately began to experiment with the California modern style that she knew from her student years at Berkeley. As she designed new types of buildings, Rice also shifted from building in stucco and adobe to using lighter board-and-batten or stone-and-brick combinations. The Arnberg House in La Jolla, a wood and brick ranch house, and the ZLAC Rowing Club, a board-and-batten structure in Mission Bay, both received awards from the San Diego chapter of the AIA. In 1938, Rice designed a wood-frame, split-level house on a hillside overlooking the Pacific Ocean for Martha Kinsey. The final building of her career and the best example of her modern style, the Kinsey House was listed on the National Register of Historic Places in 1992.

In oral histories, Rice's colleagues and students speak of her influence as both architect and teacher. She was a mentor to Sam Hamill, FAIA, one of her geometry students at San Diego State College, and supervised Olive Chadeayne (1904–2001), a 1926 Berkeley graduate and future member of the AIA, during the early years of what would become a very successful career. In the late 1930s, Rice was stricken by stomach pains and, mistakenly assuming she had stomach cancer, did not seek treatment; she died in 1938 of a ruptured appendix. At the time of her death Rice's office was working on several residences and the San Dieguito Union High School in Encinitas, California, among other buildings. Some of the unfinished projects were completed by Elinor Frazier, one of the office drafters, who was brought into the firm at Rancho Santa Fe as a student apprentice in 1924. Frazier later became an instructor of architectural drawing and design at San Diego City College and at Mesa College. In recent years there has been some controversy over the extent of Rice's contribution to Rancho Santa Fe. Although she took on the project under Requa and Jackson, sources agree that Rice was the driving force behind the community and that, in her relatively short career, she helped to shape the architectural character of San Diego. In 1991 eight of Rice's buildings at Rancho Santa Fe were named to the National Register of Historic Places.

Partial List of Buildings

1922–30s	Rancho Santa Fe, Master Plan: shops, Valenciana Apartments, Hotel la Morada (The Inn at Rancho Santa Fe), administration building, service station, garden clubhouse, school, library, residences (for Requa and Jackson), 14-mile tract northeast of San Diego, Calif.
1927	Christine Arnberg House, La Jolla Hermosa, La Jolla, Calif.
1929	Marguerite M. Robinson House, 1600 Luddington Ln., La Jolla
1932	ZLAC Rowing Club, 111 Pacific Beach Drive, Pacific Beach (remodeled in 1960s by Sim Bruce Richards), Calif.
n.d.	Rice Elementary School, Chula Vista, Calif.
1936	Paul Ecke Sr., House, Encinitas, Calif.
1938	Simard House, 9339 Lemon Ave., La Mesa, Calif. Martha Kinsey House, 1624 Luddington Ln., La Jolla (National Register)

Writings by Rice

"Architecture: A Community Asset." *Architect and Engineer* 94 (July 1928): 43–45.

"Rancho Santa Fe—A Vision." *Modern Clubwoman,* January–February 1930, 5.

"Valenciana Apartments Rancho Santa Fe, California." *Architectural Record* 67 (March 1930): 246–47.

Sources

Crosby, Bing. "Our Little Ranch in the West." *California Arts and Architecture* 48 (October 1935): 24–25.

Eddy, Lucinda L. "Lilian Jeanette Rice: Search for a Regional Ideal, the Development of Rancho Santa Fe." *Journal of San Diego History* 29, no. 4 (1983): 262–85.

Emory, Christine. "Intensive Development Applied to a Big Project." *Los Angeles Times,* January 24, 1926.

Paine, Judith. "Some Professional Roles: 1920–1960." In *Women In American Architecture,* edited by Susana Torre, 108–11. New York: Whitney Library of Design, 1977.

Seares, M. Urmy. "The Village of Rancho Santa Fe." *California Arts and Architecture* 38 (September 1930): 36, 66.

Withey, Henry F., and Elsie R. Withey. *Biographical Dictionary of American Architects.* Los Angeles: Hennessey and Ingalls, 1970. See esp. 505.

Wright, Henry. "The Place of the Apartment in the Modern Community." *Architectural Record* 67 (March 1930): 246–47 (plates showing Valenciana Apartments, Rancho Santa Fe).

"ZLAC Rowing Club, Pacific Beach, California; L. J. Rice, Architect." *California Arts and Architecture* 48 (August 1935): 27.

LOCATION OF PAPERS. The Research Library, San Diego Historical Society, holds a collection of Rice's papers, drawings, correspondence, and other archival materials from the 1920s and 1930s. Architectural drawings by Richard S. Requa are also at the San Diego Historical Society.

||||||||||||||||||||||||
Riggs, Lutah Maria (1896–1984)
||||||||||||||||||||||||

The story of Lutah Maria Riggs's rise from a struggling student teacher to one of California's most sought-after architects reads like an American rags-to-riches tale. Born in Toledo, Ohio, Riggs grew up with a chronically ill father who traveled to Southern California for his health and died there when she was nine. Riggs's mother remarried, but little is known about Riggs's stepfather, except that his search for employment brought the family to Santa Barbara in 1914. A graduate of Manual Training High School in Indianapolis, Riggs had the basic education necessary to enroll in Santa Barbara Normal School, one of the state-sponsored teacher schools and a traditional, secure path for women seeking financial independence. She spent two years at the school, working as a bookkeeper in a Woolworth's to help make ends meet. In 1917, Riggs won a contest for selling newspaper subscriptions that promised a scholarship to the University of California at Berkeley. She was able to convince the publisher of the local newspaper to finance the entire first year of her education. In 1918, the *Santa Barbara Daily News* ran an article about Riggs entitled "Winner of News Prize Is Doing Well at School."[43]

Riggs was fortunate to enter Berkeley at an exciting time, as part of a "second generation" of women graduates following in the footsteps of Julia Morgan and Lilian Rice. The school was still under the direction of its founder, John Galen Howard (1864–1931), and Riggs's class included three other women—Rose Luis, Irene McFaul, and the sculptor Elah Hale.[44] A distinguished architect with several Berkeley buildings to his credit, Howard not only taught and collaborated with Morgan but served as a mentor for Riggs. Like most major schools of architecture in America, Berkeley was modeled after the French Ecole des Beaux-Arts system, and Riggs received a traditional education with intense studio experience and instruction in the precise rendering of historical styles of architecture. Riggs, a gifted drafter, won the Alumni Prize upon her graduation in May 1919, and she continued taking graduate courses at Berkeley. The award helped finance her education, as did her work drafting for a small San Francisco architectural firm, the Riedel Building Corporation, and the San Francisco City Engineers Office, among others. Riggs's first major job began in 1920 with the architect Ralph D. Taylor in Susanville, where she worked on a range of projects including a hospital addition, public library, and mountain lodge.

In August 1921, Riggs was lucky to find work with the Santa Barbara architect George Washington Smith, a leading figure in the Spanish revival style so popular in California. Smith supported Riggs's first independent competition entry—"A Small House in Brick"—for which she won a fifty-dollar fourth prize. During the early 1920s, Riggs had a close relationship with Smith and his wife, traveling with them to Europe and engaging in other family activities. In 1924, just three years after joining the firm, Riggs became a partner and chief drafter. In 1926, Riggs designed her own house, "Clavelitos," just up the road from the Smith house and studio. She earned her license to practice architecture in California in 1928 and was on her way to becoming a full partner in the Smith firm. Then, as the Depression loomed, George Washington Smith died suddenly, in 1930. Riggs and Harold Edmondson continued the firm for about a year, primarily finishing up projects, and by January 1931 Riggs was working on her own.

During a time when jobs were scarce, Riggs was able to find work with A. E. Hanson, an artist in Los Angeles for whom she had worked with Smith. Her major project was a gated suburban community in Palos Verdes—Rolling Hills—which Hanson and Charles H. Cheney, a planner, designed and laid out in 1935. Throughout the thirties Riggs did remodeling and additions on many Smith homes and what her biographer, the architectural historian David Gebhard, calls "perhaps the most important design of her entire career," the Baron Maximilian von Romberg Villa and Estate in Montecito (1937–38).[45] The next year, Riggs was the resident consulting architect for the Rolling Hills estates, a series of ranchettes (fig. 48). She produced eighteen designs for Rolling Hills in 1939, eight of which were built. In 1941, Riggs served as president of the Santa Barbara chapter of the AIA and attended the annual meeting at Yosemite National Park, where she met fellow chapter president Marion Manley.

During the war, from 1942 to 1945, Riggs designed film sets for MGM and then for Warner Brothers. Her work in Hollywood included sets for *The White Cliffs of Dover* (1944) and *The Picture of Dorian Gray* (1945). After the war, Riggs worked in partnership with Arvin B. Shaw (from 1945 to 1951). The firm adapted to the taste of the day, addressing the preference for modernism but combining it with a regional tradition in a manner similar to that of A. Quincy Jones and Cliff May. Riggs served as president of the

FIGURE 48. Lutah Maria Riggs, n.d. This photograph was probably taken in her office on Middle Road in Montecito, California. Courtesy Santa Barbara Historical Society Museum.

AIA chapter again in 1953 and on the National Committee on Preservation of Historic Buildings in 1955. Today, Riggs is best known for her work during the late 1950s, which included the Vedanta Temple (1954–56; fig. 49) and the remodeling of El Paseo and the adjoining Suski Building in Santa Barbara. David Gebhard compares the Vedanta Temple to Lloyd Wright's Wayfarer's Chapel at Palos Verdes in terms of site, architectural design in relation to the landscape, and popularity. Riggs also worked on a major commission in Los Angeles, the design of the gardens of "Villa San Giuseppe" (1956–66) for Daniel J. Donohue. In 1960, Riggs was elected an AIA Fellow.

During the 1970s, the fashion for California residential architecture turned to traditional imagery of the Spanish west, and Riggs provided her clients with the Spanish colonial revival homes of their dreams. Although these houses used traditional forms, most often organized around a central patio, Riggs brought her sense of modernism to the designs. The Wright S. Ludington house (1973) in Montecito and her final work, the Jack C. Antrim house (1978–80) in Goleta, both show how she conceived of tradition with fresh, modern lines.

FIGURE 49. Vedanta Temple, Santa Barbara, Calif. Designed by Lutah Maria Riggs and constructed in 1954–56. Undated photo. Courtesy the Vedanta Society of Southern California.

Partial List of Buildings

This is an edited version of "Projects and Buildings (A Selected List)" in David Gebhard, *Lutah Maria Riggs, A Woman in Architecture* (Santa Barbara, Calif.: Capra Press and Santa Barbara Museum of Art, 1992), 121–26. Gebhard's list includes projects and more detailed descriptions of some buildings.

1926	Lutah Maria Riggs House, "Clavelitos," Montecito, Calif.
1930	Malcolm Douglas House, Montecito (entrance gates)
	J. Wesley Gallagher House, Montecito
	Daniel C. Jackling House, alterations, Woodside, Calif.
	George F. Steedman House (library additions and
	alterations, 1930–33), Montecito
1931	Mrs. Lester Baldwin, guest cottage, Montecito
	Mrs. Norris King Davis House, alterations, Montecito
	Mrs. Ellis Fischel House, Santa Barbara, Calif.
1932	Samuel Knight House, Montecito
1933	F. B. Edwards House, alterations, Santa Barbara
	Henry Eicheim House (alterations 1933–34, 1937), Montecito

1934	Mrs. Jeffrey S. Courtney-Ravencroft House, alterations and additions, Montecito
	Donald Myrick beach cottage, alterations and additions, Sandyland Cove, Carpinteria, Calif.
	Allen Breed Walker House (butler's cottage and glass house, 1934–35) Montecito
1935	Leon Graves House, Los Angeles
1936	William Cooper House, Montecito
1937	Biltmore Hotel, Montecito (bath house)
	Mrs. William H. Hall House, alterations, Montecito
	Kent Kane Parrot House, Montecito (with Plummer, Wurdeman, and Becket)
	Edgar Stow ranch cottage, Patera Rancho, Goleta, Calif.
	Baron Maximilian Von Romberg House, Montecito (1937–38, 1939–40)
	G. Palmer and Louise Black House, Santa Barbara (additions, 1938, 1942)
	Mrs. G. L. Spalding House, Santa Barbara (alterations)
1939	Taylor, Alexander House, Rolling Hills, Calif.
	F. N. Banta House, Rolling Hills
	Lenore Brooks House, Rolling Hills
	Gasoline Service Station, Rolling Hills
	Chadwick Seaside School, Palos Verdes (landscape design and additions, 1939–40)
	Joseph A. Denni House, Rolling Hills
	Edward C. Dudley House, Rolling Hills
	A. E. Hanson Co., Developers, Spec Residence no. 1-B, Harbor Hills, Calif.
	A. E. Hanson House, Beverly Hills, Calif. (alterations and additions; garage, 1941)
	Clifton A. Hix House, Rolling Hills
	Carl M. Johnson House, Rolling Hills
	Elwood Johnson House, Rolling Hills
	C. V. Knemeyer House, Rolling Hills
	O. W. Pearson House, Rolling Hills
	Rolling Hills Estates Administration Building, additions, Rolling Hills
	George Serpell House, Rolling Hills

Joseph Silveria House and Stable, Rolling Hills (1939–40)
1940   Lamotte Cohu House, Rolling Hills
Mrs. Charles W. Davis House, Santa Barbara
J. A. Graye House, Rolling Hills
John Percival Jefferson House, alterations, Montecito
Walter P. Limacher House, "Flying Triangle," Rolling Hills
Mrs. Walter Perkins House, Santa Barbara
Mattie Ramelli House, San Bernardino
Chester Raub House, Rolling Hills
Arthur Serns House, additions and alterations, Santa
            Barbara
Westfield, houses no. 1 and no. 2, Rolling Hills
1941   Allen Breed Walker House, alterations and additions,
            Hollywood
1942   Harry and Elsie Ravenscroft House, alterations, Goleta
Santa Barbara Botanic Gardens (library and herbarium)
1945   Arthur D. Bissell House, Santa Barbara
A. J. Comparte House, Los Angeles
Mary B. Kairne House, San Marino, Calif.
Suzanne Parsons office, alterations, Santa Barbara
Anne Stow-Fithian House, alterations and additions, Santa
            Barbara
Paul A. Hesse, farm house, Rancho Topanga, Malibu
1946   Mrs. Walter Briggs House, alterations, Santa Barbara
Percy A. Brooksbank House, Folded Hills Ranch, Gaviota,
            Calif.
Norman Foster House, alterations, Beverly Hills
John H. Green House, alterations and additions, Montecito
Katherine Harvey House, alterations, Montecito
Catherine Humphries House, Carpinteria
W. E. Hutton-Miller House, "Puerto Limon," Montecito
Mrs. Fred C. Keeney House, Santa Barbara
Donald Kellogg, beach cottage, Montecito
John Lyttle House, Ojai, Calif.
Malcolm McDuffie House, cottage addition, Montecito
Wirt Morton House, guest house addition, Montecito
Daniel Nugent, beach house, Montecito
Suzanne R. Parsons House, Santa Barbara

1947	Horace W. Armstrong House, alterations and additions, Santa Barbara
	Kent Kane Parrot houses, no. 2 and 3, Carmel, Calif.
	Herman Baer House, additions, Lompoc, Calif.
	Doyle W. Cotton House, additions, Montecito
	Leo Forbstein House, alterations, Beverly Hills
	Francis Griffin House, alterations, Bel Air, Calif.
	Mrs. William Leland Holt House, Santa Barbara
	Mrs. Elsie Johnson House, Montecito
	Mrs. Carl Lewis House, Montecito (alterations)
	Stuart O'Melveny House, Sandyland Cove, Carpinteria
	Andrew Peterson House, no. 1, Buellton, Calif.
	Santa Barbara Museum of Art, alterations and additions, Santa Barbara
1948	Earl V. Armstrong House, Montecito
	Beach Cooke House, Montecito
	Purdon Smith Hall House, Montecito
	Clinton Hollister House, additions, Santa Barbara
	Joseph J. Hollister House, Gaviota
	Howell W. Kitchell House, Montecito
	Paul Kolyn House, Santa Barbara
	J. C. Milholland House, alterations, Montecito
	Lawrence M. Nelson House, alterations, Santa Barbara
	John T. DeBlois Wack House, addition of stables, barns, and cottages, Hope Ranch, Calif.
	Harwood A. White beach cottage, alterations, Sandyland Cove, Carpinteria
1949	Ruth W. Cowlishaw House, alterations, Montecito
	Mrs. J. Langdon and Ms. Alice Erving House, Montecito
	Robert E. Gross House, Sandyland Cove, Carpinteria
	Lockwood Tower, alterations, Montecito
	Henrik Westen House, alterations and additions, Montecito
	P. Dana McMillan beach house, Sandyland Cove, Carpinteria
1950	S. R. Bill beach cottage, Sandyland Cove, Carpinteria
	G. Palmer and Louise Black House, Montecito
	A. L. Hershey and the Hershey Beverage Co., refreshment stand, Santa Barbara

Robert Mazet House, Montecito

Mrs. Floyd W. McRae House, alterations, Montecito

Lawrence M. Nelson office, Santa Barbara

Harold F. Sheets House, alterations and additions, Montecito

Guy Witter House, additions, Sandyland Cove, Carpinteria

1951   George Clifford House, Hope Ranch

Ronald Colman House, alterations and additions, Montecito

Charles Ducommun House, Los Angeles

John B. Hamilton House, Montecito

J. J. Hollister House, alterations and additions, Santa Barbara

Howard Morf House, alterations, Montecito

Daniel Nugent House, alterations, Montecito

Aldrick R. Peck House, alterations and additions, Sandyland
    Cove, Carpinteria

Austin Wynne and Mrs. John Watling House, alterations,
    Montecito

1952   Eleanor Griffith House, alterations, Montecito

Wright S. Ludington House, alterations, Montecito

Malcolm McNaughten House, alterations and additions,
    Montecito

Sterling Morton House, alterations, Montecito

1953   Harold C. Bodman House, additions, Montecito

Wallace F. Fleming House, Montecito

Mrs. M. Landreth Kelleher House, Montecito

John Boit Morse House, Montecito

Frank Nagle House, alterations and additions, Montecito

Maurice Rosenthal House, alterations and additions, Santa
    Barbara

1954   G. Norman Bacon House, alterations and additions, Hope
    Ranch

Mrs. George Merrill Davis House, Santa Barbara

Joseph Knowles House, alterations and additions, Santa
    Barbara

Miramar Hotel, alterations and additions, Montecito

Harold Plous House, Santa Barbara

Vedanta Temple, 925 Ladera Lane, Santa Barbara

1955   Richard McCurdy Ames cottage, Santa Barbara

E. Leslie Kiler House, Santa Barbara

Lobero Theater, alterations and additions, Santa Barbara

San Ysidro Ranch, alterations, Montecito

Ralph Steuard House, additions, Ventura

Byron Thornburgh House, Sandyland Cove, Carpinteria

1956   Daniel J. Donohue House, "Villa San Giuseppe,"
   Los Angeles

Packard Adobe, alterations, Santa Barbara

A. C. Pedotti House, alterations and additions, Santa
   Barbara

Austin C. Smith House, Fernald Point, Montecito

Edna A. Wiedemann House, Montecito

1957   Wright S. Ludington, "Hesperides," Montecito

Frances Colville House, Isla Vista, Goleta

C. Pardee Erdman House, Montecito

Montecito County Water District, Filter Plant building,
   alterations, Montecito

L. A. Wilkie House, alterations and additions, Montecito

1958   A. H. McCormick House, alterations and additions,
   Montecito

1959   Everett L. Harris House, alterations and additions,
   Montecito

Prynce Hopkins House, alterations and additions, Santa
   Barbara

William H. Joyce House, alterations and additions,
   Montecito

Thomas Kelland, gates, Fernald Point

M. L. Kellehed House, alterations and additions, Montecito

Margaret Mallory House, alterations and additions,
   Montecito

Alister H. McCormick House, alterations and additions,
   Montecito

Joseph H. Schaffner House, alterations and additions, Santa
   Barbara

1960   Curtis W. Hutton House, Montecito

Peter Nagel House, alterations and additions, Montecito

1961   Peter Berkey III House, Carpinteria

John Galvin House, Rancho San Fernando Rey, Santa Ynez
   Valley

Mrs. Dorothy M. Griffith House, alterations and additions, Santa Barbara

Robert M. Hutchins House, alterations and additions, Montecito

Mrs. Donald Kellogg House, "Historic Lemon House," alterations and additions, Fithian Ranch, Carpinteria

Alexander Tiers House, alterations and additions, Sandyland Cove, Carpinteria

1962   Robert Eisberg House, Santa Barbara

Santa Barbara Botanic Garden, alterations and additions to the library, Santa Barbara

S. B. Schleifer House, alterations and additions, Santa Barbara

H. Frank Swimmer House, alterations and additions, Santa Barbara

Henrik and Kay Westen Building, alterations, Santa Barbara

1963   Ruth Durney House, Santa Barbara

El Paseo Arcade Shops, Suski Building, alterations and additions, Santa Barbara

Alister H. McCormick garden, Rancho Santa Fe

Stuart S. Murray House, alterations and additions, Montecito

M. A. Silva House, alterations, Montecito

1964   Shirley C. Burden House, alterations and additions, Montecito

Wilson Forbes House, additions, Montecito

Alvan T. Fuller House, additions, Montecito

Winston Paul House (formerly Parrott House), alterations, Fernald Point, Montecito

1966–67   Ernest C. Watson House, alterations and additions, Montecito

1968   Eleanor Gooding House, alterations and additions, Santa Paula

Eva Herrmann House (Vedanta Society of Southern California), Montecito

Henrik Westen House, alterations, Montecito

1970   Daniel J. Donohue House, alterations, Montecito

1971   Ray Ordas House, alterations, Santa Barbara

1972   Roderick Nash House, Montecito

1973	Wright S. Ludington House, "October Hill," Montecito
1974	William Bradley House and barn, Santa Ynez
1975	William C. Horton House, additions, Montecito
	James Loebl House, additions, Ojai
1976	Francois Bourlon House, alterations, Montecito
	James Cronshaw House, alterations and additions, Santa Barbara
	Philip Kearny House, additions, Montecito
	Patrick McMahon House, additions, Montecito
1977	Ms. Brand House, alterations, Montecito
	Thomas W. Dibblee House, alterations and additions, Santa Barbara
	Robert Lawson House, alterations, Santa Barbara
	Jean Louis House, additions, Montecito
	Rancho San Julian Dairy, converted to house, near Lompoc
	William W. Shannon shop and guest barn, Happy Canyon, Santa Ynez
	Hallam C. Shorrock House, additions, Goleta
	John Wallop House, additions, Montecito
	Charles D. Woodhouse House, alterations and additions, Santa Barbara
1978	Jack C. Antrim House, Goleta
	Phil Kirkpatrick House, carport addition, Santa Barbara
	Mrs. Gladys Knapp House, additions, Montecito
1980	Dennis Ashley House, additions, Santa Barbara
	Gregory A. Dahlen House, terrace addition, Hope Ranch

Writings by Riggs

"Beautiful Gillespie Estate Fine Example of Mediterranean Type." *Santa Barbara News-Press,* March 17, 1940, pt. 3, 18.
"Mediterranean Sources Varied." *Santa Barbara News-Press,* March 3, 1940, pt. 3, 17.

Sources

"California Doctor's Office." *Architectural Record* 113 (May 1953): 184.
Gebhard, David. *Lutah Maria Riggs: A Woman in Architecture, 1921–1980.* Santa Barbara, Calif.: Capra Press and Santa Barbara Museum of Art and Capra Press, 1992.
———. "Obituary." *Architecture* 73 (May 1984): 378.
"House for Allen Breed Walker, Montecito, Ca." *Architectural Forum* 67 (July 1937): 34–35.
McCoy, Esther. "A Walk with Lutah Riggs." *LA Architect* 5 (July 1979): 3.

Meany, Philip J. "Winners of the Small Brick House Competition." *Pacific Coast Architect* 25 (January 1924): 6–17.

Obituary. *Progressive Architecture* 65 (May 1984): 29.

Paine, Jocelyn. "Exhibit Recognizes Women's Largely Obscured Architectural Contributions." *Los Angeles Times,* April 30, 1978, sec. 7, 20, 22–23.

Rochlin, Harriet. "A Distinguished Generation of Women Architects in California." *Journal of the American Institute of Architects* 66 (August 1977): 38–42.

Stow-Fithian, Anne. "The Home of Miss Lutah Riggs, Montecito California." *Home and Field* 40 (September 1930): 22.

Thompson, Betty. "Small Santa Barbara Homes." *California Arts and Architecture* 55 (February 1939): 18–20.

LOCATION OF PAPERS. Correspondence, personal papers, other records, and taped interviews from the 1970s related to Lutah Maria Riggs's life and work are part of the Architectural Drawing Collection, University Art Museum, University of California, Santa Barbara. Other relevant records are located in the University of California Santa Barbara Library, Special Collections; the Library of the History Committee, Montecito Association; and the Library of the Santa Barbara Historical Society. The Schlesinger Library manuscript collection, Radcliffe College, has a biographical file on Riggs.

IIIIIIIIIIIIIIIIIIIIIIIII
Roberts, Isabel (b. 1874)
IIIIIIIIIIIIIIIIIIIIIIIII

The application of Isabel Roberts to the AIA in 1921 caused considerable controversy, primarily because she was not a registered architect in Florida, the state in which she was applying. Although registration was not a requirement for AIA membership, Florida had enacted a state registration law in 1915 requiring registration for "persons claiming the title of architect." One architect who wrote a letter of endorsement for Roberts, John S. Van Bergen, pointed out that Illinois did not use registration as a criterion for institute membership and that he knew many registered architects practicing in that state who would never qualify for the AIA. Roberts's application was also heartily endorsed by H. V. von Holst, an architect for whom she had worked in Chicago. In terms of education and experience, Roberts appeared to fulfill AIA requirements: she had studied for three years at the Ecole des Beaux-Arts (1899–1901) in the atelier of M. Masqueray; from 1902 to 1914 she had worked as a drafter for Frank Lloyd Wright; and she also had spent several years drafting for the Chicago architects H. V. von Holst and William Drummond. Her partner, Ida Annah Ryan (see entry), praised her highly as a designer. Ryan commented that "twelve years of practice and design in the office of Frank Lloyd Wright in every-day contact with his personality and standards have given purity, exactitude and inspiration to a type of work that is pleasing and original."[46]

For her 1921 AIA application, Roberts listed two buildings for which she had assisted Frank Lloyd Wright: "the house built for my mother," currently known as the Isabel Roberts House (1908) in River Forest, Illinois, and the De Rhodes House (1906) in South Bend, Indiana. She also listed "Unity Chapel," which, because it was said to be "now under construction," could not be mistaken for Wright's Unity Temple (1904) in Oak Park or the earlier Unity Chapel (1886) in Hillside, Wisconsin, which belonged to Wright's family.[47]

Several AIA members sent letters expressing outrage at the fact that she might be admitted to the organization without a Florida license. Although it is unclear to what extent Roberts's gender was a factor in the discussion, she did receive one letter of recommendation that would seem to carry more weight than other, negative opinions. On August 6, 1920, Wright sent a letter from his studio, Taliesin, in Spring Green, Wisconsin. It was addressed to "Anyone, Anywhere," and attested that "Miss Isabel Roberts was my assistant in the practice of Architecture for several years and I can recommend her without reservation to anyone requiring the services of an Architect."[48] Some sources imply that Roberts was merely Wright's office manager, but his letter of recommendation suggests she had an integral role in design production.

Despite Wright's endorsement, or perhaps because of it, Roberts was denied admission to the AIA. Wright himself was never a member, a fact he noted with pride.

Ida Ryan and Isabel Roberts became partners about 1920 and worked together for at least a decade. Although Roberts did not share the title "architect" on the firm letterhead, she was an equal in the partnership. The firm contributed many buildings to the city of Orlando, including the Amherst Apartments, Veterans Memorial Library, the Old Unitarian Church, and many residences.

Partial List of Buildings

See Ida Annah Ryan entry.

LOCATION OF PAPERS. The American Institute of Architects Archives has a file on Roberts' unsuccessful AIA application and letters documenting the controversy over her membership. See membership files, Record Group 803, box 382, folder 54, American Institute of Architects Archives, Washington, D.C.

|||||||||||||||||||||||||
Rockfellow, Anne Graham (1866–1954)
|||||||||||||||||||||||||

Anne Graham Rockfellow was born in 1866, the daughter of Julia and Samuel Rockfellow, in Mount Morris, New York. Her father operated a successful mercantile business and cultivated a wide social circle. The family traveled frequently during Rockfellow's early years, visiting the major cities along the East Coast and settling briefly in Edenton, North Carolina. From the age of twelve to fifteen, Rockfellow and her family boarded at various hotels in Mount Morris and Saratoga Springs, New York. Evidently, this lifestyle afforded her many experiences not typical for young ladies of the era. As a high school student, Rockfellow paged through an MIT catalog and decided she wanted to study architecture at the institute. While she was still living at home in Rochester, New York, a local architect, William C. Walker, offered her employment in his firm upon graduation.

When MIT opened its doors to female architecture students in 1884, Anne Rockfellow was ready. She became the first woman student in the architecture department in 1885 by enrolling in the two-year course for "special students," which meant that she took an abbreviated curriculum and did not submit a thesis. Known as "Rocksy" to her classmates at the Tech, Rockfellow received a diploma in architecture in 1887, the first degree granted to a female architectural student at MIT. In an autobiographical account, Rockfellow described herself as surprising to her peers and professors, but except for sensing some mild resentment, she found her experience pleasant and the majority of fellow students encouraging. After graduation, she returned to Rochester, where William Walker kept his promise by employing her as a drafter and designer. Rockfellow worked with the firm for the next six years, until the depression of 1893 brought business to a standstill.

In 1895, Rockfellow decided to try her luck in Tucson, where her brother, John, had settled in 1879 and joined the faculty of the University of Arizona. Through this family connection, Rockfellow secured a position teaching English, history, and geography in the university's preparatory department. Although she found teaching these subjects difficult, she enjoyed tutoring a few students in architecture and drawing. After her two-year contract expired, Rockfellow embarked on a four-month bicycle trip through continental Europe and Great Britain, her personal version of the Grand Tour. Upon her return to the United States in 1898, she established a private practice in her birthplace, Mount Morris. Rockfellow worked on her own and for firms in Detroit and Buffalo until 1909. "The Nutshell," a residential design by Rockfellow, had been featured in the January 1905 issue of *Good House-keeping* magazine, and evidently this publicity resulted in other domestic commissions. Rockfellow spent the next two years with her dying father in Arizona, and after his death in 1911 she opened a private office in Rochester. During this time, she designed a house for her brother in Tucson, where she had already established important business connections.

During one of her family visits to Tucson, a local architect, Henry O. Jaastad, asked Rockfellow to collaborate on a competition entry for a YMCA in Miami, Arizona. The design won the commission, and Jaastad offered Rockfellow a job. Before committing herself, Rockfellow completed a few unfinished projects and visited the Panama-California Exposition in San Diego, an experience that influenced her future architectural designs. In 1916, Rockfellow became a member of Jaastad's office. She would go on to spend twenty-two years with the firm, "taking part in all the work and supervision, but principally the designing."[49] Although she acquired many domestic commissions, Rockfellow preferred commercial work, and her contributions to the architecture of Tucson include the El Conquistador Hotel, the Desert Sanitorium, La Fonda Buena Provecho, and the Safford School. According to one of her grand nieces, Rockfellow considered the El Conquistador Hotel her greatest achievement. The *Tucson Citizen* described the hotel's opening in 1928 as a "blaze of social splendor" and praised the décor, layout, and elegance of its Arizona mission style.[50] Unfortunately, the opulent El Conquistador suffered the effects of the Depression, went bankrupt in 1935, and was razed in 1964.

Rockfellow retired from Jaastad's firm in 1938 and moved to Santa Barbara, California, a coastal city known for its Spanish architecture. When Rockfellow died, on January 17, 1954, the *Santa Barbara News-Press* ran an obituary declaring that "Rocky . . . lived here with the same independent spirit that marked her career and was frequently seen hiking along the water front wearing a skipper's cap." She was remembered as the first woman to receive a degree in architecture at MIT and as "a leader in the ideas embodying the historical and scenic feeling of Arizona architecture."

Partial List of Buildings

This list is based on drawings in the Henry O. Jaastad Collection at the College of Architecture of the University of Arizona in Tucson. For more information about the criteria used to identify Rockfellow's drawings, see Kimberly Ann Oei Kunasek, "Anne Graham Rockfellow: Who Was She? What Was Her Contribution to the History of Architecture?" (M.A. thesis, University of Arizona, 1994). Lisa Bunker, a librarian at the Pima County Public Library, used Kunasek's thesis and research materials at the Arizona Historical Society and the University of Arizona archives to compile a more complete list of Rockfellow's work. Her biographical Web site on the Rockfellow family, and Anne in particular, can be found at http://www.rockfellowfamily.com (accessed October 10, 2007).

1918	Stafford School, 300 Fifth Ave., Tucson, Ariz.
1919	Inspiration Grammar School, Miami, Ariz.
1919–20	Menaul School, Albuquerque, N.M.
ca. 1920	Comstock Hospital, addition, Tucson
1920	Eric Wick House, Tucson
1922–24	Allison-James School, Santa Fe, N.M.
1923	George Martin House, 202 E. Speedway, Tucson
1924	Girls' School, Lutheran Apache Mission, White River, Ariz.
	High School, Superior, Ariz.
	Hospital, Apache Powder Co., Benson, Ariz.
1925	Lone Star District #20, Graham County, Ariz.
1926	W. E. Rudasill House, Tucson
1926–29	Desert Sanitorium (now Tucson Medical Center), Tucson
	Elementary School, Benson
1927	J. C. Wright House, Safford, Ariz.
1928	El Conquistador Hotel, Tucson
	Caroline Marshall House, E. Broadway, Tucson
	E. S. Jackson House, Tucson
1929	Hayward Hoyt, Broadway and Wilmot, Tucson
	Hotel, Safford
1929–35	Mortuary chapel, Reilly Undertaking, 102 W. Pennington, Tucson
1929–36	YWCA building, University and N. Fifth Ave., Tucson
1931	La Fonda Buena Provecho Inn, 1325 E. Speedway, Tucson
1932	R. P. Bass House, Tanque Verde Rd., Tucson
1932	J. Ivancovitch, building facade, Tucson
1935	Inspiration Home, Tucson
n.d.	Arizona Children's Home, Tucson
	Bank building, Safford
	Casa Grande Women's Club, Casa Grande, Ariz.
	Church, Miami, Ariz.
	Elementary School, St. David, Ariz.

First Church of Christ Scientist, 904 N. Stone Ave., Tucson
Houses (four), Lee St., Tucson
Methodist Episcopal Church, Safford
Pinal County Hospital, Florence, Ariz.
V. G. Presson House, 1317 N. Stone, Tucson
William P. Haynes House, Tucson
Warren Grossetta House, 1645 E. Speedway, Tucson
Southern Arizona Bank and Trust Co., Tucson

Writings by Rockfellow

"Architectural Alphabet." *Better Homes and Gardens,* undated clipping in Rockfellow file, Arizona Historical Society, Tucson.
"The Nutshell." *Good Housekeeping,* January 1905, 116–18.

Sources

"Anne Graham Rockfellow." In *American Women, 1935–1940,* edited by Durwood Howes, vol. 2, 768. Detroit: Gale, 1981.
"Anne Graham Rockfellow" (obituary). *Santa Barbara News-Press,* January 18, 1954.
Architect and Engineer 133 (June 1938): 53.
Bever, Marilynn A. "The Women of MIT, 1871–1941: Who They Were, What They Achieved." B.S. thesis, MIT, 1976. See esp. 38.
Kunasek, Kimberly Ann Oei. "Anne Graham Rockfellow: Who Was She? What Was Her Contribution to the History of Architecture?" M.A. thesis, University of Arizona, 1994.
O'Donnell, Kathleen. "Woman Architect Has Local Career of Unusual Interest." *Arizona Daily Star,* February 8, 1933.
"Tucson Architecture Held Region's Finest." *Arizona Daily Star,* November 1949.

LOCATION OF PAPERS. Drawings by Rockfellow are in the Henry O. Jaastad Collection, College of Architecture, University of Arizona. The Arizona Historical Society Archives in Tucson has the Rockfellow Photographs, 1919–1938, a collection of many photographs of buildings designed by Rockfellow. A biography of Rockfellow, part of the Arizona Writers' Project, is at the Arizona State Library in Phoenix.

|||||||||||||||||||||||||
Rogers, Eliza Jacobus Newkirk (1877–1966)
|||||||||||||||||||||||||

Eliza J. Newkirk, a native of Wyncote, Pennsylvania, entered Wellesley College as an art and mathematics major in 1896. Upon her graduation in 1900,

Newkirk taught at a local girls' school for two years. A Wellesley fellowship in architecture allowed her to attend courses at MIT and the Museum of Fine Arts, Boston, from 1902 to 1904 and to spend fifteen months in Italy working on her thesis, "Domes of the Renaissance in Italy." When she returned to the United States, Newkirk taught in the art department at Mount Holyoke for a year. In 1906 she completed her thesis at Wellesley and taught art history and drawing there, receiving her master's degree in 1907 (fig. 50).

While she continued as an instructor at Wellesley, Newkirk pursued professional interests. Over the next ten years, she worked for the firm of Prince and McLanahan in Philadelphia and for Kendall, Taylor, and Stevens in Boston. She was also briefly employed by Lois Lilley Howe, an 1890 MIT graduate, who established a Boston firm in 1907.

Newkirk opened her own Boston architectural firm in 1913 and appears

FIGURE 50. Eliza Newkirk Rogers. Courtesy Wellesley College Archives.

to have found clients immediately. Early projects included residential commissions and a dormitory for the Walnut Hill School in Natick, Massachusetts. She worked as a consultant for Frank Miles Day when he served as supervising architect for Wellesley, which was rebuilding after a severe fire. As her firm prospered over the next decade, Newkirk found time for travel and scholarship. She visited England with a fellow Wellesley instructor, Eleanor Manning (see entry), and wrote about English domestic architecture for *House Beautiful*.

From 1915 to 1916, Newkirk collaborated with Woldemar H. Ritter on a remodeling and addition to the Stowe House at Walnut Hill School. During this time she was also working on a house for Caroline B. Thompson at Leighton Road in Wellesley and remodeling the residence of Mr. and Mrs. C. C. Beebe at 188 Grove Street. During the 1920s, her commissions increased, particularly those at Wellesley College and Walnut Hill; both campuses required remodeling and new buildings. Newkirk also worked with other architects on planning the Walnut Hill School campus.

Newkirk's marriage in 1924 to George B. Rogers, the headmaster of Phillips Exeter Academy in New Hampshire, did not significantly alter her professional life. She split her time between Exeter and Boston, continuing her work at Walnut Hill and her writing on domestic architecture and travel abroad. When her husband died in 1936, Rogers joined family in Philadelphia. She taught at Rosemont College, lectured on architectural topics, and played a major role in establishing the Elfreth's Alley Association, a historic preservation group. Upon her death in 1966, Rogers left behind forty-six buildings and countless students inspired to pursue the study of architecture.

Partial List of Buildings

1913–15	Dormitory, Walnut Hill School, Natick, Mass.
1915–16	Alterations and addition to Stowe House, Walnut Hill School, Natick (with Woldemar H. Ritter)
ca. 1915	Caroline B. Thompson House, Leighton Rd., Wellesley, Mass.
1916	Mr. and Mrs. C. C. Beebe House, remodel, 188 Grove St., Wellesley
1917	Apartment House for Julius Buhlert and Helena Magee, Appleby Rd., Wellesley
1917	Ella Wilson House, Denton Rd., Wellesley
1920–21	Bigelow House, Walnut Hill, Natick (with George F. Marlowe)

1920–21	Highland Hall, addition, Walnut Hill, Natick (with George F. Marlowe)
1921	Stone Hall, remodel, Wellesley College
1921	Agora Society House (Slater International Center), remodel and rebuilding of Alpha Kappa Chi House (Harambee House), Wellesley College
1922	Horton House, faculty club house, Wellesley
1922–23	Hallowell, faculty apartment complex, Wellesley
1923	Homestead, renovations and additions, Wellesley
ca. 1923	Ridgeway, Eliot House, and Dower dormitories, remodel, Wellesley College
ca. 1923–25	Eliot Dormitory, Walnut Hill School, Natick
ca. 1923	The Playhouse, Walnut Hill School, Natick
1929	Curtis House, 60 Dover Rd., Wellesley
1929	28 Dover Rd., house, Wellesley
ca. 1928–30	Gymnasium, Walnut Hill School, Natick
1930	Shepard Faculty Apartments, Wellesley College
1930–31	Wessel House, experimental project, Windsor, Canada

Writings by Newkirk/Rogers

"An Analysis of the Appropriate Forms That Have Been Utilized in House Design for Centuries, Here Especially Considered in Relation to Mass." *House Beautiful,* September 1926.

"French Farm and Manor Houses and Minor Chateaux of the 15th, 16th, and 17th Centuries." *House Beautiful,* December 1926.

"The Georgian Houses." *House Beautiful,* November 1926.

"Individual Expression in the Smaller Houses in England and America." *House Beautiful,* January 1918, 78–81.

"Richelieu, An Example of 17th Century Town Planning in France." *Journal of the American Institute of Architects* 15, no. 1 (January 1927): 22–25.

"Spanish Houses and Villas of the Renaissance." *House Beautiful,* January 1926.

"The Tudor and Elizabethan Cottages and Manor Houses." *House Beautiful,* October 1926.

"War-Time Housing." *House Beautiful,* September 1918, 196.

Sources

Folger, Martha. "Eliza Newkirk Rogers, Architect, 1877–1966." Paper, Wellesley College, 1989.

LOCATION OF PAPERS. Class letters, newspaper clippings, photographs, and employment records documenting the life and work of Eliza J. Newkirk are held in the archives, Wellesley College, Wellesley, Mass.

IIIIIIIIIIIIIIIIIIIIIII
Ryan, Ida Annah (1873–1950)
IIIIIIIIIIIIIIIIIIIIIII

When Ida Annah Ryan applied for AIA membership in 1921, she noted that her collegiate and practical experience included "about eighteen or twenty years of office work, both training and independent practice."[51] The first woman to receive a master's degree from MIT (1906; BA, 1905), Ryan worked throughout her undergraduate and graduate years; won several honors, including a coveted traveling fellowship; and earned the best academic record in her class. As a recent college graduate in 1907, Ryan had applied for AIA membership and was rejected by a margin of nine votes.

In 1909, Ryan established a firm in Waltham, Massachusetts, with a fellow MIT graduate, Florence Luscomb (MIT, 1909). The firm of Ryan and Luscomb, one of the country's earliest partnerships of female architects, continued until the outbreak of World War I. From 1912 to 1913, Ryan was acting superintendent of the Public Buildings Department in Waltham. She resumed her firm with a new partner in 1915 and worked in Nashua, New Hampshire, and Waltham. In 1917, she moved to Orlando, Florida, and established a partnership with Isabel Roberts, the former office manager and drafter to Frank Lloyd Wright. By 1929, the firm of Ryan and Roberts was operating out of studios at Kenilworth Terrace in Orlando, Florida, with Ryan listed as the architect and Roberts as the landscape architect in charge of "architectural development." Ryan resigned her membership in the Florida chapter of the AIA that year, stating that her firm was without "means to function," due to the "paralysis and failure of several financial institutions which hold our funds, together with almost complete stagnation in the architectural field."[52] Evidence suggests that the firm did not survive the Depression.

Partial List of Buildings

1922	Amherst Apartments, 325 W. Colonial Dr., Orlando, Fla.
	Veterans Memorial Library, St. Cloud, Fla.
1923	Tourist Club House, 608 Florida Ave., St. Cloud
1924	Eola Bandshell, Eola Park, Orlando
n.d.	Old Unitarian Church, Rosalind and E. Central, Orlando
	Matilda Fraser House, Lake Formosa, Fla.
	Cottages, Kenilworth Terrace, Orlando
	Old Hollywood Land and Water Company, alterations, 10 N. Orange, Orlando

Sources

Bever, Marilynn A. "The Women of MIT, 1871–1941: Who They Were, What They Achieved." B.S. thesis, MIT, 1976. See esp. 38.

"Ida Annah Ryan." In *American Women, 1935–1940,* edited by Durwood Howes, 784. Detroit: Gale, 1981.

Koenigsberg, Lisa M. "Professionalizing Domesticity: A Tradition of American Women Writers on Architecture, 1848–1913." Ph.D. diss., Yale University, 1987. See esp. 96–97.

McQuaid, Matilda. "Educating for the Future: A Growing Archive on Women and Architecture." In *Architecture: A Place for Women,* edited by Ellen Perry Berkeley, 256–57. Washington, D.C.: Smithsonian Institution Press, 1989.

Smith, Marcia F. "Amherst Worth Saving to Honor an Orlando Pioneer." *Orlando Sentinel,* October 31, 1985, 3.

LOCATION OF PAPERS. The Albert M. Ryan Collection at the Waltham Public Library in Waltham, Mass., contains papers relating to Ida Annah Ryan, daughter of Albert M. Ryan, and other members of the Ryan family. There is also correspondence in the AIA Archives, Washington, D.C., dealing with Ryan's membership in the organization.

|||||||||||||||||||||||||||||
Salomonsky, Verna Cook (1890–1978)
|||||||||||||||||||||||||||||

A native of Spokane, Washington, Verna Cook Salomonsky was the daughter of a newspaper editor and a concert singer. She not only chose the unusual occupation of architect, but traveled across the country and the Atlantic Ocean to gain her education. Salomonsky studied at Columbia University's School of Architecture and at the Ecole Speciale d'Architecture in Paris. From 1913 to 1915, she worked as a junior drafter in the office of William Knighton in Salem, Oregon. She then moved to New York City and found a position as a general drafter and designer in the office of Dwight James Baum. During her three years at Baum's firm, she also completed jobs for Howard Major and Electus D. Litchfield. She married a fellow Columbia graduate, Edgar Salomonsky, and in 1920 the couple opened an office. A plan by the Salomonskys was included in Henry Atterbury Smith's *500 Small Houses of the Twenties* (1923). After Edgar's death in 1929, Salomonsky continued the firm on her own, advertising her specialty as residences in the Georgian, colonial, and English styles.

In 1937, the year Salomonsky became an AIA member, the *New York Times* mentioned her work in an article on women architects. At this point,

Salomonsky was a registered architect in New York, Connecticut, and Pennsylvania, and had designed hundreds of houses in the New York suburbs of Westchester, Berkley, and Scarsdale. She attributed her success to her diligence at finding materials—from floor coverings to fixtures and hardware—appropriate to each residential design. She also described her good relationships with workmen and gave an example of an "Old-World custom" that she practiced to celebrate the completion of each new home. The roof tree was hoisted up and nailed to the ridge pole of a house under construction, and the workmen were invited inside as guests of the owner. They lit a bonfire of leftover timber and gathered around with pretzels and beer. Salomonsky's residential commissions ranged from a $100,000 twenty-room house to a child's lakeshore playhouse. At this time, she was the only female member of the Architectural League of New York.[53] Salomonsky served as an architectural critic at the School of Design for Women in Philadelphia for one year and at the New York School of Interior Decoration for three years.

Salomonsky's success as a residential architect led to her selection as the designer of *House and Garden* magazine's first "Ideal House" in 1936. Three years later, her "Garden Home, #13" was exhibited as a model home in the "Town of Tomorrow" at the World's Fair in New York. Her design was intended for middle-class suburban residents such as Dwight and Kate Wade, who visited the fair on their honeymoon. The couple selected Salomonsky's home from about twenty choices and sent for architectural plans that were used by the builder Fred McMahan to construct the house. The design was not only economical but featured aspects of modernist style, such as an emphasis on natural light and spaciousness. According to the Tennessee Historical Society, the Wade House is the only Town of Tomorrow replica home known to exist.[54]

After her marriage to Warren Butler Shipway, an architectural engineer, Salomonsky moved to California in 1947. The Shipways traveled to Mexico on a vacation that led to a new collaborative experience for the designers. Together, the couple published five books on Mexican architecture and design. Salomonsky herself wrote many articles that appeared in *House and Garden, House Beautiful,* and other popular magazines under her married name. Verna Salomonsky Shipway died in La Jolla, California, in 1978.

Partial List of Buildings

1929	George M. Waugh Jr. House, Scarsdale, N.Y.
	Margaret Owen Hiss House, Bedford-Four-Corners, N.Y.
1933	C. Ernest Greenwood House, Scarsdale

1935	Philip M. Davis House, Greenwich, Conn.
1936	House and Garden Ideal House, Scarsdale
1939	New York World's Fair, model home (demolished)
1940	Dwight and Kate Wade House, Sevierville, Tenn.
n.d.	Algernon Brown House, Scarsdale
	M. F. Griffin House, Scarsdale
	C. G. Novotny House, Scarsdale
	Alexander Crane House, Scarsdale

Writings by Salomonsky (as Verna Shipway)

Decorative Design in Mexican Homes (1966, with Warren Shipway). Reprint. New York: Architectural Book Publishing Co., 1991.

Houses of Mexico: Origins and Traditions (1970, with Warren Shipway). Reprint. New York: Architectural Book Publishing Co., 1991.

Masterpieces of Furniture Design. Grand Rapids, Mich.: Periodical Publishing Company, 1931; reprint, New York: Dover, 1953.

Mexican Homes of Today (1964). Reprint. New York: Architectural Book Publishing Co., 1990.

Mexican House, Old and New (1960, with Warren Shipway). Reprints. New York: Architectural Book Publishing Co., 1965; Santa Monica, Calif.: Hennessey and Ingalls, 2007.

Mexican Interiors (1962, with Warren Shipway). Reprints. New York: Architectural Book Publishing Co., 1991; Santa Monica, Calif.: Hennessey and Ingalls, 2007.

"Woman Architect Gives Views." *Southwest Builder and Contractor* 88 (August 14, 1936): 19.

Sources

"Ernest Greenwood House at Scarsdale, New York." *House and Garden,* September 1936, 137.

"Formal Georgian House." *Pencil Points* 16 (February 1935): 75.

Petersen, Anne. "Women Architects Few but Versatile." *New York Times,* April 11, 1937, 92.

LOCATION OF PAPERS. The Verna Cook Shipway Papers, 1904–79, are in the Mandeville Special Collections Library at the University of California San Diego, La Jolla, California. The papers include correspondence, travel diaries, sketches, plans and photographs of her homes, newspaper and magazine clippings, and manuscripts. The Library of Congress Prints and Photography Division, Washington, D.C., has a drawing of a residence at 424 Madison Ave., New York, by Shipway.

|||||||||||||||||||||||
Sawyer, Gertrude (1895–1996)
|||||||||||||||||||||||

Born in Tuscola, Illinois, in 1895, Gertrude Sawyer attended secondary school in Indianapolis. Like many early women architects, Sawyer pieced together her higher education at several institutions. In 1918, she graduated with a B.S. in landscape architecture from the University of Illinois at Urbana-Champaign. Sawyer then moved to Cambridge, Massachusetts, and spent the next year as a special student in town planning with Professor Pray, during the early years before the more formal organization of the Cambridge School. She was one of eleven women (six of them, architects) to receive a certificate from the Cambridge School and may have stayed on as a student until 1922. One of Sawyer's fellow graduates was Eleanor Raymond, with whom she maintained a friendship throughout her career. In 1930, Sawyer reported to the Cambridge School alumnae bulletin that she was an associate of the architect Horace W. Peaslee in Washington, D.C., and had recently given a summer lecture course in the history of architecture at Vassar College in Poughkeepsie, New York.

Sawyer described her practice as primarily residential, "with particular emphasis on country estates."[55] One of her first commissions, Washington's Junior League building, was the only Art Deco building on Dupont Circle and stands in sharp contrast to the Point Farm compound she began designing at the same time. In the early 1930s, Jefferson Patterson, a foreign service diplomat and heir to the National Cash Register Company, hired Sawyer to design Point Farm at Peterson's Point, Maryland, above the Patuxent River. Sawyer designed and oversaw the construction of twenty-six buildings on the property, most of which is now Jefferson Patterson State Park. The buildings ranged from an elegant family residence and guest houses to a show barn for Black Angus cattle and similar structures that demanded technical expertise. Sawyer officially established her own firm in 1934, after receiving her master's from Smith College (which had since absorbed the Cambridge School). Sawyer became an AIA member in 1939 and was a registered architect in the District of Columbia, Ohio, Florida, Maryland, and Pennsylvania.

During World War II, Sawyer worked in the engineering department of Fairchild Aircraft Corporation and was one of two female officers in the navy's Engineer Corps Reserves, achieving the rank of lieutenant commander. She supervised the building of four thousand temporary homes for military families in Washington, D.C. In 1957, Sawyer was the only woman officer in the Seabees Reserve Corps and maintained an architectural office on Wisconsin Avenue in Washington, D.C. She retired from practice in 1969.

Like most successful women architects, Sawyer refused to complain about any poor treatment due to her gender. In her essay "Educating for the Future," Matilda McQuaid described an interview in which Sawyer mentioned "that several women's organizations had contacted her, knowing her to be one of the pioneer women architects. But when she told them, 'I was always treated fairly, and throughout my career had a very good time building and designing,' they never called back."[56]

Partial List of Buildings

1931–33   Junior League Building (now Kossuth House, Hungarian Reformed Federation), Dupont Circle, Washington, D.C.

1932–55   Point Farm, Mr. and Mrs. Jefferson Patterson House, St. Leonard, Md. (National Register of Historic Places)

pre-1948   Mr. and Mrs. Nathan Scott II House (now the official residence for the president of American University), Washington, D.C.

1950   Tudor Hall remodel, Tudor Place and Breton Bay Road, Leonardtown, Md.

Sources

Alumnae News Journal (The Cambridge School), vol. 3 (1930). Sophia Smith Collection, Smith College Archives.

McQuaid, Matilda. "Educating for the Future: A Growing Archive on Women and Architecture." In *Architecture: A Place for Women,* edited by Ellen Perry Berkeley and Matilda McQuaid, 249. Washington: Smithsonian Institution Press, 1989.

"A Thousand Women in Architecture." *Architectural Record* 103, part 2 (April-June): 1948.

"University of Illinois Semi-Centennial Alumni Record." June 4, 1918. University of Illinois, Archives.

LOCATION OF PAPERS. The University of Illinois at Urbana-Champaign has a file on Sawyer with clippings and alumni record forms. A photograph of an unidentified Sawyer house is in the Prints and Photographs Division, Library of Congress. The Architectural Records Collection, American Architectural Foundation, Washington, D.C., has some drawings by Sawyer.

IIIIIIIIIIIIIIIIIIIIIIIIIII
Schenck, Anna Pendleton (d. 1915)
IIIIIIIIIIIIIIIIIIIIIIIIIII

Anna Pendleton Schenck studied architecture in Paris under a Monsieur Aubertin. She is remembered as the partner of Marcia Mead (see entry) in what has erroneously been called the first firm of women architects. Although Gannon and Hands preceded Schenck and Mead by eighteen years (the former established an office in 1896), the latter partnership gave every promise of being a more enduring firm. Unfortunately, Schenck's sudden death in 1915 ended the partnership. At the time of her death, the office had accepted commissions for country houses in New York and New Jersey, a neighborhood center for children, and the Ellen Wilson Memorial Homes in Washington, D.C. (fig. 51). Marcia Mead went on to have a prosperous career.

Sources

"The Bridgeport Housing Development." *American Architect* 113 (February 6, 1918): 129–48.

"More Women Architects." *Architect and Engineer* 36 (April 1914): 116.

Paine, Judith. "Some Professional Roles." In *Women in American Architecture,* edited by Susan Toore, 68. New York: Whitney Library of Design, 1977.

Prather-Moses, Alice I., comp. *The International Dictionary of Women Workers in the Decorative Arts.* Metuchen, N.J.: Scarecrow Press, 1981. See esp. 146.

Withey, Henry F., and Elsie R. Withey. *Biographical Dictionary of American Architects.* Los Angeles: Hennessey and Ingalls, 1970. See esp. 538–39.

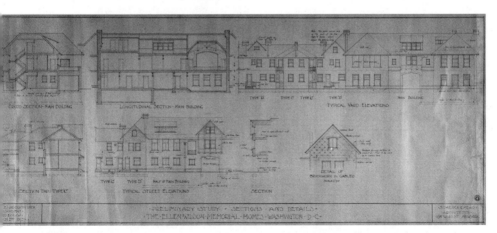

FIGURE 51. Ellen Wilson Memorial Homes, Washington, D.C., 1915, designed by Anna Schenck and Marcia Mead. The designs for these apartments were accepted by the United States Housing Corporation but not executed until after World War I. Courtesy Library of Congress, Prints and Photographs Division.

||||||||||||||||||||||||
Spencer, Margaret Fulton (1882–1966)
||||||||||||||||||||||||

Born in Philadelphia in 1882, Margaret Fulton Spencer was the niece of two painters, Thomas Alexander Harrison (1853–1930), celebrated for his marine nocturnes, and Birge Harrison (1854–1929), known as "the painter of snows." Although a capable artist herself, Spencer was determined to use her artistic talents as an architect. She spent two years at Bryn Mawr College before transferring to MIT. After graduating in 1911, she studied interior decoration and landscape architecture at the New York School of Applied Design for Women. In 1912, she was employed by the successful Philadelphia architect Frank Miles Day (1861–1918). The firm was known as Day Brothers and Klauder until 1912, when the retirement of Day's brother, H. Kent Day, altered staff arrangements.

Today, Spencer is most often remembered as a painter who was part of an artists' colony in New Hope, Pennsylvania, and the wife of the American impressionist painter Robert Spencer (1879–1931). According to one account, Margaret Spencer took up painting because her husband did not encourage her architectural career. Robert Spencer suffered from severe depression and committed suicide in 1931.

After Robert's death, Margaret Spencer worked for an American architectural firm in Paris and exhibited some of her work at the Salon. In 1935, she applied to the American Institute of Architects, noting that she had been in practice for twenty years. She was a registered architect in Pennsylvania and New Jersey. Her AIA membership application included the plans and photographs of two unidentified completed buildings. During the 1930s, Fulton became known as a specialist in the restoration of vernacular fieldstone farmhouses; one example of this work is the Chimney Hill Bed and Breakfast in Lambertville, New Jersey.

Spencer was elected to AIA membership in 1936. The next year, she notified the AIA that she had moved to Arizona and was a registered architect practicing in Tucson. Sometime in the late 1930s, Spencer bought a two-hundred-acre ranch in the Arizona desert and designed sixteen cottages for the property. Las Lomas Estates featured native colored stones in the floors and walls and attracted wealthy vacationers during the 1940s and 50s. After Spencer's death in 1966, her desert retreat was severely damaged by fire.

Partial List of Buildings

1930s   Chimney Hill Bed and Breakfast, 207 Goat Hill Rd.,
               Lamberville, N.J.

n.d.   Isaac Clothier House, alterations and additions, Gwynedd
               Valley, Montgomery County, Pa.

Sources

AIA membership files, Record Group 803, box 427, folder 77. Archives, American Institute
of Architects, Washington, D.C.

LOCATION OF PAPERS. The MIT Museum and Special Collections has alumni records documenting Spencer's attendance. Short biographies of Spencer are located on the Web sites
of Philadelphia Architects and Buildings, http://www.philadelphiabuildings.org/pab/
app/ar_display.cfm/77090 (accessed September 25, 2007), and the James A. Michener
Art Museum, http://www.michenermuseum.org/bucksartists/artist.php?artist=87 (accessed September 25, 2007).

||||||||||||||||||||||||||
Steinmesch, Harriet Mae (1893–1979)
||||||||||||||||||||||||||

H. Mae Steinmesch is remembered as one of the founders and the inaugural
president of the Association for Women in Architecture (AWA), the first
professional organization for women architects. In 1915, Steinmesch and three
of her classmates at the School of Architecture at Washington University in
St. Louis founded a sorority, La Confrerie Alongiv (the latter word, Vignola
spelled backwards). Steinmesch graduated from Washington University with
a bachelor's degree in architecture in 1916, but she remained dedicated to
creating a full-fledged sorority. By 1922, the group had established Alpha
Alpha Gamma, with chapters at the University of Texas, the University of
Minnesota, and the University of California at Berkeley. In 1934, the Association for Women in Architecture was founded by alumnae of the student
groups. By this time there were additional student chapters at the University
of Illinois, the University of Michigan, and Cornell University, and alumnae
groups in Minneapolis/St. Paul, California, and St. Louis. As first president
of the AWA, Mae Steinmesch realized the importance of keeping historical
records documenting her organization, and her determination led to the collection of archival records now held by the International Archive of Women in
Architecture. Today, the only active chapter of the AWA is in Los Angeles.

During World War II, Steinmesch worked for the U.S. Army Corps of Engineers at Scott Field, Belleville, Illinois, and for the navy in St. Louis. At an unknown date, she moved to the Bay Area and became associate building director for the western division of USO Building Services and a planner for the San Francisco Redevelopment Agency. She drew the layout for a city college campus in California (fig. 52), and while living in the Bay Area she

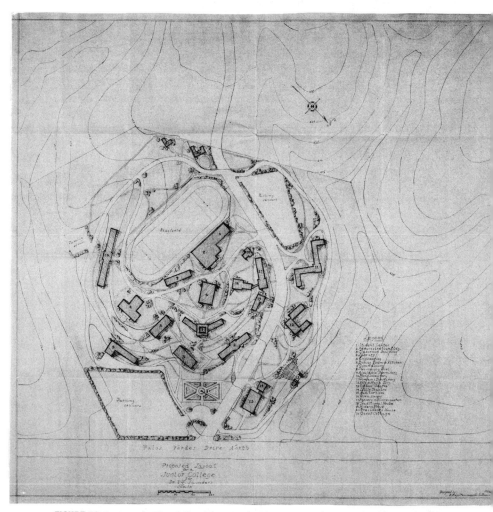

FIGURE 52. Layout of a City College. Drawing by Mae Steinmesch, 1946. Courtesy International Archive of Women in Architecture.

also assisted the architect Henry Higby Gutterson (1884–1954), an important practitioner of the Arts and Crafts style. The details of Steinmesch's private architectural practice are unknown.

Partial List of Buildings

n.d.   Model of City of St. Louis, showing past and future city
            planning projects
1946   Proposed Layout for a Junior College in California

Sources

A short biography and information on Steinmesch's work as a founder of the Association for Women in Architecture can be found at the Web sites of the IAWA, http://spec.lib.vt.edu/IAWA/news/news7.html (accessed September 25, 2007), and the Association for Women in Architecture, http://www.awa-la.org/History.htm (accessed September 25, 2007).

LOCATION OF PAPERS. The International Archive of Women in Architecture holds the Association for Women in Architecture Papers, 1928–92, which include files on Steinmesch, as well as two images, a portrait and a drawing of a proposed junior college. The IAWA is part of the University Libraries, Virginia Polytechnic Institute and State University.

|||||||||||||||||||||||||
Waterman, Hazel Wood (1865–1948)
|||||||||||||||||||||||||

As an aspiring art student at Berkeley in the early 1880s, Hazel Wood Waterman probably never imagined pursuing a career in architecture. Her first exposure to design may have occurred in 1901, when she and her husband hired the well-known modern architect Irving Gill to work on their home. According to legend, Gill praised Waterman for her architectural eye. Following the death of her husband in 1903, Waterman took a correspondence course in drafting and found employment with the firm of Hebbard and Gill.

After a few years working in Gill's office, Waterman decided to open her own business. Her first commission was a series of three houses for Alice Lee, a friend, and involved some supervision by Gill, who was working at a site across the street. Just three years later, Waterman received a high-profile project: restoration of the famous Estudillo House in Old Town, San Diego (fig. 53). John D. Spreckles commissioned the project, which had gained notoriety from its description as Ramona's marriage place in Helen Jackson's bestselling novel *Ramona* (1884). In restoring the adobe, Waterman consulted archival manuscripts, photographs, and other artifacts to determine specifications for adobe bricks and the orientation of rooms and gardens. When the historic structure was recorded by the Historic American Buildings Survey in 1937, Waterman's role as architect of "the design and construction" of the restoration was included in a short history of the property.

After her reputation as a domestic architect was established, Waterman received a commission for the Wednesday Club of San Diego, a women's civic group of which she had been a member for over twenty years. She hired Lilian Rice (see entry), a recent Berkeley graduate, to work on the drawings. From 1912 to 1925, Waterman worked on the Administration Building for the Children's Home in Balboa Park, San Diego. Waterman's design for a garden commissioned by Julius Wangenheim received a certificate of honor from the San Diego chapter of the AIA.

In her busy office, Waterman employed Frank Hope Sr. and Sam Hamill, FAIA, among other drafters. Waterman's daughter, Helen G. Waterman, a 1914 Berkeley graduate, collaborated with her mother on several commissions.

FIGURE 53. John Antonio Estudillo House, "Ramona's Marriage Place," Old Town, San Diego. Renovation by Hazel Waterman, 1909. Photo by Henry F. Withey, 1937. Courtesy Library of Congress, Prints and Photographs Division, HABS.

Partial List of Buildings

1905	Alice Lee houses, San Diego, Calif. (for Hebbard and Gill)
1906	Alice Pratt House, n.p.
1907	William Clayton House, 6th and Laurel, San Diego
	Mrs. George Barney, cottage developed from a barn, n.p.
1908–9	Mrs. Smith and Miss Friese House, n.p.
1909	Estudillo House ("Ramona's Marriage Place") restoration, Old Town San Diego
1910–11	Wednesday Club, 6th and Ivy Lane, San Diego
1912	Home for Babies, Children's Home Association of San Diego, Balboa Park (demolished)
1912?	Captain and Mrs. Albert A. Ackerman residence, 3170 Curlew Street, San Diego
1914–15	Mrs. Churcher House, La Jolla, Calif.
1917–20	Julius Wangenheim, city garden, San Diego
1920	Leisenring House, n.p.
1923	Lucy Newkirk, shop building, n.p.
1924–25	Children's Home, Administration Building, Balboa Park, San Diego
1928–29	Judge Walton J. Wood House, n.p.
1929?	Waldo Dean Waterman, cottage, n.p.

Writings by Waterman

"A City Garden in Southern California—Possessing the Charm of Adaptability to the Out-of-Door Habits of Life." *House and Garden,* August 1920, 54–55, 82.

"A Granite Cottage in California." *House Beautiful,* March 1902, 244–53.

"The Influence of an Olden Time." *House Beautiful,* June 1903, 3–9.

"On My Friend's Porch." *House Beautiful,* September 1902.

Sources

Birnbaum, Charles A., and Lisa E. Crowder, eds. *Pioneers of Landscape Design: An Annotated Bibliography.* Washington, D.C.: U.S. Department of the Interior, 1993. See esp. 23–24.

Kessler, D. E. "The Restoration of Ramona's Marriage Place," *Pacific Monthly* (Portland, Ore.), June 1910, 585–88.

Paine, Judith. "Pioneer Women Architects." In *Women in American Architecture,* edited by Susana Torre, 64, photo. New York: Whitney Library of Design, 1977.

Rochlin, Harriet. "Distinguished Generation of Women Architects in California." *AIA Journal* 66 (August 1977): 39–40.

Thornton, Sally Bullard. *Daring to Dream: The Life of Hazel Wood Waterman.* San Diego, Calif.: San Diego Historical Society, 1987.

Walsh, Victor A. "Una Casa del Pueblo—A Town House of Old San Diego." *Journal of San Diego History* 50, nos. 1–2 (Winter–Spring 2004): 1–16.

LOCATION OF PAPERS. Waterman's notebooks, working drawings, and papers are in the Hazel Waterman Papers, San Diego Historical Society Research Archives, San Diego, California. Old Town State Historic Park, District Headquarters, San Diego, also has some records.

||||||||||||||||||||||||
Whitman, Bertha Louise Yerex (b. 1892)
||||||||||||||||||||||||

Bertha Yerex Whitman is remembered as the first woman to graduate with a B.S. in architecture from the University of Michigan (1920), but her college education began at Eastern Michigan University, where she received a teaching certificate in 1911. Whitman taught in her native town of Newago, Michigan, for three years before deciding to change careers. She enrolled in a correspondence course in mechanical drafting and in 1914 became a student in the architecture program at the University of Michigan. When many of her classmates left for World War I, Whitman found her own way to participate in the war effort by becoming the first female drafter for the Dodge Company in Detroit. She and her class graduated in 1920.

After graduation, Whitman moved to Chicago in the hope of finding better opportunities, and she joined the office of Perkins, Fellows, and Hamilton. Whitman married in 1921 but remained at the firm until the birth of her first child in 1924. She earned her license to practice architecture in Illinois in the fall of 1926, when pregnant with her second child. The Great Depression altered Whitman's life permanently when her husband's business collapsed and he deserted the family sometime after 1929. Left to support her two young children, Whitman went to work as a social worker for the City of Chicago. After about three years, she became a state employee responsible for designing all types of office buildings. Although Whitman's architectural practice had been compromised, she was able to maintain a limited residential practice, designing more than fifty houses between 1928 and 1967. Throughout these years, she recalled working for a Mr. Jansson on churches, a Mr. Reed on homes, and Perkins, Fellows, and Hamilton on schools, while maintaining her private office. Projects attributed to Whitman include the H. W. Dring House, the R. W. Pervier House, and the Fred Johnson House (1929), but very little is known about them. Recognition for Whitman's work included a "Better Homes Award" presented by the contractors association for the B. G. Lawrence residence (1930) in Chicago.

A world traveler, Whitman studied architecture in Europe, Egypt, Tokyo, and Africa and received many "Neptune certificates" for crossing the equator and the Arctic Circle. After circling the world in 1965–66 she wrote *A Tyro Takes a Trip.*

Partial List of Buildings

1930	John Strom House, Evanston, Ill.
	B. G. Lawrence House, 2710 Payne St., Evanston
1931	Raymond L. Scheid House, Glencoe, Ill.
	Otto Schultz House, Evanston

LOCATION OF PAPERS. The Bertha Yerex Whitman Papers are part of the Bentley Historical Library at the University of Michigan. The collection includes a series of interior and exterior photographs of buildings by Whitman.

||||||||||||||||||||||||||||
Wilburn, Leila Ross (1885–1967)
||||||||||||||||||||||||||||

The second woman to receive a license to practice architecture in Georgia (after Henrietta Dozier), Leila Ross Wilburn was a prolific residential designer with an unusual talent for promoting her work. She was born in Macon, Georgia, the eldest of five children, and moved with her family to Atlanta in the mid-1890s. After two years at the Agnes Scott Institute, she gained an apprenticeship as a drafter in the office of Benjamin R. Padgett, before establishing her own Atlanta office in 1909. Wilburn's practice was residential, but at a large scale, including apartments and designs for extensive housing developments. Wilburn advertised a variety of home styles in the seven plan books she wrote, including *Southern Homes and Bungalows* (1914), *Brick and Colonial Homes,* and *Ideal Homes of Today.* Before 1920 she had designed at least eighty residences, twenty apartment buildings, and twenty-four duplexes. Wilburn offered her services to the middle class at the right moment, when the Atlanta suburbs of Inman Park, Ansley Park, Midtown, Boulevard, and Druid Hills were expanding and when the demand for office workers created a need for inexpensive apartments. By working for real estate developers, such as Ansley, Goldsmith, Reid, and McCall and Rausenberg, Wilburn capitalized on the area's dramatic growth, providing what is now considered Atlanta's vernacular architecture. During World War II, Wilburn worked for three years as an engineering drafter in Tampa and Washington, D.C. After the war, Wilburn responded to the vicissitudes of public taste with her version of a new style, the ranch home.

Like other early women architects, Wilburn did not encourage others of her gender to work in the profession. She told a reporter for the *Atlanta Journal* that women in the office annoyed her because they sat around waiting to be told what to do, while men got right down to business. At the same time, she believed that women had an innate talent for designing domestic architecture, and she used this popular notion in her promotional literature. During her fifty-five-year career, Wilburn was extraordinarily successful in spreading her personal residential style, designing more than three hundred structures and creating a series of model plans for others to copy.

Partial List of Buildings

ca. 1907	YMCA gym building, Georgia Military Academy (now Woodward Academy), College Park, Ga. (National Register)
1912	Gordon Street Baptist Church, Atlanta, Ga.
1913	The Rosslyn, apartments, 344 Ponce de Leon, Atlanta
1914	The Piedmont Park Apartments, 266 11th St., Atlanta
1918	The Regal Apartments, 640 Boulevard, Atlanta
1920	North Apartments, 60 Parkway Dr., Atlanta
1925–27	William B. King House, 604 Elm St., Conway, S.C.
1927	House, 4652 Collins Ave., Acworth, Ga. (National Register)
1928	Webb-Adams House, 223 Jennings Ave., Greenwood, S.C. 125 Greenwood Pl., Decatur, Ga.

Writings by Wilburn

Brick and Colonial Homes: A Collection of the Latest Designs, Featuring the Most Modern in Domestic Architecture. Atlanta, Ga.: n.p., 1920.

Ideal Homes of Today (n.p.: n.d.).

New Homes of Quality (n.p.: n.d).

Ranch and Colonial Homes (n.p.: n.d.).

Sixty Good New Homes (n.p.: n.d).

Small Low-Cost Homes (n.p.: n.d.).

Southern Homes and Bungalows: A Collection of Choice Designs. Atlanta, Ga.: By the author, 1914.

Sources

"Atlanta Women Have Man-Size Jobs." *Atlanta Journal,* August 24, 1924, 7.

Jennings, Jan. "Leila Ross Wilburn: Plan-Book Architect." *Woman's Art Journal* 10 (Spring/ Summer 1989): 10–16.

"Leila Ross Wilburn (1885–1967)." New Georgia Encyclopedia, http://www .georgiaencyclopedia.org (accessed September 24, 2005).

Smith, Susan Hunter. "Women Architects in Atlanta, 1895–1979." *Atlanta History Journal* 23, no. 4 (Winter 1979–80): 85–108.

Wells, John E., and Robert E. Dalton. *The South Carolina Architects, 1885–1935.* Richmond, Va.: New South Architectural Press, 1992. See esp. 205–6.

LOCATION OF PAPERS. The Leila Ross Wilburn Collection is held by the Atlanta History Center. It includes 338 sets of architectural drawings, photographs, and slides. Information on Wilburn projects is in the survey files of the South Carolina Department of Archives and History, Columbia.

IIIIIIIIIIIIIIIIIIIIIIIIIIIII
Williams, Emily (1869–1942)
IIIIIIIIIIIIIIIIIIIIIIIIIIIII

When a Craftsman-style house in San Jose, California, associated with a prominent politician was nominated for the National Register of Historic Places, local historians uncovered an unknown female architect named Emily Williams. A native of San Jose, Williams began her professional life as a teacher. After graduating from San Jose State Normal School, she taught in local schools for several years. At some point in her twenties, Williams decided to pursue her interest in architecture and took drafting courses at James Lick School of Arts and Crafts in San Francisco.

With the help of her lifetime partner, Lillian McNeill Palmer, Williams was able to launch her own architectural office. Little is known of Williams's career, which seems to have been centered around residential commissions, but her work was identified in 2003 in the Naglee Park neighborhood of San Jose. The Arthur Monroe Free House, designed in 1905, is a Craftsman-style house that was assumed to have been designed by Julia Morgan, but it was in fact the work of Williams. The two-story brown shingle home was built for Palmer, a renowned Arts and Crafts metalworker. The couple appear to have moved by 1910, when Palmer opened the Palmer Copper Shop in San Francisco. Later in life, Williams and Palmer moved to Los Gatos and founded the National Federation of Business and Professional Women's Clubs.

Partial List of Buildings

1905   Arthur Monroe Free House (former Palmer House), 66
            South 14th St., San Jose (National Register)
n.d.   Walter McIntire House, 117 South 17th St., San Jose
            Reverend George Foote House, 475 Spencer Ave., San Jose
            Gertrude Austin House, 2728–30 Union St., San Francisco
            Emily Williams House, 1037–39 Broadway, San Francisco

Sources

Douglas, Jack. "Emily Williams, Architect and Feminist." *Advisor,* June 2003, 8; http://
    gems.es-designs.com/newsite/AdvisorSpr2003.pdf (accessed September 25, 2007).
———. "Lillian McNeill Palmer: Naglee Park Artisan." *Advisor,* Spring 2001, 4.
Horton, Inge S. "Emily Williams, San Jose's First Woman Architect." *Continuity* 17, no. 4
    (Winter 2006):15–16; http://preservation.org/newsletters/winter2006.pdf (accessed
    September 25, 2007).

|||||||||||||||||||||||||||
Young, Helen Binkerd (1877–1959)
|||||||||||||||||||||||||||

In 1900, Helen Binkerd Young graduated from Cornell University's architecture program and began to look for work in the field. Although Young
appears to have been financially self-sufficient, she was unable to establish
herself in the architectural profession immediately, and in 1910 she returned
to Cornell to teach in the Department of Home Economics. Young had hoped
to become a design instructor, but she found much of her knowledge of architecture applicable to the field of "household arts," which included residential
planning and interior design. Young's papers from 1911 to 1919 include plans
signed "Helen Binkerd Young, arch't" for a remodeled farmhouse, a pantry-
less kitchen for a servantless house, and other designs focused on easing the
housekeeper's burdens. In 1921, Young left Cornell and was able to work as
an architect. According to alumni records she designed homes at Cornell
and in Cayuga Heights, near Ithaca, New York, throughout the 1920s. Plans
and photographs of her residence, "Hidden Home," were published in the
American Architect in 1927.

Partial List of Buildings

1921   "Hidden Home," Ithaca, N.Y.

Writings by Young

"The Arrangement of Household Furnishings." Farmhouse Series. *Cornell Bulletin for Homemakers,* part 3, vol. 4, no. 15 (April 1, 1915): 141–50.

"Economics of a Sound House." Thrift Series. *Cornell Bulletin for Homemakers,* part 4, no. 131 (July 1919): 1–6.

"Household Decoration." *Cornell Bulletin for Homemakers,* part 3, vol. 1, no. 5 (December 1911): 43–63.

"Household Furnishing." *Cornell Bulletin for Homemakers,* part 3, vol. 1, no. 7 (January 1912): 65–84.

"Planning the Home Kitchen." Cornell Bulletin for Homemakers, part 4, no. 108 (July 1916): 3–19.

"The Relation of House Planning to Home Economics. *Journal of Home Economics* 6, no. 3 (June 1914): 229–33.

Sources

Information on Young can be found at the Web site for Cornell University Library, Division of Rare and Manuscripts Collections, under "home economics," http://rmc.library. cornell.edu/homeEc/bios/helenbinkerdyoung.html (accessed September 25, 2007).

APPENDIX 1
Female Graduates of Architecture Schools, 1878–1934

Although this chronological list of university graduates was assembled from a variety of sources, including alumni records, online thesis records, and biographies, it remains incomplete. A thorough search for early women architectural graduates would require primary research at each potential institution. The list is presented here to illustrate that numerous women who graduated from architecture programs either did not go on to practice or remain unknown as architects. The list does not include individuals who obtained certificates from the Ecole des Beaux-Arts, graduated from the Cambridge School, or undertook academic training that did not result in a degree.

NAME	SCHOOL	DEGREE	DATE
Margaret Hicks	Cornell	A.B., B. Arch.	1878, 1880
Mary Louisa Page	Illinois	B.S. in Arch.	1879
Marian Sara Parker	Michigan	B.S. in Civil Eng.	1885
Anne Graham Rockfellow	MIT		1887
Mary Wardwell	Cornell		1888
Sophia Hayden	MIT	B.S. in Arch.	1890
Lois Lilley Howe	MIT		1890
Marion Mahony	MIT	B.S. in Arch.	1894
Julia Morgan	UC–Berkeley		1894
Mabel Warren Sawyer	MIT	B.S. in Arch.	1894
Ethel Bartholomew	MIT	B.S. in Arch.	1895
Helen Chamberlin	MIT	B.S. in Arch.	1896
Marion L. Lewis	MIT	B.S. in Arch.	1896
Lucy D. Thomson	MIT	B.S. in Arch.	1896
Frances E. Henley	RISD[1]		1897
Mel Dora Ice (Stritesky)	Illinois	B.S. in Arch.	1897
Eva H. Crane	MIT	B.S. in Arch.	1898
Henrietta C. Dozier	MIT	B.S. in Arch.	1899
Ethel F. Fifield	MIT	B.S. in Arch.	1900
Helen Binkerd Young	Cornell		1900

NAME	SCHOOL	DEGREE	DATE
Greta Gray	MIT	B.S. in Arch.	1901
Edna D. Stoddard	MIT	B.S. in Arch.	1903
Eliza Codd	MIT	B.S. in Arch.	1904
Eliza Newkirk	MIT		1904
Linda S. Fraser	MIT	B.S. in Arch.	1904
Ethel Ricker	Illinois	B.S. in Arch.	1904
Alice Hartzel Clark (Myers)	Illinois	B.S. in Arch.	1905
Nora Barney	Cornell		1905
Edith Leonard	Illinois	B.S. in Arch.	1906, M.S. 1910
Ida Annah Ryan	MIT	B.S. in Arch.	1905, M.S. 1906
Eleanor Manning (O'Connor)	MIT	B.S. in Arch.	1906
Helen Jane Van Meter (Alyea)	Illinois	B.S. in Arch.	1906
Helen McClellan-Wilson (Atwater)	Drexel[2]		1906
Emily Helen Butterfield	Syracuse	B. of Arch.	1907
Maude Frances Darling (Parlin)	MIT	B.S. in Arch.	1907
Helen Augusta Lukens	Drexel		1908
Helen McGraw Longyear	MIT	B.S. in Arch.	1909
Florence Luscomb	MIT	B.S. in Arch.	1909
Arselia Bessie Martin (Swisher)	Illinois	B.S. in Arch.	1909, M.S. 1910
Lahvesia Paxton Packwood	MIT	B.S. in Arch.	1909
Rebecca H. Thompson	MIT	B.S. in Arch.	1909
Lilian Rice	UC–Berkeley		1910
Anna Wagner Keichline	Cornell		1911
Margaret Alexina Fulton Spencer	MIT	B.S. in Arch.	1911
Charlotte V. Simonds	MIT	B.S. in Arch.	1913
Marcia Mead	Columbia		1914
Helen G. Waterman	UC–Berkeley		1914
Elizabeth G. Pattee	MIT	B.S. in Arch.	1916
Charlotte Lewis Phelps	MIT	B.S. in Arch.	1916
Marion Manley	Illinois	B.S. in Arch.	1917
Elisabeth Coit	MIT	B.S. in Arch.	1919
Lutah Maria Riggs	UC–Berkeley		1919
Bertha Yerex Whitman	Michigan	B.S. in Arch.	1920
Helene Kuykendall Deadman	Oregon	B.A. in Arch.	1922
Phebe Elisabeth Gage Hayslip	Oregon	B.A. in Arch.	1922
Juliet Peddle	Michigan	B.S. in Arch	1922
Marjorie Pierce	MIT	B.S. in Arch.	1922, M.S. 1923
Mary Margaret Goodin Fritsch	Oregon	B.A. in Arch.	1923
Alberta Pfeiffer	Illinois	B.S. in Arch.	1923, M.S. 1925
Elsa Mathilda Bussard	Carnegie[3]	B.A.	1924
Olive Tjaden	Cornell		1925
Georgina Pope Yeatman	MIT	B.S. in Arch.	1925
Olive Chadeayne	UC–Berkeley		1926
Edith Amelia Hollander	Cornell	B. Arch	1926

NAME	SCHOOL	DEGREE	DATE
Edith Mortensen Northman	USC[4]		1930
Mary Ann Elizabeth Crawford	MIT	B.S. in Arch.	1929, M.S. 1932
Gertrude E. Ebbeson	MIT	B. Arch.	1933
Margaret Kelly	MIT	B. Arch.	1933
Hazel Weld	MIT	B. Arch	1933
Nina Perera Collier	MIT	B. Arch	1934
Virginia D. Davidson	MIT	B. Arch	1934
Elisabeth Hilde Scheu	MIT	B. Arch.	1934

1. Rhode Island School of Design.
2. Drexel Institute of Art, Science, and Industry (now Drexel University).
3. Carnegie Institute of Technology (now Carnegie Mellon University).
4. University of Southern California.

APPENDIX 2
Female Members of the American Institute of Architects, 1857–1950

The list is in chronological order by the year each woman first joined the AIA. For those who became Fellows, "FAIA" followed by year, in the membership column, refers to the date each woman was elevated to Fellowship in the institute. This list was compiled by Nancy Hadley, AIA archivist and records manager, as part of an effort to create a complete list of AIA members from the original membership records. Members were coded as women if they had unambiguously feminine names, or if they were listed as Miss or Mrs. A number of ambiguous names (such as Leslie or Marion) were individually checked for gender using the membership files. The very few members who used only initials were not checked. List printed by permission of the American Institute of Architects Archives.

NAME	STATE	AIA JOIN DATE
Louise Blanchard Bethune	NY	1888, FAIA 1889
Lois Lilley Howe	MA	1901, FAIA 1931
Henrietta C. Dozier	FL; GA	1905
Marcia Mead	NY	1918
Theodate Pope (Riddle)	CT	1918
Agnes Ballard	FL	1921
Julia Morgan	CA	1921
Ida Annah Ryan	FL	1921
Eleanor Manning O'Connor	MA	1923
Katharine Cotheal Budd	NY	1924
Eleanor A. Raymond	MA	1924, FAIA 1961
Mary Almy	MA	1926
Marion I. Manley	FL	1926, FAIA 1956
Emily H. Butterfield	MI	1927
Elizabeth Kimball Nedved	IL	1927
Alice Walton	MO	1927
Elisabeth Coit	NY	1929, FAIA 1955
Carina Eaglesfield Milligan (Mortimer)	CT	1930
Georgina Pope Yeatman	PA; NC	1930

NAME	STATE	AIA JOIN DATE
Lilian J. Rice	CA	1931
Marion Frances Blood	MI	1932
Elizabeth Greenleaf Pattee (Comey)	MA; RI	1933
Margaret Goodin Fritsch	OR; AK	1936
Lutah Maria Riggs	CA	1936, FAIA 1960
Margaret F. Spencer	PA; AZ	1936
Verna Cook Salomonsky	NY	1937
Louise Leland	KY	1938
Olive Frances Tjaden (Johnson)	NY; FL	1938
Elizabeth Hirsh Fleisher	PA	1939
Larch Campbell Renshaw	CT	1939
Gertrude Sawyer	DC	1939
Elizabeth Ayer	WA	1940
Margaret Burnham Kelly Geddes	RI; DC	1940
Lottie B. Helwick	OH	1942
Elsa Gidoni	NY	1943
Helen Chittenden Gillespie	NY	1943
Elisabeth A. Martini	MI	1943
Florence Ward Stiles	MA; DE	1943
Hilda Young (Wilson)	OH; AZ	1943
Elsa Mathilda Bussard	CA	1944
Olive Kingsley Chadeayne	CA	1944
Rose Connor	CA	1944
Natalie Griffin de Blois	NY; IL; TX	1944, FAIA 1974
Victorine du Pont Homsey	DC, DE	1944, FAIA 1967
Ellamae Ellis League	GA	1944, FAIA 1968
Irene McFaul Pierce	CA	1944
Christine Fahringer Salmon	IL; OK	1944, FAIA 1978
Esther Schwinck	MI	1944
Elmira Sauberan Smyrl (Scott)	TX	1944
Marjorie Katherine Wright	NY	1944
Florence England Bishop	NY	1945
Elizabeth Boyter	CA	1945
Ruth Louise Dines	MA	1945
Dorothy Gray Harrison	MI; CA	1945
Edla Muir Lambie	WA; CA	1945
Edith Mortensen Northman	CA	1945
Alice S. Pardee	MI	1945
Juliet Alice Peddle	IN	1945
Lillian Polly Povey Thompson	MA; OR	1945
Alexzena Raines Watson	TX	1945
Barbara Friedman Bayard (Tocker)	TX	1946
India Boyer	OH	1946
Katherine Gibbs (Ericsson; Stone)	DC; OR	1946

NAME	STATE	AIA JOIN DATE
Mary Alice Hutchins	OR; HI	1946
Elizabeth Pennock Kinne	WI; OR	1946
Miriam Frank Logan	TX	1946
Lucille Bryant Raport	CA	1946
Chloethiel Woodard Smith	DC	1946, FAIA 1960
Mary Jane Blackburn	TX	1947
Jean Washburn Cobb	KS; AL	1947
Mary Clare Hogg	LA; NY; DC	1947
Mary Morrison Kennedy	MA	1947
Mary Frances Knee	CA; DC	1947
Grace Wilson	IL	1947
Marjorie McLean Wintermute	OR	1947
Mary Caroline Cole	OK	1948
Melissa Minnich Coleman	PA	1948
Ruth Reynolds Freeman	VT	1948
Bernice Ropiequet Goedde	IL	1948
Jean League Newton	GA	1948
Irene Artemia von Horvath	NY; NM	1948
Ida Brown Webster	NY	1948
June Wood Wicker	GA	1948
Alice McKee Armstrong	TN	1949
Mary Ann Elizabeth Crawford	IL	1949
Jean Bodman Fletcher	MA	1949
Helen Douglass French	CA	1949
Rossie Moodie Frost	HI	1949
Janet Estelle Hooper	LA	1949
Barbara Carstairs Lewis	NY	1949
Rose E. Luis	CA	1949
Annette Yates Maier	DE	1949
Ruth Harriett Perkins	IL	1949
Anna Loretta Robb Peters	MI	1949
Margaret Merrell Bond	AL	1950
Katherine Cutler Ficken	MD	1950
Mary Louise Grace	NM	1950
Eugenia Lane	IL; WA	1950
Roslyn Ittelson Lindheim	NY; CA	1950
Helen Graham Park	NY	1950
Anne Griswold Tyng	PA	1950, FAIA 1975

NOTES

Introduction

The remark by Henrietta C. Dozier that forms the epigraph for this book comes from an interview with Dozier conducted by Rose Shepherd, March 10, 1939, that appears in "American Life Histories: Manuscripts from the Federal Writers' Project, 1936–1940." The histories are transcriptions of interviews done as part of the Folklore project at the Federal Writers' Project during 1936–40. They are in the collection of the Library of Congress and are available online at http://lcweb2.loc.gov/wpaintro/wpahome.html (accessed October 8, 2007).

1. The epigraph for this introduction comes from a letter in the AIA membership files, Record Group 803, box 19, folder B (pt. 2), American Institute of Architects Archives, Washington, D.C. (hereafter AIA Archives).

2. See Emily Adams Perry, "Marion Isadore Manley: Pioneer Woman Architect," in *Florida Pathfinders,* ed. Lewis N. Wynne et al. (Saint Leo, Fla.: Saint Leo College Press, 1994), 32. The letter is in the AIA Archives.

3. See Kathryn H. Anthony, *Designing for Diversity: Gender, Race, and Ethnicity in the Architectural Profession* (Urbana: University of Illinois Press, 2001).

4. Quoted in Doris Cole, *Eleanor Raymond, Architect* (Philadelphia: Art Alliance Press, 1981), 20.

5. "Women in Architecture: One Who Has Been Successful in It Talks to Other Women," *Buffalo Morning Express,* March 7, 1881, 6. Bethune did believe that there was a special need for women in the fields of medicine and law.

6. Although the details of her early career are unknown, Ethel Bailey Furman (1893–1976) began her career working for her father in 1915 and went on to design more than two hundred buildings. One should assume that other African American women participated in the design of vernacular architecture at an early date. Amaza Lee Meredith (1895–1984), founder of the fine arts department at Virginia State University, had established a practice by the 1940s. Her achievements include Azurest South (1939), one of the few International style buildings in Virginia, and Azurest North, a resort complex at Sag Harbor.

7. From 1897 to 1899, Caroline E. Ashley worked at 191 Broadway. Laura H. Charsley had an office at 24 West Twenty-second Street. See Dennis Francis, *Architects in Practice: New York City, 1840–1900* (New York: Committee for the Preservation of Architectural Records, 1980).

8. Richard Ellison Ritz, *Architects of Oregon: A Biographical Dictionary of Architects Deceased—19th and 20th Centuries* (Portland, Ore.: Lair Hill Publishing, 2002).

9. Courtlandt Van Brunt, President, Kansas City Chapter, AIA, to Frank C. Baldwin, Secretary, AIA, Washington, D.C., February 14, 1927, Record Group 803, box 391, folder 52, AIA Archives.

10. The book is dedicated to "farmers and mechanics." See Catharine Sedgewick, *Scenes and Characters Illustrating Christian Truth. No. III. Home* (1835; reprint, Boston: James Munroe, 1841).

11. Francis Wright, *Views of Society and Manners in America* (1821; reprint, Cambridge, Mass.: Belknap Press of Harvard University Press, 1963), 48.

12. Francis Trollope, *Domestic Manners of the Americans* (London: Whittaker, Treacher, 1832), 210.

13. Among Fuller's earliest art-related contributions to that journal were "A Record of Impressions Produced by the Exhibition of Mr. Allston's Pictures in the Summer of 1839," *The Dial* 1 (July 1840): 73–84, and "The Athenaeum Exhibition of Painting and Sculpture," *The Dial* 1 (October 1840): 260–64.

14. See Corlette R. Walker and Adele M. Holcomb, "Margaret Fuller (1810–1850): Her Work as an Art Critic," in *Women as Interpreters of the Visual Arts, 1820–1979,* ed. Claire Richter Sherman (Westport, Conn.: Greenwood, 1981), 123–46.

15. Louisa Tuthill, *The Young Lady's Home* (New Haven, Conn.: S. Babcock, 1839), 83.

16. Tuthill to Carey and Hart, February 15, 1841, Gratz Collection, Historical Society of Pennsylvania, Philadelphia. In the preface to one of her translations, Cresy noted that "there being in the English language no biographical history devoted to Architects, either ancient or modern, it appeared, that a translation from the best work, embracing such subjects, would be an acceptable addition to the libraries of both architects and amateurs." See Mrs. Edward Cresy, trans., Francesco Milizia, *The Lives of Celebrated Architects,* vol. 1 (London: J. Taylor Architectural Library, High Holborn, 1826), preface.

17. The author of Tuthill's *Architecture. Part I. Ancient Architecture* (1831) was unnamed at publication, but the work has been erroneously attributed to its publisher, Hezekiah Howe. Though the *History* does not contain entire pages from *Architecture,* Tuthill repeats several quotations and selected sentences. An engraving of the "Indra Subba, at Ellora," by Nathaniel and Simeon Jocelyn, appeared on the title page of Tuthill's *Ancient Architecture* and as plate 3 of her *History.*

18. For more information about Ithiel Town and Louisa Tuthill's use of his library, see Sarah Allaback, "Louisa Tuthill, Ithiel Town, and the Beginnings of Architectural History Writing in America," in *American Architects and Their Books to 1848,* ed. Kenneth Hafertepe and James F. O'Gorman (Amherst: University of Massachusetts Press, 2001), 199–215.

19. Louisa Tuthill, *History of Architecture from the Earliest Times* (Philadelphia: Lind-

say and Blakiston, 1848), viii. William Hickling Prescott (1796–1859) and George Bancroft (1800–1891) were two of the most famous historians of the day. Prescott had recently completed his extensive *History of the Conquest of Mexico* (1843) and Bancroft was in the midst of his ten-volume *History of the United States* (1834–75).

20. Louisa Tuthill, ed., *The True and the Beautiful in Nature, Arts, Morals, and Religion* (New York: John Wiley), 1858. Tuthill also edited two additional collections of Ruskin's work: *Precious Thoughts: Moral and Religious* (New York, 1866) and, in the year before her death at age eighty-one, *Pearls for Young Ladies* (1878).

21. *Proceedings of the Franklin Institute* (Philadelphia), April 19, 1850, 23, entry dated April 9.

22. Even earlier a woman identified only as "Miss Ludlow" attempted to improve national aesthetics in the field of art appreciation with her book *A General View of the Fine Arts, Critical and Historical* (New York: Putnam, 1851). Her patron, Daniel Huntington, introduced the volume as "intended to diffuse a taste . . . for the study of fine arts."

23. Peabody is considered the first successful woman publisher. For more information about her role in art education, see Robert Saunders, "The Contributions of Horace Mann, Mary Peabody Mann, and Elizabeth Peabody to Art Education in the United States" (Ph.D. diss., Pennsylvania State University, 1961).

24. See Harriet Monroe, "Corn as a National Emblem," in *Columbia's Emblem: Indian Corn*, ed. Candace Wheeler (Boston and New York: Houghton Mifflin, 1893).

25. For more information on women who wrote about architecture, see Lisa Koenigsberg, "Professionalizing Domesticity: A Tradition of American Women Writers on Architecture, 1848–1913" (Ph.D. diss., Yale University, 1987). Koenigsberg's dissertation includes a section on Mary Northend (1850–1926), photographer, journalist, and author of many books on architectural subjects, primarily historic homes and furnishings.

26. Charlotte Perkins [Stetson] Gilman, *Women and Economics* (Boston: Small, Maynard, 1899), 243.

27. Kathleen D. McCarthy, *Women's Culture* (Chicago: University of Chicago Press, 1991), 67.

28. Bethune's article was part of a talk she gave at the Women's Educational and Industrial Union in Buffalo on March 6, 1891. See Louise Bethune, "Women and Architecture," *Inland Architect and News Record* 17, no. 2 (March 1891): 20. See also Minerva Parker Nichols, "A Woman on the Woman's Building," *American Architect and Building News*, December 10, 1892, 169.

29. Alice Severance, "Talks by Successful Women, IX.—Miss Gannon and Miss Hand on Architecture," *Godey's Magazine* 133, no. 795 (September 1886): 314–16.

30. For information about Harriet Warner, see Phebe A. Hanaford, *Daughters of America; or Women of the Century* (Augusta, Me.: E. E. Knowles, 1882), 315–16.

31. For more information on the history of design schools for women, see Sarah Allaback, "Better Than Silver and Gold: Design Schools for Women in America, 1848–1860," *Journal of Women's History* 10, no. 1 (Spring 1998): 88–107.

32. "For Women Who Earn a Living," *New York Times*, July 25, 1892, sec. 4–4. In 1944 the New York School of Applied Design for Women merged with the Phoenix Art Institute to become the coeducational New York Phoenix School of Design. Pratt Institute

took over the school in 1974 and renamed it Pratt–New York Phoenix School of Design, which in turn became the Pratt Manhattan Center in 1979.

33. Although I have been unable to locate the San Francisco hospital, several contemporary sources reported its existence. An unidentified newspaper fragment shows a bit of the first-floor elevation of the building and reports that "it is now erected and considered, from a sanitary point of view, the most complete on the Pacific coast. Funding for the building was provided by a Dr. Stanstonstall and his partner, Mr. Ward." Collection of the author.

34. "They Are Talented Girls," *New York Times,* October 7, 1894, 20.

35. Lord's partner, J. Monroe Hewlett, was an instructor in the architectural department of the New York School of Design by 1896. The firm of Lord and Hewlett is best known for the Second Battalion Armory, constructed for the naval militia in 1904 at 5100 First Avenue, New York.

36. Louise Hall, "A Pivotal Group in Architecture," in *Architecture: A Place for Women,* ed. Ellen Perry Berkeley and Matilda McQuaid (Washington, D.C.: Smithsonian Institution Press, 1989), 79–86.

37. Dorothy M. Anderson, *Women, Design, and the Cambridge School* (West Lafayette, Ind.: PDA Publishers Corp., 1980), 1–23.

38. For details of graduates' lives after their time at the Cambridge School, see "Alumnae News Notes," *Alumnae Bulletin,* vols. 3–6, 1930–33, Archives, Smith College, Northampton, Massachusetts.

39. For a brief discussion of coeducation at the Graduate School of Design, see Anthony Alofsin, *The Struggle for Modernism: Architecture, Landscape Architecture, and City Planning at Harvard* (New York: Norton, 2002), 175–76.

40. "Nolanum," *The New Century for Women,* Philadelphia, August 19, 1876, 115.

41. Mrs. E. D. Gillespie, *A Book of Remembrance* (Philadelphia, 1901), quoted in John Maass, *The Glorious Enterprise* (Watkins Glen, N.Y.: American Life Foundation, 1973), 121.

42. For details about the controversy over a woman's building at the Columbian Exposition, see Jeanne Madeline Weimann, *The Fair Women* (Chicago: Academy Chicago, 1981).

43. Although defeated in its bid for a place at the exposition, the Isabella Society found a site a few blocks from the fair for a clubhouse and the Isabella Hotel. The Isabella Club and Conference Hall was an eleven-story building (later reduced to six) of brick and stone by Jenney and Mundie (1892). See Frank A. Randall, *History of the Development of Building Construction in Chicago,* 2nd ed., revised and expanded by John D. Randall (Urbana: University of Illinois Press, 1999), 146, 203. Harriet Hosmer's statue of Queen Isabella became part of the 1894 California Midwinter Exposition in San Franciso after the sculptor turned down Bertha Palmer's request to exhibit it in the Woman's Building in Chicago. See Weimann, *Fair Women,* 68–70.

44. Bethune, "Women and Architecture," 21.

45. *American Architect and Building News,* November 26, 1892.

46. Although the national AWA was dissolved in 1969, many of its chapters continued to grow. Today, the AWA-LA in Los Angeles, California, is the largest such chapter, with over one hundred eighty members.

47. Bertha Yerex Whitman, University of Michigan Alumni Association Alumnae Survey, 1924, Bertha Yerex Whitman entry, box 109, University of Michigan Alumni Association records, Bentley Historical Library, University of Michigan, Ann Arbor.

48. Bertha Yerex Whitman, "My Life with Perkins, Fellows, and Hamilton, Architects," unpublished manuscript, May 1977, p. 6, Bentley Historical Library, University of Michigan, Ann Arbor.

49. Harriet Rochlin, "A Distinguished Generation of Women Architects in California," *AIA Journal* 66 (August 1977): 38–42.

50. Henry Atherton Frost and William R. Sears, "Women in Architecture and Landscape Architecture," *Institute for the Coordination of Women's Interests* 7 (1928): 12, Record Group 60, Archives, Smith College.

51. Anne Petersen, "Women Architects Few but Versatile," *New York Times,* April 11, 1937, 92.

52. For more information about twentieth-century women planners, see Eugenie Ladner Birch, "Woman-made America: The Case of Early Public Housing Policy," in *The American Planner,* ed. Donald A. Krueckeberg (New York: Methuen, 1983), 149–75.

53. Whitman, "My Life with Perkins, Fellows and Hamilton, Architects," 2.

54. Ibid., 3–4.

55. International Archive of Women in Architecture (IAWA) *Newsletter* 2 (Fall 1990): 1–2. This source can be found online at the IAWA Web site at http://spec.lib.vt.edu/IAWA/news/news2.pdf (accessed September 18, 2007).

56. "Interview with Mary Ann Crawford," interview by Betty J. Blum, Chicago Architects Oral History Project, May 17, 1983, Art Institute of Chicago, http://www.artic.edu/aic/libraries/caohp/crawford.pdf (accessed August 2, 2007).

Biographical Entries

1. Bethune, "Women and Architecture," 21.

2. "A Woman Who Builds Homes," *Ladies Home Journal,* October 1914, 3.

3. "Prize-Winning Home Plans Stress Compact Layouts," *New York Times,* February 26, 1933, RE1.

4. Arnold Berke, *Mary Colter, Architect of the Southwest* (New York: Princeton Architectural Press, 2002), 55.

5. David Gebhard, "Architecture and the Fred Harvey Houses," *New Mexican Architect* (July/August 1962): 16.

6. Ibid.

7. Rose Connor, AIA membership files, Record Group 803, box 33, folder 17, AIA Archives.

8. "Maude Darling-Parlin Architecture in Fall River," National Register of Historic Places, National Register Travel Itineraries, Places Where Women Made History, http://www.nps.gov/history/nr/travel/pwwmh/ma73.htm (accessed October 9, 2007).

9. Interview by Rose Shepherd, March 1, 1939, "American Life Histories: Manuscripts from the Federal Writers' Project, 1936–1940," Library of Congress, online at http://lcweb2.loc.gov/wpaintro/wpahome.html (accessed October 8, 2007).

10. Frances E. Willard, *Occupations for Women* (Cooper Union, N.Y.: The Success Company, 1897), 366.

11. Jacob Riis, *A Ten Years' War* (1900; reprint, Freeport, N.Y.: Books for Libraries Press, 1969), 96. See also James Ford, *Slums and Housing* (Westport, Conn.: Negro Universities Press, 1936); the "Elevation and patio tenements for 25' lot" by Gannon and Hands is figure 118, page 681, and the plans are in appendix, pl. 7, G.

12. Bethune, "Women and Architecture," 21. The article includes the note "Portions of a talk before the Women's Educational and Industrial Union, Buffalo, March 6, 1891."

13. The Wasmuth Portfolio was published as *Ausgeführte Bauten und Entwürfe von Frank Lloyd Wright* (Berlin: E. Wasmuth, 1910).

14. Quoted in Dave Weinstein, "Signature Style: Leola Hall on Spec," *San Francisco Chronicle*, August 2, 2003, E-1.

15. Severance, "Talks by Successful Women," 316.

16. Erik Larson, *The Devil in the White City* (New York: Vintage Books, 2003), 143.

17. Hanaford, *Daughters of America*, 286; Gwendolyn Wright, "On the Fringe of the Profession: Women in American Architecutre," in *The Architect*, ed. Spiro Kostof (New York: Oxford University Press, 1977), 293.

18. C. H. Blackall to Glenn Brown, September 7, 1907, AIA membership files, Record Group 803, box 10, folder 2, AIA Archives.

19. Mrs. Charles Almy, quoted by Doris Cole and Karen Cord Taylor, *The Lady Architects: Lois Lilley Howe, Eleanor Manning, and Mary Almy, 1893–1937* (New York: Midmarch Press, 1990), 18 (first quote); Graham Gund, quoted, ibid., 26 (second quote), 28 (third quote).

20. Madeleine B. Stern, *We the Women: Career Firsts of Nineteenth-Century America* (New York: Artemis, 1962), 60.

21. "Woman Invades Field of Modern Architecture," *New York Times*, November 17, 1907, SM11.

22. Marion Manley, quoted in David Gebhard, *Lutah Maria Riggs: A Woman in Architecture* (Santa Barbara, Calif.: Santa Barbara Museum of Art and Capra Press, 1992), 22.

23. School of Architecture, University of Miami, Coral Gables, Florida, http://www.arc.miami.edu/school/FACILITIES/Facilities.html (accessed August 8, 2007).

24. Perry, "Marion Isadore Manley," 21.

25. See Cole and Taylor, *The Lady Architects*.

26. "Why I Chose Westwood Park for My Bungalows" (advertisement), *San Francisco Chronicle*, June 5, 1920.

27. "Girl Architects Organize a Firm," *New York Times*, March 8, 1914, 15.

28. This paragraph is based on information in an article by Albert M. Tannler, "Wagner Built a Career as Designer at Turn of the Century," originally published for the *Tribune Review*, Sunday, May 9, 2004. It is posted on the Pittsburgh History and Landmarks Foundation News "Blog Archive" at http://wordpress.phlf.org/wordpress/?p=394 (accessed September 11, 2007).

29. Mary Temple Jamison, quoted in Tannler, "Wagner Built a Career," 3.

30. Ibid.

31. Wormser's recollections appear in Sara Holmes Boutelle, *Julia Morgan: Architect*

(New York: Abbeville Press, 1995), 44. Information about her can be found in the *Julia Morgan Architectural History Project,* ed. Suzanne B. Riess, vol. 2, Regional Oral History Office, Bancroft Library, University of California at Berkeley.

32. Washington, House of Representatives, House Resolution no. 2005–4654, Representatives Dunn, Ahern, and McCune (Olympia, Wash.), April 15, 2005.

33. Harriet Rochlin, "Among the First and Finest: California Architects Julia, Hazel, Lilian, and Lutah," manuscript, 15, San Diego Historical Society, San Diego, Calif.

34. Mark Hammons describes Marion Parker in a biographical essay in "Guide to the William Gray Purcell Papers," www.organica.org/peteam2.htm. See also "Biographical Note by William Gray Purcell" on Marion Parker, www.organica.org/peparker4.htm. Purcell's reminiscences of the Charles I. Buxton Bungalow are also part of Hammons's guide to the Purcell Papers. Purcell's entry for April 2, 1912, can be found at www.organica .org/pejn154_1.htm (all accessed September 12, 2007).

35. Purcell quoted in Hammons, "Guide to the William Gray Purcell Papers," www .organica.org/pejn158_1.htm (accessed September 12, 2007).

36. International Archive of Women in Architecture (IAWA) *Newsletter* 2 (Fall 1990): 2. This source can be found online at the IAWA Web site at http://spec.lib.vt.edu/IAWA/ news/news2.pdf (accessed July 12, 2007).

37. Theodate Pope to McKim, Mead, and White, September 1898, McKim, Mead, and White records, New-York Historical Society Archives, New York.

38. Cass Gilbert to Professor Laird (University of Pennsylvania), August 26, 1912, Theodate Pope Riddle Papers, Archives, Hill-Stead Museum, Farmington, Conn.

39. Theodate Pope to Ada Brooks Pope, March 11, 1915, no. 860, Archives, Hill-Stead Museum.

40. Theodate Pope Riddle to William Stanley Parker, June 10, 1918, Record Group 803, box 230, folder 29, AIA Archives.

41. Cole, *Eleanor Raymond, Architect,* 26.

42. Federal Writers' Project of the Works Progress Administration, *The WPA Guide to California* (1939; reprint, New York: Pantheon, 1984), 407.

43. This entry is based on David Gebhard's biography *Lutah Maria Riggs.* For the article about Riggs's university progress, see "Winner of News Prize Is Doing Well at School," *Santa Barbara Daily News,* May 20, 1918, sec. 2, 7.

44. Irene McFaul [Pierce] (1897–1979) graduated from Berkeley with an M.A. and worked as a drafter in the San Francisco area before opening her own practice. She went on to become chief drafter in the office of Walter R. Hagedohm. Her "model of a church for a small town," designed while working for Hagedohm, is pictured in the June 1949 *Architectural Record.* An example of McFaul's residential work, a "House for Mr. and Mrs. Milton J. Poppett" in Santa Ana, was published, with a photograph and plan, in 1940. See "A Thousand Women in Architecture," *Architectural Record* 103 (June 1948): 108–15, and "House for Mr. and Mrs. Milton J. Poppett, *California Arts and Architecture* 57 (September 1940): 37.

45. Gebhard, *Lutah Maria Riggs,* 17.

46. Ida Anna Ryan to William Stanley Parker, Secretary, AIA, October 29, 1921, Record Group 803, box 38, folder 54, AIA Archives.

47. Nothing more is known about this reference to "Unity Chapel." In the AIA application, Roberts did explain that she chose to cite the house for her mother and Unity Chapel as "exhibits" satisfying membership requirement because they were the only works of which she had photographs in her Orlando, Florida, office. She included the De Rhodes House without photographs. See Isabel Roberts, Orlando, Florida, to William Stanley Parker, Secretary, AIA, September 11, 1921, in "Isabel Roberts," Record Group 803, box 382, folder 54, AIA Archives.

48. Frank Lloyd Wright to "Anyone, Anywhere," August 6, 1920, in "Isabel Roberts," Record Group 803, box 382, folder 54, AIA Archives.

49. Anna Graham Rockfellow, "The Professional Life of a Pioneer Co-Ed" (1938), quoted in Kimberly Ann Oei Kunasek, "Anne Graham Rockfellow: Who Was She? What Was Her Contribution to the History of Architecture?" (M.A. thesis, University of Arizona, 1994), 37.

50. Effie Leese Scott, "Hotel Will Open Tonight in Blaze of Social Splendor," *Tucson Citizen,* November 22, 1928.

51. AIA membership files, Record Group 803, box 383, folder 50, AIA Archives.

52. Ida Annah Ryan to F. J. Kennard, December 9, 1929, Orlando, Fla., AIA membership files, Record Group 803, box 383, folder 50, AIA Archives.

53. Petersen, "Women Architects Few but Versatile," 92.

54. "Fred McMahan, 1895–1980," "Tennessee Encyclopedia of History and Culture," online at http://tennesseeencyclopedia.net/imagegallery.php?EntryID=MO54 (accessed October 8, 2007).

55. Gertrude Sawyer to James C. Colvin, editor, *Alumni News,* May 27, 1957, University of Illinois Archives, Urbana, Illinois.

56. Matilda McQuaid, "Educating for the Future: A Growing Archive on Women and Architecture," in Berkeley and McQuaid, *Architecture: A Place for Women,* 249.

ANNOTATED BIBLIOGRAPHY

The following sources are limited to books and online offerings about the history of early women architects and designers in related fields. During the 1970s and early 1980s, scholarship on women's history focused on discovering women of achievement and adding them to the historical record. One recent study, *Women's Places: Architecture and Design 1860–1960* (2003), edited by Brenda Martin and Penny Sparkles, describes this as the "hidden from history approach" (xi) and calls the identification of practitioners a first step in understanding the impact women have made on architecture in society.

Foremost among pioneering texts are Doris Cole's *From Tipi to Skyscraper* (1973); *Women in American Architecture* (1977), a series of essays edited by Susana Torre; and Gwendolyn Wright's essay "On the Fringe of the Profession: Women in American Architecture" in *The Architect: Chapters in the History of the Profession* (1977), edited by Spiro Kostof. "Women in American Architecture" was a major exhibition that opened at the Brooklyn Museum in 1977, and the Whitney Library of Design sponsored the companion book of the same title as its catalog, with the majority of Judith Paine's master's thesis, "Pioneer Women Architects" (1975), appearing as a central essay. *Women, Design, and the Cambridge School* (1980), by Dorothy M. Anderson, deals almost exclusively with the history of the school founded in 1917 and provides insight into the social barriers confronting potential architects in the early twentieth century. A Ph.D. dissertation by Rochelle Martin, "The Difficult Path: Women in the Architectural Profession" (1986), includes a general historical introduction but focuses on the career experiences of six architects working after World War II. The AIA Women in Architecture Committee celebrated Louise Bethune's membership in the AIA with an exhibition, "That Exceptional One: Women in American Architecture, 1888–1988," which included a brief catalog. The catalog provided the first documented list of women who had practiced architecture in the United States prior to 1988. In addition, the Smithsonian Institution Press published *Architecture: A Place for Women* (1989), edited by Ellen Perry Berkeley and Matilda McQuaid, to honor Bethune and to further research on women in architecture. The volume includes McQuaid's essay entitled "Educating for the Future," on the AIA Archive of Women in Architecture, which identifies Katharine C. Budd among several women who would be "excellent subjects for monographs, articles, theses, or dissertations" and would "someday be well known" (254).

The most extensive historical research on early women architects in the last two decades has appeared in the form of biographies. Foremost among these is Sara Holmes Boutelle's *Julia Morgan, Architect,* published in 1988 and revised and updated in 1995. Sandra L. Katz has written *Dearest of Geniuses* (2003), an account of the life and work of Theodate Pope Riddle. The latest book on Mary Colter, Arnold Berke's *Mary Colter: Architect of the Southwest* (2002), is considered the most complete biography to date and joins two earlier works, *The Uncommon Perspective of M. E. J. Colter* (1992), by Lynne Avadenka, and *Mary Colter: Builder Upon the Red Earth* (1980), by Virginia L. Grattan. Recent books on Marion Mahony Griffin include a collection of essays edited by Anne Watson, *Beyond Architecture: Marion Mahony and Walter Burley Griffin: America, Australia, and India* (2000) and a volume edited by Debora Wood, *Marion Mahony Griffin: Drawing the Form of Nature* ((2005), which was the catalog for an exhibition at Northwestern University. David Gebhard's *Lutah Marie Riggs: A Woman in Architecture, 1921–1980* (1992) is an important catalog of the Southern California architect's work. Doris Cole wrote two biographies after her early history—*Eleanor Raymond, Architect* (1981) and, with Karen Cord Taylor, *The Lady Architects: Lois Lilley Howe, Eleanor Manning, and Mary Almy, 1893–1937* (1990). Another biography of this era, *Daring to Dream: The Life of Hazel Wood Waterman* (1987), by Sally Bullard Thornton, is appreciative of Waterman's achievement but does not focus on architectural analysis of her buildings. Scholarly work on women architects includes "Anne Graham Rockfellow: Who Was She? What Was Her Contribution to the History of Architecture?" (1994), a master's thesis by Kimberly Ann Oei Kunasek, and a Ph.D. dissertation by Nancy Beth Gruskin, "Building Context: The Personal and Professional Life of Eleanor Raymond, Architect, 1887–1989" (1998).

Although there has been recent scholarly interest in women architects, the most comprehensive reference book on the topic remains a 1988 bibliography by Lamia Doumato, *Architecture and Women: A Bibliography Documenting Women Architects, Landscape Architects, Designers, Architectural Critics and Writers, and Women in Related Fields Working in the United States.* In an effort to show the breadth of women's participation in the field of architecture, Doumato includes a wide range of professions without any discrimination based on achievement. Doumato's groundbreaking bibliography serves her purpose of providing a starting point for further research, listing sources on women in design, home economics, and literature. Her work represents a new trend in study about women and architecture—the idea that women have always influenced design and the built environment in a variety of "nonprofessional" ways. This inclusive approach assumes that women have consistently participated in design through work such as quilting and pottery and has opened up the field to an understanding that the amateur and the consumer are active shapers of "nonmodernist" design. A more recent collection of essays edited by Pat Kirkham, *Women Designers in the USA: Diversity and Difference* (2000), illustrates this broader outlook by featuring a range of designers who demonstrate women's participation in the field.

All efforts to study the history of women in architecture will be furthered by the International Archive of Women in Architecture (IAWA), which was established in the Special Collections division of the University Libraries of Virginia Polytechnic Institute and State University (Virginia Tech) in Blacksburg, Virginia, in 1985. The archive, founded by Milka Bliznakov, describes itself as a joint program of the College of Architecture and Urban Studies and the University Libraries. The IAWA is a useful online source of biographical information on early women architects and includes a limited number of digital images. See the Web site at http://spec.lib.vt.edu/IAWA. Virginia Tech owns valuable manuscript collections relating to individual women and architectural organizations and is working to promote its archive.

In 2007, the Beverly Willis Architecture Foundation (BWAF) established a Web site focusing on women architects from 1950 to 1980. Although this source was not consulted in the writing of this book, readers may wish to view the BWAF timeline of women in architecture with biographical information about selected practitioners before 1920. See http://www.bwaf.org/timeline.

During the production of *The First American Women Architects,* many valuable and reliable original sources about women architects have been digitized and made available on the Internet. Libraries, archives, and other institutions are rapidly making their collections accessible electronically as funding becomes available. The present book is only a starting point in the pursuit of information about women architects. Readers are encouraged to use search engines to check frequently with the ever-expanding electronic research library.

INDEX

SARAH ALLABACK is an architectural historian based in Charlottes-ville, Virginia. She has worked for the National Park Service, the National Historic Landmarks Program, and the Historic American Buildings Survey/Historic American Engineering Record (HABS/HAER). She is the author of *Mission 66 Visitor Centers: The History of a Building Type.* Her articles have appeared in journals such as *Nineteenth Century* and the *Journal of Women's History.*

The University of Illinois Press
is a founding member of the
Association of American University Presses.

Composed in 10.5/13 Minion Pro
with Helvetica Neue display
by Jim Proefrock
at the University of Illinois Press
Designed by Kelly Gray
Manufactured by Sheridan Books, Inc.

University of Illinois Press
1325 South Oak Street
Champaign, IL 61820-6903
www.press.uillinois.edu